THE AIR FIGHTERS

Other National Historical Society Publications:

THE IMAGE OF WAR: 1861-1865

TOUCHED BY FIRE: A PHOTOGRAPHIC PORTRAIT OF THE CIVIL WAR

WAR OF THE REBELLION: OFFICIAL RECORDS
   OF THE UNION AND CONFEDERATE ARMIES

OFFICIAL RECORDS OF THE UNION AND CONFEDERATE NAVIES
   IN THE WAR OF THE REBELLION

HISTORICAL TIMES ILLUSTRATED ENCYCLOPEDIA OF THE CIVIL WAR

CONFEDERATE VETERAN

THE WEST POINT MILITARY HISTORY SERIES

IMPACT: THE ARMY AIR FORCES' CONFIDENTIAL HISTORY
   OF WORLD WAR II

HISTORY OF UNITED STATES NAVAL OPERATIONS IN WORLD WAR II
   by Samuel Eliot Morison

HISTORY OF THE ARMED FORCES IN WORLD WAR II
   by Janusz Piekalkiewicz

A TRAVELLER'S GUIDE TO GREAT BRITAIN SERIES

MAKING OF BRITAIN SERIES

THE ARCHITECTURAL TREASURES OF EARLY AMERICA

For information about National Historical Society Publications, write:

The National Historical Society, 2245 Kohn Road, Box 8200,
Harrisburg, Pa 17105

THE ELITE
The World's Crack Fighting Men

THE AIR FIGHTERS

Ashley Brown, Editor
Jonathan Reed, Editor

Editorial Board

Lisa Mullins, Managing Editor, NHS edition

A Publication of
THE NATIONAL HISTORICAL SOCIETY

Published in Great Britain in 1986 by Orbis Publishing

Library of Congress Cataloging-in-Publication Data
The Air fighters.
    (The Elite: the world's crack fighting men; v. 1)
    1. Fighter plane combat—History.   2. Air warfare—
History. I. Brown, Ashley.   2. Reed, Jonathan.
III. Series: Elite (Harrisburg, Pa.); v. 1.
UG700.A57 1989   358.4'3   88-36224
ISBN 0-918678-39-0

CONTENTS

INTRODUCTION

We have always thought they were special men, from the days of the Sopwith Camel to the Stealth Fighter, from the Flying Circus to the Flying Tigers. The Airfighters. The men who got into their cockpits and flew off alone into the skies to attack enemy ground positions, to protect the heavy bombers with their awesome loads, or to battle one-on-one with others of their own kind, not for land or territory, but for a piece of the sky, and perhaps for glory.

Nowhere else in the broad range of warfare has one man and one machine been so intimately linked. Each would have been nothing without the other, from the "Red Baron" to "Pappy" Boyington. And besides the airplanes that themselves became legendary—the Mustang, the P-38, the Zero, the MiG, and more—and the individuals who achieved renown in them, there were the great groups of men and machines, the squadrons. The Tuskegee Airmen, America's first black fighter pilots, the Flying Tigers, the Shark Squadron, the Warthogs and Wild Weasels, Zemke's Wolfpack, and even the dreaded and tragic Kamikaze.

Here in the pages of THE ELITE's *Airfighters,* all these great men and aircraft come to life once again, from World War I through Vietnam and beyond, not to glorify warfare, but to recognize the heights to which ordinary men can rise when extraordinary times call upon them for uncommon bravery against all the odds. There are no right or wrong sides when a man and his fighter are locked in a life or death battle of wits and technology above the clouds. There are only instinct, reflex, and courage—things that transcend nations and ideologies, qualities that separate the ordinary from THE ELITE.

Overstretched along the Eastern Front, and in the face of vast odds, the pilots of JG 52 established an astounding combat record

JAGDGESCHWADER 52 ended World War II as the Luftwaffe's highest scoring fighter unit, with a total of over 10,000 aerial victories to its credit. Five of the Luftwaffe's top 10 aces served with the unit, including the three highest scorers: Major Erich Hartmann with 352 victories, Major Gerhard Barkhorn with 301 victories and Major Günther Rall with 275 victories. More than 30 of the unit's most successful fighter pilots had personal scores in excess of 100 kills. JG 52 fielded some of the Luftwaffe's most colourful and effective pilots and, between them, they established a remarkable and unprecedented combat record which no fighting formation of comparable size has ever come close to equalling.

By the spring of 1941, the Third Gruppe (III/JG 52) was stationed in Romania, responsible for the defence of the vital oil-wells and installations at Ploiesti, and the remainder of the Jagdgeschwader, under its Kommodore Major Hans Trübenbach, shortly afterwards followed it to Eastern Europe – in preparation for the assault on the Soviet Union.

On 22 June 1941, II/JG 52, operating from Suwalki in Poland, carried out a series of ground-attack missions and fighter sweeps over Soviet territory without encountering any fighter opposition. 'Still no sight of any Russians in the air,' noted Leutnant (Second Lieutenant) Heinz Knoke of 6 Staffel on the following day. 'Not until afternoon is any encounter with the Ratas [Polikarpov I-16s] reported. Then comrades from 4 Staffel tell of an engagement with Russian fighters near Grodno. They note the primitive flying technique of the Ivans. Their aircraft are slow, but surprisingly manoeuvrable.' Later in the same month III Gruppe began intercepting unescorted Soviet bomber raids over the Black Sea, aimed at Romanian oil targets. Getting into their stride, the German pilots claimed some 50 enemy aircraft destroyed.

during a period of only five days. Like the Soviet fighters met by II Gruppe, these raiders possessed very little tactical skill and they fell easy prey to the Bf 109Es. In the words of Gunther Rall, 'since they had no fighter escort, it was simple.'

In August 1941, III Gruppe began offensive operations in support of the advancing German armies on the southern sector of the Eastern Front. At this auspicious moment in the unit's fortunes 28-year-old Leutnant Hermann Graf began his operational career, having previously served as a flying instructor. His rise to fame was meteoric, for within little more than a year of combat flying he became the first Luftwaffe ace to achieve the distinction of 200 victories. In October 1941 Graf took command of 9/JG 52, the Karaya (Sweetheart) Staffel, which had as its emblem a red heart pierced by an arrow. By January 1942 Graf's personal score stood at 42 victories and his remarkable prowess in air combat earned him the Knight's Cross. A number of up-and-coming NCO pilots prospered under Graf's tutelage in 9 Staffel, notable amongst them being Oberfeldwebel (Sergeant-Major) Heinrich Füllgrabe (65 victories), Feldwebel (Senior Sergeant) Alfred Grislawski (133 victories), Oberfeldwebel Leopold Steinbatz, Graf's wingman, (99 victories) and Oberfeldwebel Ernst Suss (70 victories).

The astonishingly high victory claims by Luftwaffe pilots operating on the Eastern Front were in marked contrast to the more modest scores of the top British and American aces of World War II. This was partly due to the Luftwaffe's practice of keeping pilots on combat duty indefinitely, while the western Allies adhered to a system of carefully regulated combat tours. In addition, opportunities for running up high scores were far greater on the Eastern Front – as Rall has testified:

'Tactics were different in Russia. The Russian pilots liked to fly in large masses. And at the beginning of the war, we had experience and it was easy. Later it became much more difficult. They didn't have the individual initiative of pilots we fought on the Western Front. But the Red Banner Guard Regiments were very good.'

Although the pilots of JG 52 faced easier opposition than their Luftwaffe colleagues on the Western Front, they nonetheless entered combat with the knowledge that to be captured meant at best imprisonment under extremely grim conditions. In response to Germany's changing fortunes on the Eastern Front, the Jagdgeschwader was obliged to operate from bases where accommodation was invariably spartan and the makeshift airstrips at the mercy of the harsh Russian climate. Rall remembers their

Despite being the idol of the Nazi propaganda machine, Oberst Hermann Graf (below), earned the respect of his colleagues as a superb fighter pilot and a cool-headed leader. Right: The youthful, confident profile of Major Erich Hartmann

JG 52

Soviet Il-2 Shturmoviks patrol the icy wastelands of the Eastern Front (far left). Below: A Messerschmitt Bf 109 in mid-flight.

Bottom left: Hauptmann Hans Marseille gained his combat experience with JG 52, and then went on to become Germany's top-scoring ace in the west.

PRIDE OF THE LUFTWAFFE

Jagdgeschwader 52's I Gruppe was formed in August 1939 as a single-seat fighter unit, flying the Messerschmitt Bf 109E. When the German assault in the west began, in the spring of 1940, JG 52 was up to full strength with three Gruppen of Bf 109E's. Deployed to the Channel coast in July 1940, the unit came under the command of Jagdfliegerführer 2, Oberst Theo Osterkamp.

During the Battle of Britain, JG 52's fortunes were mixed. The inexperienced III Gruppe suffered particularly heavy losses during the convoy battles of July, losing the Gruppenkommandeur, Hauptmann Wolf von Houwald, and one Staffelkapitän on the 24th and a further Staffelkapitän the following day. Such was the severity of III Gruppe's mauling by the RAF that it was withdrawn to Germany in August with orders to re-form and re-train.

Major Günther Rall, who served with the ill-fated III Gruppe during this period recalled that: 'In the Battle of Britain we in 52 were very inexperienced...we really wasted our fighters. We didn't have enough to begin with and we used them in the wrong way.'

The Geschwader's I Gruppe was somewhat more successful, claiming 72 RAF aircraft destroyed for the loss of 26 of its own pilots.

Above: The Luftwaffe's daytime interceptor pilots' qualification clasp.

first winter in the Soviet Union with horror – mild autumn weather changed dramatically within the space of two days, bringing temperatures of minus 30°C.

Incredibly, the only respite from combat flying that the majority of Luftwaffe pilots could expect were the periods spent in hospital recovering from wounds or sickness. In November 1941, Rall's fighting career was almost finished due to the severe injuries he sustained during an intense dogfight between Rostov and Taganrog in the southern Ukraine. After shooting down one Soviet fighter, his 36th victory, Rall suffered a vicious surprise attack from another enemy aircraft and was forced to bring his crippled Bf 109F down for a crash-landing behind German lines. Paralysed, Rall was pulled from the wreckage of his fighter and doctors discovered that

his back had been broken in three places. Told by the physicians that he would never fly again, Rall stubbornly fought his way back to health and in August 1942 rejoined III/JG 52 in Russia. Despite the enforced nine-month break from combat, Rall soon regained his form and in November 1942 gained his 100th victory. By the end of the war he had flown 800 combat missions and, with 275 victories to his credit, was the third-highest scoring German ace.

'I could see fire glaring redly under the engine cowlings. There wasn't much time for action'

By no means all of the Luftwaffe's top-scoring aces gained their victories during the early years of the war against the Soviet Union, when conditions were comparatively easy. A marked improvement in the capabilities of the Soviet fighter force was evident after the Kuban battles in the spring of 1943. Increasing supplies of Lend-Lease aircraft and more effective Soviet-built machines improved the quality of the fighter opposition and the odds against the Luftwaffe pilots rose steadily. The top-scoring ace Erich Hartmann, who had gained only 11 of his eventual total of 352 victories by the end of April 1943, flew an average of four sorties a day. Combats were frequent and by April 1944 his score had risen to over 200 victories.

Below: The Messerschmitt Bf 109Es of III Gruppe JG 52 stand ready, their pilots awaiting orders to take to the skies in defence of the Ploești oilfields and installations. Left: Pride of II Gruppe and one of the Luftwaffe's highest scoring fighter pilots, Major Gerhard Barkhorn. Seen here wearing the coveted Knight's Cross, Barkhorn positively relished combat and ended the war with 301 aerial victories to his credit. Bottom: One of the JG 52's groundcrew adds the finishing touches to a service check on Barkhorn's aircraft.

By mid-1943 German pilots were sometimes facing odds as great as 30-1 in the air, yet such heavy odds often provided the opportunity for remarkable feats of arms. For example, during the air battles over Kursk, Hartmann scored four victories on 5 July 1943, seven on 7 July and four on the following day. In the finest traditions of the Luftwaffe, this performance was bettered by two other pilots of JG 52. Hauptmann (Captain) Johannes Wiese gained no fewer than 12 victories on 5 July, despite having force-landed five times during the action. Oberleutnant (Lieutenant) Walter Krupinski was close behind him with 11 kills. The ebullient and reckless Krupinski, nicknamed 'Graf (Count) Punski' because of his love of high living, ended the war with 197 victories, 177 of which he gained when flying with JG 52.

One of the most difficult Soviet aircraft to shoot down was the heavily armoured Ilyushin Il-2 Shturmovik, as this account by Hartmann illustrates:

'Our position was behind and above our enemies. We . . . attacked in a steep dive, firing through the fighters and attacking the bombers. I attacked the aircraft on the extreme left, closing in very fast and opening fire at about two or three hundred feet. I saw numerous hits, but the bullets and shells ricocheted off the Il-2. The heavy armour plating on those Il-2s resisted even 20mm cannon shell hits.

'I began my second attack on the same machine, starting with a steep dive and coming up on him from behind and below. This time I closed in even closer before opening fire. A hit in the oil cooling system! Black smoke belched from the Il-2 followed by rapidly lengthening tongues of flame. The fire swept back under the fuselage. I was alone at this time because the aircraft I had attacked had pulled out of formation and was trying to escape to the east.

Eastern Front 1942-1944

The German summer offensive of 1942 ground to a halt in the Caucasus and at Stalingrad.
The winter of 1942-1943 saw a dramatic reverse on the Eastern Front with the invading Germans driven back across the Don. German efforts to eliminate the Kursk salient in July were a costly failure, and from then onwards the Soviets advanced inexorably towards Germany

Key
→ Soviet forces
····· Front line, Nov 1942
--- Front line, July 1943
Front line, Nov 1943
Front line, Aug 1944

'I was still sitting behind him and we were both in a shallow dive. Then there was an explosion under his wing, and simultaneously there was a heavy explosion in my own aircraft. Smoke billowed back into the cockpit and I could see fire glaring redly under the engine cowlings. There wasn't much time for action.

'Quickly I went through the drill. Altitude: low level and still on the German side of the lines. Fast, power back, fuel master switch off and ignition switch off in quick order. None too soon. I bellied into a field, raising a huge shower of dirt and dust which quickly extinguished the fire. Just as I clambered out of the cockpit, my first kill crashed thunderously three kilometres away.'

In September 1943, following in Graf's footsteps, Hartmann became Staffelkapitän of 9/JG 52 – the Karaya Staffel. The following month he gained his 150th victory and was awarded the Knight's Cross. Like Graf before him, Hartmann was anxious to foster any new talent in the pilots under his command and he found a particularly adept pupil in his wingman, Leutnant Hans-Joachim Birkner. Birkner scored his first victory on 1 November 1943 and by July the following year his score had risen to 98 kills – earning him the Knight's Cross. However, Birkner's career came to an untimely end in December 1944 when he was killed during an accident at take-off.

Hartmann developed a fighting technique that was particularly suited to the conditions of the Eastern Front in the later war years. He stressed to his pilots the necessity of weighing up the tactical situation before making an attack – always seeking to put the enemy at a disadvantage. He particularly favoured a diving attack on his victims, from above and astern, closing in to minimum range before firing. 'I opened fire only when the whole windshield was black with the enemy', he recalled. 'The further you get away from the enemy the less impact and penetration your projectiles have.' Hartmann always avoided dogfighting. If his initial attack did not bring down the enemy, he would use the speed built up during his dive to climb for altitude, then reassess the situation before making a second attack.

This cautious approach to air fighting, similar to the philosophy of the great World War I ace, Manfred von Richthofen, brought Hartmann through the war unscathed, despite being forced down on 16 separate occasions. Once he was briefly captured by Soviet soldiers, but by feigning injury Hartmann was able to escape and rejoin his unit. His friend and rival, Gerhard Barkhorn, was less fortunate. The illustrious Barkhorn was wounded twice during his combat career of over 1100 missions. Nor was Barkhorn so reluctant to engage in dogfighting – in one notable air combat with a LaGG-3, he engaged the enemy for 40 minutes, with both pilots forced to conduct violent manoeuvres, before the encounter finally ended in stalemate.

Bottom: Fighting machine – the Bf 109K belonging to Major Erich Hartmann. Armament consisted of one 30mm and two 15mm machine guns, with provision for underwing cannon or rockets. Beneath the cockpit canopy is the red heart of the 'Sweetheart' Staffel, to which pilots often added the names of their wives or girlfriends. Chalked on the Messerschmitt's tail is Hartmann's current victory tally – in excess of 300 kills. Below: A formation of heavily armoured Soviet Shturmoviks, known as 'flying tanks', fly in low to fulfil their combat assignment.

The career of the sixth-ranking Luftwaffe ace, Major Wilhelm Batz, was perhaps most remarkable for its extremely sluggish start. A pre-war Luftwaffe pilot, Batz served as a flying instructor from 1937 until late 1942, amassing a total of 5000 flying hours. Thus, when he was posted to JG 52 in December 1942, he was a far better pilot than many of his contemporaries. Yet success in combat constantly eluded him. His first victory was gained in March 1943, yet by the spring of 1944 his score had only risen to 15 kills. 'I was a good adjutant, but a bad fighter', he recalls of this period. Batz's appointments as Staffelkapitän in May 1943, and then Kommandeur of III/JG 52 a year later were on the grounds of seniority rather than combat performance. However, in mid-1944 Batz at last found his form and thereafter began to build up an impressive number of victories in an astonishingly short period. During the summer of 1944 he was claiming an average of two to three victories every day and, on one of these days, he shot down a phenomenal 16 enemy aircraft. Batz's final score was 237.

By early 1944, the increasing demands of German home defence units had considerably depleted the fighter forces operating in the Soviet Union. With relatively limited resources, the Luftwaffe was hard-pressed to cover an extensive front which had been weakened by Soviet counter-offensives. Units were frequently forced to change their bases at short notice in response to fast-changing tactical demands. During the first five months of 1944, III/JG 52 operated from 14 different airfields. In April 1944, both Rall and Krupinski left JG 52 for home defence units in Germany. The inexorable advance of the Soviet armies exerted further pressures on the German fighter forces; JG 52's Bf 109Gs covered the final evacuation of the Crimea in May 1944 and then, stripped of their radios and armour plate, each carried two groundcrew to safety from the beleaguered peninsula. Later that same month JG 52 was in action against the bombers and escort fighters of the US Fifteenth Army Air Force over the Romanian oil refineries. Operating under the command of its Kommodore, Oberst Dieter Hrabak (himself a 125-victory ace), the unit performed admirably against a much better-trained and well-equipped air force than its usual enemy. Hartmann succeeded in adding seven North American P-51 Mustangs to his

ERICH HARTMANN

Born at Weissach in Wurttemberg on 19 April 1922, Erich Hartmann (below left) was a proficient glider pilot by the age of 14. He enlisted in the Luftwaffe in October 1940 and, after being commissioned as a Leutnant, was assigned to fighter pilot training at Jagdfliegerschule 2 at Zerbst-Anhalt.

Hartmann's first posting to an operational unit came in October 1942, when he joined III/JG 52's 7 Staffel on the Eastern Front. His Gruppenkommandeur was Major Hubertus von Bonin, a veteran of the Condor Legion in Spain, and his fellow pilots included such distinguished aces as Leutnant Edmund Rossman (93 victories) and Oberleutnant Josef Zwernemann (126 victories). The youthful appearance of the 20-year-old Hartmann earned him the nickname 'Bubi' (the boy), but he was soon to demonstrate his uncanny ability as a fighter pilot.

Gaining his first victory on 5 November 1942, by April 1943 Hartmann was considered sufficiently experienced to lead a Rotte of two fighters. On 3 August he gained his 50th kill and the following month was made Staffelkapitän of 9/JG 52.

October 1943 witnessed Hartmann's 150th kill and he was awarded the Knight's Cross. His victory streak continued unabated and by August 1944 his total exceeded 300. In November 1944 Hartmann was appointed Gruppenkommandeur of I/JG 52 and by the end of hostilities had achieved the remarkable total of 352 enemy aircraft destroyed, the highest score of any fighter pilot.

Hartmann then endured nine years' imprisonment in the Soviet Union and after his release served in the West German Luftwaffe, retiring as an Oberst (Colonel) in 1973.

Right: A Messerschmitt Bf 109 banks in pursuit of the enemy. Below right: Oberstleutnant Helmut Bennemann, who served with I/JG 52 from June 1940 until October 1943, during which time he rose to command the Gruppe. Following this, he commanded JG 53 on home defence operations and ended the war with 92 victories to his credit.

victory list. However, operations against the Americans were not without loss. On 4 June 1944 JG 52 claimed nine enemy aircraft destroyed, one of the victims falling to the 203-victory ace Hauptmann Helmut Lipfert, but five German pilots had been lost.

By July 1944 the numerical superiority of the Soviet air force had become greater than ever. In one month of hectic fighting, from 20 July to 22 August, Hartmann shot down 32 enemy aircraft. On 23 August he gained eight kills in three missions, bringing his total to 290 victories. Yet such was the strength of the opposing air forces that the skill of individual German pilots counted for relatively little. The wide dispersal of limited Luftwaffe forces over the vast extent of the Eastern Front can be illustrated by the assignments of JG 52 in January 1945. III Gruppe was assigned to Luftflotte 4 in Hungary, whereas I and II Gruppe were serving under Luftflotte 6, covering the front from East Prussia to the Carpathians. In October 1944 Oberst (Colonel) Hermann Graf relieved Hrabak as Kommodore of JG 52. He remained with the unit until Germany's final surrender and accompanied his men into captivity in the Soviet prison camps.

THE AUTHOR Anthony Robinson was formerly on the staff of the RAF Museum, Hendon. He has written and edited a number of books.

Oberleutnant, Eastern Front, 1944

This officer wears a fur-collared windcheater, a Luftwaffe field cap, service breeches and black leather and suede flying boots. An altimeter is carried on his belt.

ZEMKE'S
WOLFPACK

Hubert Zemke's 56th Group was the ace fighter unit of the US Eighth Air Force in World War II

Below: Dogfight in progress – Thunderbolts protect a bomber stream of B-17s, while a Bf 109 goes down in flames (inset).

TWENTY THOUSAND FEET above the North Sea, Lieutenant-Colonel David Schilling leaned forward in the cockpit of his P-47 Thunderbolt so that he could see down over the wing's leading edge. He watched the coastline of Hitler's *Festung Europa* (Fortress Europe) appear out of the blue haze; the Group was on schedule. Gently easing the 'stick' from side to side, Schilling induced a rocking movement of the fighter's wings, the signal for the other 36 red-nosed Thunderbolts of the first wave to spread out into battle formation. It was just past noon and 40 minutes flying time to the rendezvous with the leading formation of the B-17 Flying Fortress bomber column bound for Berlin. Two days before, the American bombers had made their first major assault on the enemy capital and had met fierce opposition. The bombing was poor and today, 8 March 1944, the bombers were returning to finish the job. Headquarters of the US Eighth Army Air Force anticipated the Luftwaffe appearing in strength again and had assigned their most successful fighter group, the 56th, to a position ahead of the B-17s when they penetrated deep into Germany. Command was not mistaken, for as Schilling, the group air executive (deputy commander), led his Thunderbolts along

Colonel, 56th Fighter Group, England 1943-44

Colonel Hubert Zemke was one of the outstanding fighter commanders of World War II. Besides being a brilliant combat pilot – scoring 17 air victories with the 56th – he was a thoughtful tactician and an inspiring leader of men. In this illustration Zemke has just returned from a mission over Germany and is kitted-out in flying overalls, carrying his seat-type parachute within the standard fighter-pilot harness. Alongside US goggles and inflatable life-vest he wears two items of British origin, a Type C flying helmet and Type F oxygen mask.

Below: A side view of a P-47M of 62nd Squadron, a late Mark of the Thunderbolt series – in contrast to the P-47D of First Lieutenant Frank Klibbe (below right). Main picture: The burst of flame on the starboard wing of an FW 190 signals the end of another defender of *Festung Europa* at the hands of the USAAF. 56th Fighter Group was made up of 61st, 62nd and 63rd Fighter Squadrons which together accounted for some 1000 enemy aircraft destroyed.

the bomber stream, ground control in England reported radio intercepts of German aircraft assembling in the area between Dummer and Steinhuder. Reaching the leading B-17s, the three squadrons of the 56th prepared to meet the inevitable German assault. This was not long in coming and the vapour trails of some 20 to 25 enemy aircraft were seen at around 30,000 feet, approaching the Fortresses.

'This is Yardstick, bogies at 5 o'clock high. Woodfire squadron follow me.' Schilling's command received, throttles were advanced as the Thunderbolts began a curving climb towards the oncoming vapour trails. But what the American pilots had not seen was the large 'gaggle' of enemy fighters flying below vapour-trail level. With advantages in surprise and altitude an FW 190 staffel launched an attack on Schilling's squadron, shooting down two P-47s on the initial pass. In an effort to evade them, the Thunderbolts pulled into tight defensive turns and a far-ranging air battle ensued. The radioed commands and warnings from the P-47 pilots locked in combat were heard by a second wave of 56th Group which had taken off 10 minutes after the first. Led by Lieutenant-Colonel Francis Gabreski, the 36 Thunderbolts of the second force were soon speeding to join the fight. After 15 minutes the Luftwaffe assault on the leading bombers was dispersed with the Americans gaining the upper hand. The 56th's mission was not only to escort the bombers, but to destroy enemy fighters, and to this end the Group had another ploy. As the German pilots made for airfields to refuel and rearm, so they were followed down by Thunderbolts and several unwary Bf 109 and FW 190 pilots were caught and shot down. Where airfields were seen, some 56th flights swept down in firing passes to shoot up aircraft on the ground. Three hours and 40 minutes after take-off most of the Group's Thunderbolts were back over their Halesworth base in Suffolk. Many of the aircraft had precious little fuel remaining, as full-throttle air fighting had consumed gasoline at a rate of around 300 gallons per hour.

Debriefing revealed claims of 30 enemy aircraft destroyed, a new record for a fighter group on one mission, and one which took the total of 56th Group's victories over the 300 mark. Individual scores on this day included two FW 190s and a Ju 88 downed by Captain Walker 'Bud' Mahurin, then leading Eighth AAF ace, while Captain Gerald Johnson and Lieutenant Robert Johnson each destroyed two Bf 109s. The day's battle had seen 56th Group take its heaviest losses– five P-47s (including one to flak) – as well as

its largest number of victories. Nevertheless, it was yet further confirmation of the Group's prowess, bolstering its standing as the most successful American fighter unit in the European theatre of operations.

Much of the achievement could be attributed to the 56th's commander, Colonel Hubert 'Hub' Zemke, through his aggressive leadership, considered tactics and emphasis on air discipline. The 56th gained this position not without some setbacks, however, particularly during the early days of its combat operations.

The 56th Fighter Group, together with its three component squadrons – the 61st, 62nd and 63rd Fighter Squadrons – was formed early in 1941 at Savannagh, Georgia, during the hasty pre-war expansion period of the US Army Air Corps. It remained under-manned and with only a handful of aircraft during its first year of existence until, in January 1942, the group was selected to be the first to be equipped with the new Republic Aviation Corporation high-altitude fighter, the P-47 Thunderbolt. Under the leadership of Colonel Zemke, teething troubles were sorted out, and by the end of 1942 – when orders for movement to the UK were received – the group's proficiency in the P-47 was high.

Despite the 56th's trouble-shooting in the USA, technical troubles still dogged the Thunderbolt, notably engine ignition interference with VHF radio reception. Correcting this so delayed the type's operational employment that the 56th was only finally equipped and ready for combat on 8 April 1943. While 56th Group pilots may have had more confidence in the P-47 than those in other units similarly equipped, their early combat experiences were the least creditable. A first encounter with the enemy resulted in two P-47s being shot down through poor tactics and control. In May the group made its first claim for an enemy shot down, only to discover that the victim was an RAF Spitfire (the pilot survived), while on 26 June the 56th was again severely trounced by the Luftwaffe when three P-47s went down and two others were so badly shot up as to be

written-off on return to England.

While the 56th had little success during the first four months of operations, with higher losses than victories, its pilots did, however, gain valuable experience. Moreover, Zemke's leadership began to have effect. His demand for strict air discipline was gradually acknowledged by even the wildest pilots. Zemke also instilled into his team an appreciation of tactics: he reasoned that success hung on exploiting the advantages of the P-47's performance and minimising its weaknesses. The aircraft was heavy, and had poor acceleration and rate-of-climb in comparison with its principal adversaries, the Bf 109 and FW 190. Nor was it a match for the enemy types in slow-speed turning fights. On the other hand, at altitudes above 25,000 feet, when the engine turbo-supercharger came into its own, the P-47 could out-run both enemy types in level flight and, providing speed was not allowed to drop below 360 km/h, also out-turn them. Further, because of its weight, the P-47 could easily dive away from both the Bf 109 and FW 190, using the momentum attained to 'zoom climb' back to high altitude. Thus the tenets of air fighting with the P-47 were to avoid climbing combats, only engage in turning fights at high speed, and use the advantage in diving speed to attack and escape.

Eight 0.5in Brownings unleashed over 100 rounds per second

The firepower of the P-47 was formidable; eight 0.5in Browning machine guns, from which a one-second burst unleashed over 100 rounds, sufficient to damage critically or destroy a German fighter. As the guns were wing mounted, fire converged at a set point and Zemke impressed on his pilots the importance of range estimation in obtaining a kill. Such assessment of how to use the Thunderbolt to maximum advantage was soon to pay rich dividends.

On 17 August 1943 the Eighth AAF launched its initial mission to bomb the ball-bearing plants at Schweinfurt. On its second support mission that day, the 56th found the returning B-17s, over Belgium, under attack by the Luftwaffe. Zemke positioned his P-47 squadrons above the bombers and as the Bf 109s

The Republic P-47 Thunderbolt was the largest and heaviest single-seat fighter in mass production to see service in World War II. Despite its size and a number of deficiencies in manoeuvrability, it was an exceptional warplane, highly capable when employed either as a high-altitude interceptor or as a ground-attack aircraft. The P-47 went through a whole series of Marks during the course of the war, incorporating improvements gained through technical development and combat experience. The P-47D was the standard Thunderbolt used by the 56th during the first year of operational employment. It was powered by a 2000hp Pratt and Whitney R-2800-21 engine, capable of a maximum speed of 450mph, with a ceiling of 42,000ft. Firepower was provided by eight 0.5in Browning machine guns. The Thunderbolt was an exceptionally resilient aircraft, capable of absorbing a tremendous level of punishment, and in the event of a crash its rugged structure frequently allowed the pilot to escape unharmed.

Some of the great aces of the 56th. Gerald Johnson in the cockpit (left) with the groundcrew of his plane 'In The Mood' (far left). Below, from left: Gabreski celebrates his 28th kill; 56th aces test the strength of the P-47; Robert Johnson rests his elbow over 25 victories; 'Bud' Mahurin clambers out of the cockpit, with 14 enemy aircraft to his credit – one of the 'wild men' of the 56th, he was to score seven more air victories.

and FW 190s turned in to make their attack runs, so he despatched his pilots down to intercept them. Some hard fighting ensued with the loss of three P-47s but the 56th returned to base with claims of 19 enemy aircraft destroyed, a record for an Eighth AAF group. Two days later Zemke was able to repeat these fruitful tactics, achieving 10 victories for only one loss. Further successes followed in September but the 56th really got into its stride during the following month.

Someone dubbed the 56th 'Zemke's Wolfpack' and the name stuck

The availability of auxiliary 'belly' fuel tanks, which provided an extra half to three-quarters of an hour endurance, allowed the P-47s to range further into Germany. On 5 November the 56th was credited with its 100th victory and had now firmly established itself as the most successful fighter group flying from England. On a mission to Emden at the end of that month, the group set yet another new record when 23 victories were claimed. In this fight Captain Bud Mahurin shot down three enemy aircraft and became the first Eighth AAF ace to take his total personal score into double figures – 11. Mahurin had been one of the 'cautioned' flyers in the 56th, incur-

ring Zemke's displeasure when he 'buzzed' and collided with a B-24 Liberator over England. The Liberator kept flying while Mahurin had to bail out from a tailless Thunderbolt. Other 56th pilots who had reached 'ace' status by late-November 1943 were David Schilling and Gerald Johnson with eight kills apiece, Zemke with seven, Robert Johnson and Walter Cook with six each, and Francis Gabreski with five. Someone dubbed the 56th 'Zemke's Wolf-pack', and the name stuck.

The winning streak continued in the following winter months with the group's victory score running into double figures on five occasions. By mid-March Robert Johnson had become leading Eighth AAF ace with 22 victories and other 56th pilots were close to this total. While the ratio of victories to losses was extremely good there were, inevitably, some re-verses, mostly as a result of ground strafing attacks on airfields when German light flak took its toll. To encourage the destruction of enemy aircraft on the ground, Eighth AAF rated these equal to victories in the air. On 27 March the group lost two of its leading aces: Gerald Johnson went down to ground fire while strafing, but survived as a POW, and Bud Mahurin's aircraft was hit by return fire from a Dornier bomber he was attacking. Mahurin evaded capture and later returned to England with the help of the French Resistance.

In April the 56th moved to Boxted, Essex, vacating Halesworth for a bomber group to move in. This coincided with the general decline of the Luftwaffe fighter force at the hands of American long-range fighters, and thereafter the rate of the group's victor-ies declined. Another factor which contributed to the fall-off in kills was that several Eighth AAF fighter groups were now equipped with the P-51 Mustang which had a far better endurance than the P-47. The Mustang groups could fly all the way with the bom-bers to distant targets, whereas the Thunderbolts were limited to a maximum radius of action of 720km, and that only when encumbered with two wing-carried drop tanks. In the spring of 1944 it was the Mustang units that usually got into the big air fights.

Nevertheless, the enterprising Zemke devised a plan to improve the 56th's chances of meeting the enemy. His plan involved the group flying to a predetermined point over Germany in advance of a bomber mission, and then a number of aircraft would fan out over 180 degrees in search of the enemy. If contact was made by one of these searching flights it could radio for assistance to a stronger force of P-47s which would be centrally placed and ready to go in. On 12 May 1944, when Eighth AAF opened its campaign against the German oil industry, the 'Zemke Fan' was put into practice with startling results. In fact, the group had more action than it could comfortably deal with and Zemke had a nar-row escape himself when his flight was 'bounced'. In some hard fighting three P-47s were lost, but on return to Boxted the group's tally of victories added up to 18, taking the cumulative total past 400.

In May Robert Johnson had taken his personal score to 28 air victories, a total which was equalled in July by Francis 'Gabby' Gabreski, and stood as the highest individual score figure for US fighter pilots in Europe for the whole war. Having completed his tour of duty, Johnson returned to the USA. Gabreski was not so fortunate, having to crash-land his aircraft while ground strafing and eventually joining other

GABRESKI AND JOHNSON

Of the many fighter aces produced by the 56th Fighter Group, the two leading scorers were Francis Gabreski and Robert Johnson, both credited with 28 aerial victories. Gabreski was the son of Polish immigrants to America, and on his arrival in England in January 1943 with the 56th he was assigned to 315 Squadron RAF (Polish) and flew 13 operational sorties in Spitfires. In February he returned to the 56th as a flight leader in the 61st Fighter Squadron. His first victory was an FW 190 shot down over France in August 1943 and during the next 11 months another 27 German aircraft fell to his guns. Shot down over Germany on 20 July 1944, he attempted to evade capture, but after five days on the run he was caught and spent the rest of the war in a POW camp. After the war he continued to serve as a fighter commander and scored 6½ air victories in the Korean War. Robert Johnson saw service in both 61st and 62nd Fighter Squadrons. He flew a total of 91 combat missions, his victories scored between June 1943 and May 1944, before being returned to the United States. An excellent pilot and fighter tactician, Johnson was able to exploit the fighting qualities of the P-47 to the full against his German opponents.

(The insignia of the US Eighth AAF is shown above)

former 56th flyers in a German POW camp. The opportunities for high personal scores while flying P-47s were gone by the summer of 1944, although Fred Christensen achieved 22 victories before finishing his tour. The last six of these were transports he surprised in a traffic pattern. With D-Day and the subsequent Allied ground offensive in France and the Low Countries, the 56th found itself increasingly assigned to ground-attack missions to which the rugged Thunderbolt was better suited than the Mustang with its vulnerable liquid-cooled engine.

In August 1944, Zemke moved to take over another group about to convert to P-51s, but eventually he too was to end up as a POW. The effervescent David Schilling was given command of the 56th which was now largely manned by replacement pilots, most of the originals who had survived their tours having gone home. Supporting the airborne landings at Arnhem in September, the 56th was to experience its most disastrous mission when it was given the dangerous job of 'flak busting' – locating and strafing light anti-aircraft batteries. Poor visibility helped conceal the quarry but not the hunter, with the result that 16 P-47s failed to return to Boxted.

During a period of bad weather in mid-December 1944, the Germans launched a major counter-offensive in the Ardennes area. When the weather improved, this campaign was supported by the Luftwaffe in strength, providing the 56th with its most distinguished action. On 23 December Schilling led 56 P-47s on a sweep and patrol in the Bonn area of Germany. Under microwave early warning radar control, the Wolfpack was vectored towards an estimated 250 FW 190s and Bf 109s, stacked in several formations at a lower altitude. With height advantage, Schilling ordered attacks which resulted in massive claims of 37 of the enemy shot down against a loss of three. Schilling distinguished himself personally by destroying three Bf 109s and two FW 190s in the melée which raised his total individual score to 22.

For most of 1945 the 56th saw only limited action, partly because of technical problems with the new P-47M model, which were not rectified until the end of March. During the last few weeks of the war,

Above: Thunderbolts of the 56th fly over England, heading for Germany. American fighters had two main functions: firstly, to protect the bombers (B-17s, below) and secondly to secure overall air superiority by destroying the Luftwaffe in the air.

enemy aircraft were rarely seen in the air and the group's last two air victories, Me 262 jet aircraft, were claimed on 7 April. On 13 April the group carried out its most successful strafing attack when, at Eggebek airfield near Hamburg, 90 Luftwaffe aircraft were shot up and destroyed – although by this time the Germans probably had little or no fuel available at this airfield for flying. The last mission of the 56th was flown on 21 April, an uneventful sweep ahead of bombers in the Munich area.

The totals of enemy aircraft destroyed by US fighter groups in Europe were amended after the cessation of hostilities when former POW pilots were available for interrogation. Overall, the 56th had credits of just over 1000 destroyed, in the air and on the ground; in the final analysis a figure slightly less than the total for the 4th Group. However, in air fighting the 56th stood unchallenged, its 675 con-

firmed victories being far ahead of the group in second position. Further, it had by far and away the best victory-to-loss ratio, with only 128 aircraft missing in action (the 4th Group had 241 missing). Not only were the two top ranking US aces in the European theatre (Gabreski and Johnson) 56th pilots, but so were six of the top ten. No less than 18 awards of the Distinguished Service Cross, the second highest US honour for valour, were awarded to 56th Group pilots.

The kill figures attributed to the 56th Fighter Group were a measure of its achievement in the destruction of the German Air Force, a feat of arms which ensured that the Allies had air superiority over Europe during the last year of the war – a vital factor in the overall Allied victory against Nazi Germany.

THE AUTHOR Simon Clay is a leading authority on the history of the US Air Force in World War II and has written numerous books on the subject. He also advises and contributes to television documentaries on aviation topics.

Equipped with P-51 Mustangs, the 354th Fighter Group despatched the Luftwaffe with unrivalled tenacity

'BANDITS 3 O'CLOCK level, 30 plus ME one tens.' It was the kind of chilling message Major Allison Brooks had been expecting to come crackling out of his headphones. He looked out over the starboard wing and the sight that greeted him confirmed his worst fears; about 30 or 40 Messerschmitt Bf 110 twin-engine fighters were ranging round the formation of B-17 Flying Fortresses he was leading, preparing to attack. Brooks was already aware that their mission – to strike important enemy aircraft manufacturing facilities in north central Germany – was not going as planned. The weather front, that had to be crossed to reach clear skies forecast for the target areas, was found to be near 25,000ft, far higher than predicted. This obstacle was disrupting the formations to such a degree that the US Eighth Army Air Force had sent out a recall signal. By this time, however, the leading 1st Division was within 100 miles of Oschersleben, and was allowed to continue in the hope that it would be able to reach the target before the weather closed in. What Brooks did not know was that of the two P-38 Lightning and single P-51 Mustang fighter groups assigned to give target area support, only a few of the P-38s and the 49 P-51s had been able to clear the cloud over Germany.

Bottom: Sitting astride drop tanks, groundcrew watch a P-51 Mustang coming in to land at Boxted. Below: Major James Howard (left) was a fighter ace of extraordinary ability. He is seen here on the wing of his Mustang, talking to a colleague who is painting yet another confirmed kill on the fuselage.

Calls for fighter assistance had so far gone unanswered and now, as Brooks and his 401st Bomb Group prepared to face the enemy attack, the situation looked critical. Brooks knew that armed with rocket projectiles, the Bf 110s would be able to launch an assault from well outside the range of the B-17s' defensive 0.5in machine guns. The Forts would be sitting ducks.

As the enemy began its attack, a crew member exclaimed, 'Hey, look at him!' Major Brooks peered up through the cabin plexiglass in time to see one of the new long-range P-51 Mustangs manoeuvring to attack a Messerschmitt. The bombers' radio calls had been answered; but where were the other escort fighters? Only this lone Mustang could be seen in the vicinity of the Fortress formations.

MUSTANG PIONEERS

354TH FIGHTER GROUP

The 354th Fighter Group was activated in November 1942, forming and training at bases on the west coast of America for 10 months before being despatched overseas. Composed of three squadrons, the 353rd, 355th and 356th, the group was part of the Ninth Army Air Force – a purely tactical organisation tasked to support land forces participating in the cross-channel invasion.

Upon arrival in southern England, pilots were sent to Greenham Common and Membury where they began their conversion training on Mustang P-51As, borrowed from a USAAF reconnaissance unit. When the first production batch of P-51Bs arrived, they were allocated to the Ninth Army Air Force. However, the Eighth Army Air Force, based in England, was in desperate need of a long-range fighter to save its ailing bombing offensive. The controversy which raged between the two air forces was eventually settled by letting VIII Fighter Command have control of P-51 units assigned to the Ninth. Until further Mustangs arrived in England, the 354th Fighter Group was to escort the bombers of the Eighth Army Air Force on long-range missions over Germany.

As the success of the Normandy landings became evident, the 354th moved to a series of landing strips in France. From here the group was deployed in a multitude of roles in addition to their escort duties: ground strafing in advance of land forces; fighter bomber missions on enemy targets; and air superiority patrols over the front lines.

Intermittently, as the battle raged, one of Brooks' gunners would report the Mustang's presence; above, below and to the side, attacking enemy fighters and driving them off. This American fighter pilot could not deflect every enemy assault on the bombers, but his timely arrival appeared to have scattered the vulnerable Bf 110s. For around half an hour, while the 401st and the other 50 B-17s in the three combat wings bombed their target, and then withdrew, the solitary P-51 was present.

On return to their home bases, the B-17 crews were full of praise for the pilot who had put up such a magnificent fight on their behalf – 'a one man air force' as they called him. The combat wing led by the 401st had sustained heavy losses, but Brooks and its other leaders were emphatic that, but for the endeavours of the single Mustang, many more B-17s would have gone down. 'It was a case of one lone American against what seemed to be the entire Luftwaffe,' Brooks commented. 'For sheer determination and guts it was the greatest exhibition I've ever seen. They can't give that boy a big enough reward.'

Brooks' opinion was shared by higher authority, and the pilot's heroic action resulted in the only award of the Congressional Medal of Honor to a fighter pilot in the European Theatre of Operations. The recipient was Major James H. Howard, commander of the 356th Fighter Squadron of the 354th Fighter Group, the first and, at that time, the only organisation equipped with the long-range P-51B Mustang. The development and deployment of this aircraft would save the American daylight bombing campaign, and

The 353rd Squadron of the 354th attained a victory tally unsurpassed by any other squadron in the USAAF. Top left: Pilots of the 353rd next to one of their beloved charges, the P-51B Mustang. Captain Don Beerbower (wearing a white flying scarf) is flanked by the squadron leader, Captain Wallace Emmer (left), and Captain Jack Bradley (right). Top right: All systems go for Major Glenn Eagleston as he completes a final instrument check. Above: 'Time out' for the bomber crews of the 401st to admire one of their guardian angels – a P-51B Mustang. During the B-17s' long-range missions over Germany, these remarkable fighters helped to keep the Luftwaffe at bay.

play an unprecedented role in the achievement of air supremacy over Germany.

On the eventful Oschersleben mission of 11 January 1944, Howard had been leading his squadron when a mass of Bf 110s were spotted preparing to attack the B-17s. He ordered an interception, but in the mêlée that followed, he became separated from the rest of his squadron. Climbing back towards the Fortresses, Howard called over the radio for the rest of his squadron to join him, but bad visibility prevented the other P-51 pilots from locating the particular bomber formation that their leader was defending. Howard had shot down a Bf 110 in his first fight and, during the next half-hour, while he conducted his vigil over the bombers, he had five further encounters at altitudes ranging between 21,000 and 15,000ft, involving both twin and single-engine enemy aircraft. Many of his interceptions were, in fact, feints, because during his second combat two of the Mustang's four guns jammed. When Howard fired at a third Messerschmitt, another gun failed and from then on he had only one functioning weapon, until finally he ran out of ammunition.

Initially, the primary role of the 354th Fighter Group, under the control of VIII Fighter Command, was to escort the bombers of the Eighth Army Air Force to their targets. Based at Boxted, near Colchester, pilots were introduced to their new charges – the P-51B Mustang. Following three weeks of intensive training, the 354th was alerted for its first mission, an introductory sweep over Belgium on 1 December 1943. The group was led by Colonel Don Blakeslee, an ex-RAF Eagle Squadron pilot with considerable experience flying Merlin-powered

Left: Mustangs from the 354th Fighter Group scramble from their base at Boxted. In 1956 the P-51s were replaced by F-100 Sabres and the group was designated the 354th Tactical Wing. In 1978 the wing was equipped with A-10 tank-busters, and now operates from Myrtle Beach, South Carolina.

aircraft in operations over Europe. Since all but a few of the 354th's pilots were 'green' second lieutenants straight out of flying school, their experience level was raised by assigning to the group a handful of pilots with Spitfire experience. Even so, the nature of the operation that the 354th was about to undertake represented a new experience for all the pilots. Never before had a single-engine fighter possessed such long-range capability.

The 354th's second mission was also the group's first bomber escort, albeit one of comparatively short range. On 11 December, again under the eye of Blakeslee, the P-51Bs began to push out over hostile territory, providing bomber support over Emden. Enemy aircraft were encountered for the first time during this operation, and the 354th lost one pilot, whose aircraft suffered engine trouble and failed to return to base. Two days later, the group accompanied their charges 500 miles to Kiel – the longest mission ever before undertaken by single-engine fighters. The long 500-700 mile flights put a heavy strain on the pilots. Cooped up in a cockpit for up to seven hours, and flying in the dismal weather conditions of northwest Europe, they faced the prospect of severe physical and mental fatigue. One of the major complaints heard from pilots returning from these missions was sore buttocks, and one squadron in the group, the 356th, christened itself the 'Red Ass Squadron' and adopted a red donkey motif.

Above: Two RAF pilots flying with the group inspect the deadly armament of a P-51B. Right: Mechanics perform routine maintenance on one of the 'Mighty Mustangs'.

The 354th waded into several formations of enemy fighters, mainly twin-engine Bf 110s

On 16 December, en route to Bremen, Lieutenant Charles Gumm of the 355th Squadron made the group's first confirmed kill. On the next raid to Bremen, four rocket-carrying Bf 110s were destroyed as the 354th got into its stride. Although on the balance sheet losses still exceeded claims, many of these were due to mechanical and allied problems rather than enemy action. The teething troubles of the Mustang were numerous, and primarily the result of the low temperatures experienced at high altitudes. Of particular concern were the fluid leaks caused by perished seals, and the frosting of cockpit glazing which impaired visibility. In addition, until modifications could be made, pilots were forced to maintain level flight whilst loosing off machine-gun fire, as the Brownings tended to jam when the aircraft was put through a tight turn.

On 5 January, near Kiel, the 354th waded into several formations of enemy fighters, mainly twin-engine Bf 110s and, with the enemy undoubtedly stunned to see single-engine fighters so far from home, arrived back at base with 18 kills and no losses.

Six days later at Oschersleben, ranged against superior numbers, the group claimed 15 kills, again without loss. Another month was to pass before a second P-51 group could be brought into operation, and meanwhile the 354th continued to shoulder the brunt of the escort duties on the long bomber missions.

The P-47 Thunderbolts were still the USAAF's most numerous aircraft, a situation which proved an added hazard for the 354th. Many P-47 pilots persisted in the belief that a single-engine fighter with square cut wings was a Bf 109E. As a result, there were many instances of Mustangs being 'bounced' by Thunderbolts. One such incident, on 10 February, nearly caused the death of Lieutenant Glenn Eagles-

ton. Managing to nurse his badly shot-up P-51 back to home base, Eagleston was finally forced to bale out of his crippled plane – parachuting to safety. On the same day, the group ran up eight kills for the loss of two aircraft. Two enemy fighters were credited to Colonel Martin, the group CO, making him the second man in the group behind Jim Howard to achieve ace status. On 11 February, while leading a mission to Frankfurt, Martin took on a Bf 109 in a head-on attack. Neither pilot would give an inch and, in the ensuing collision, both aircraft went down. Despite a badly injured leg, Martin managed to extricate himself from the falling wreckage and open his parachute, his safe descent eventually leading to POW confinement. During the dogfight that continued to rage overhead the 354th claimed 14 of the enemy, with Captains Jack Bradley and Richard Turner reaching ace status. With the loss of Colonel Martin, Howard took over command of the group and was promoted to Lieutenant Colonel, while Richard Turner took his place as CO of the 356th Squadron.

There was no let-up in the action during March

Above: A converted P-51, used by the USAAF for reconnaissance operations over Europe. Two K-24 cameras would have been mounted in the fuselage, and the 'Malcolm' hood afforded the pilot greater visibility. Right: The new Merlin V liquid-cooled engine gave the Mustang a range double that of any other single-engine fighter.

DISTINGUISHED SERVICE

The North American P-51 Mustang is generally acknowledged as the best all-round fighter of World War II. Built to RAF specifications for a photo-reconnaissance and ground-attack role, the Mustang made its first production flight on 16 April 1941. The US air planners, recognising its potential as a long-range fighter, made several modifications designed to improve the aircraft's performance. The P-51A's Allison engine was replaced with a Packhard-built Merlin. The result of this conversion was the P-51B, with high-altitude capability and a top speed boosted to 441mph. Streamlined wing racks increased range by allowing the carriage of drop-tanks containing 224 gallons of fuel. Later, a one-piece perspex hood was fitted to the cockpit allowing greater visibility. Fins were also modified to improve directional stability. Armament comprised six 0.5in Browning machine guns and up to 2000lb of bombs, or 10 5in rockets. Capable of climbing to 20,000ft in seven minutes, the Mustang's upper ceiling was 41,900ft. As the P-51B, C and D the Mustang saw action in Europe and Southeast Asia; on 7 April 1945 it made the first land-based fighter strikes against Tokyo. Over 15,000 Mustangs were built, and of the 19,000 enemy aircraft destroyed, the P-51 claimed 8,000. During the Korean war the P-51D, with underwing attachments for bombs and rockets, was used for low-level strafing among Korea's hills and twisting valleys. Although slower than the enemy jets, the Mustang's greater manoeuvrability was a distinct advantage. One of the P-51s even managed to destroy a North Korean MiG-15. The Mustang continued in US service until being replaced in 1957 by the F-86 Sabre.

and April, when Captain Don Beerbower became the group's leading ace and the 354th victory total passed the 200 mark. In mid-April the Ninth Air Force decided that Colonel James Howard should be taken off operations and his expertise used at headquarters. Colonel George Bickell, at one time commanding officer of the 353rd Squadron, took over command of the 354th, remaining in that position until the end of hostilities.

On 17 April the group reluctantly moved to a makeshift airstrip at Lashenden in Kent. There was little doubt among personnel that they were being prepared for the expected cross-channel invasion, and the 354th fully expected to take on a tactical role in support of the land forces. Although the group had flown its first ground attack mission in late March – dropping bombs from the Mustangs' wing racks on the airfield at Creil, near Paris – for the most part the 354th continued to fly long-range escort missions in support of Eighth Army Air Force heavy bombers. From mid-May, however, the number of missions to Germany declined and operations became increasingly centred over France.

During the ground forces' break-out at St Lô, a dozen Mustangs of the 353rd took on over 40 Bf 109s

After D-day, patrols over the battle area proved a frequent and boring chore in comparison to the action-filled days earlier in the year. Only 11 days after the Allies set foot in Normandy, the 354th began to use a hastily constructed landing strip at Criqueville, less than 10 miles from the front line. The move was spread over three weeks with the rear elements remaining at Lashenden until the beginning of July. During their time among the Kent orchards, some engineers in the group had converted one of the older Mustangs into a two-seater. By removing the radio equipment and auxiliary fuel tank behind the pilot, they created a second cockpit. This aircraft was to prove unexpectedly useful when, on 4 July, General Eisenhower, the Supreme Allied Commander, used it – with Major General Pete Quesada as his pilot – to view the confused battle situation around Cherbourg. Following this flight a wit painted 'The Stars Look Down' as a nickname on the P-51.

Patrols, fighter-bombing and ground strafing operations over the battle area occupied the 354th during the summer months, and only occasionally did the group have a chance to get into an air fight. When such an opportunity arose, its 353rd Squadron frequently stole the battle honours, building a total of victories far in excess of the other two squadrons. During the ground forces' break-out at St Lô, a dozen Mustangs of the 353rd took on over 40 Bf 109s that were intent on disrupting American air support for its armies. In a fierce low-altitude engagement, 10 of the enemy were despatched without loss. The squadron leader, Captain Wallace Emmer, was credited with three of these victories. On other occasions, however, the squadron did suffer losses, notably Captain Don Beerbower, at the time the Group's leading ace with more than 15 victories.

For their next assignment the 354th was tasked to work with General George Patton's Third Army and during early August, in the wake of Patton's lightning advance through northwest France, they were moved to the captured Luftwaffe base airfield at Gael in Brittany. While supporting Patton's drive, the group experienced its most successful day of air

Above: The tall, unassuming figure of Lieutenant-Colonel James Howard (left). Having flown Curtiss P-40s against the Japanese, his experience was a vital asset to the 354th Fighter Group. Following Howard's transfer to headquarters, Major George Bickell (right of picture) was given command of the group.

combat. On 25 August, in the course of six, separate fighter sweeps over the Beauvais area, a total of 37 Bf 109s and Fw 190s were shot down, and several more destroyed by ground strafing. On 9 September the group completed its 500th combat mission. Whereas it had taken six months to complete the first 100 missions, the next 400 had been flown in just three months, illustrating the pace of operations over northern France.

To keep up with the advancing ground forces, in September the 354th left their pleasant surroundings in Brittany and moved east, to an advanced landing ground at Orconte, near St Dizier. In early November the Marne river flooded to such an exent that the Mustangs temporarily moved to another airfield at St Dizier itself. Morale took a heavy blow later that month when, because of a shortage of P-51s in the Eighth and Fifteenth Army Air Forces, the 354th was forced to part with its beloved charges in return for P-47 Thunderbolts. Although the 'Thunderbuckets' were better suited to the ground attack role which had now become the 354th's principal mission, the change provoked such a storm of protest that the group was assured of a return to Mustangs once

supplies improved. Few enemy aircraft were shot down while flying the heavy P-47, but in February, the arrival of 36 P-51Ds caused great excitement among the pilots. Once again, the 354th could live up to its reputation as the 'Pioneer Mustang Group'.

Reunited with the P-51 Mustang and operating from Rosières-en-Haye, north of Toul, the group started to run up large claims of enemy aircraft. On 1 April the 354th moved to Ober Olm in Germany. Frequently assigned air superiority patrols over the front lines, there was ample opportunity to engage the Luftwaffe and, during the last two months of hostilites, 157 aircraft were shot down. Most of these were Bf 109 and Fw 190 fighters and fighter bombers, but several Me 262 jets also fell to the 354th.

By VE-day, 8 May 1945, the 354th Fighter Group had acquired a victory tally that was unequalled by any other fighter group in the USAAF. The 354th – Pioneer Mustang Group – had established itself in the annals of American air force history.

THE AUTHOR Simon Clay is a leading authority on the history of the US Army Air Forces in World War II and has written numerous books on the subject.

Top left: A Mustang from the 354th Fighter Group despatches a Bf 110 which plummets to the ground in a ball of flame. Above: Lieutenant Robert Stephens of 355 Squadron, a fighter ace with 13 victories. Below: The indefatigable Mustangs were christened 'little friends' by the hard-pressed bomber crews.

COMBAT HONOURS OF THE 354TH FIGHTER GROUP

Equipped with the Mustang P-51, one of the truly great aircraft of all time, the tenacious pilots of the 354th Fighter Group relished their combat duties. The group's roll-call of battle honours reflects their eagerness to do battle with the Luftwaffe; 39 air aces were credited to the group, representing over half of the Ninth Army Air Force total. Leading the hunt for enemy kills was Major Glenn Eagleston with 18½ confirmed victories. Colonel Bradley, who took command of the group at the end of the war, followed closely behind with a score of 15. All but one of the pilots in the Ninth Army Air Force with a score in double figures, flew with the 354th Fighter Group. By the end of the war, the 354th had claimed 701 enemy aircraft destroyed. Although this figure was subsequently revised, the success of the 'Pioneer Mustang Group' was unparalleled. Its 353rd Squadron was credited with 290 kills –

higher than any other squadron in the USAAF.

The complete record of destruction wrought by the 354th during hostilities reads as follows: 1543 military vehicles destroyed and 691 damaged; 96 armoured vehicles destroyed and 54 damaged; 532 locomotives destroyed and 52 damaged; 1465 rail wagons and coaches destroyed and 3817 damaged; 26 bridges destroyed and 29 damaged; 75 gun emplacements silenced and 37 damaged; 11 ammunition stores destroyed and four damaged; 13 aircraft hangars destroyed and 24 damaged; 623 strategic buildings destroyed and 211 damaged; 230 rail lines cut; 69 roads obstructed; 18 marshalling yards and nine airfields attacked. In achieving this success 27,052 sorties were flown, but not without loss. From the group's first mission on 1 December 1943, to the end of the war, 187 aircraft went missing in action and 92 pilots were killed in combat duty. A further nine pilots were killed in flying accidents.

Formed as a counter to the 'Fokker scourge' of the winter of 1915, the French Groupe de Chasse No.12 – the Storks – was to include some of the greatest air aces of World War I

IN THE HOUR before dawn on 7 August 1916, three Nieuport XVII scouts of the French air service took off from a simple grass airstrip, the first aircraft aloft on the dawn patrol. The Battle of the Somme was now in full swing and the aircraft of both sides were fully committed to providing aerial reconnaissance for the ground forces. In addition, the fledgling aviation branches were exploring a new role – direct attack upon the enemy, whether in the air or on the ground. The three French aircraft were heavily laden with ammunition in preparation for a ground-attack sortie.

This was no ordinary patrol, however. An examination of the Nieuports revealed a stork insignia painted onto the fuselages, the emblem of France's elite fighter group, Groupe de Chasse No.12 – les Cigognes (the Storks). More than this, the three Nieuport pilots were top aces in the French air service. Leading the patrol was Lieutenant Alfred Heurtaux, commander of Escadrille N. No.3 (his final score, 21 confirmed kills), while flying alongside him were Lieutenants René Dorme (23 kills) and Georges Guynemer (53 kills).

Their target was a German encampment just behind the opposing front lines. Flying at tree-top level, the trio approached the enemy position unobserved. The single 0.303in Vickers machine guns mounted on each aircraft were then cocked and, following a wave from Heurtaux, the Frenchmen opened fire. Reveille had just been blown and the half-awake Germans were caught completely unawares. 'The Boches,' recalled Heurtaux, 'ran widely in all directions like a swarm of fear-crazed ants.' The Nieuports swept up and down the encampment, raking all that moved with accurate bursts of machine-gun fire. An attempt by the Germans to set up their machine guns was dealt with ruthlessly; the dead and wounded were left slumped over their broken weapons.

The German encampment wrecked, the Nieuports set off to find new targets. A road full of trucks was raked from end to end before one of the pilots spotted a stationary troop train in the distance. Packed with soldiers, it was a virtual sitting duck. The French aces flew up and down the length of the train, pumping it with the remainder of their ammunition. They flew so low that the pilots could see each other's aircraft through the windows of the coaches. Ammunition expended, the Nieuports turned for home, another successful mission completed.

Exploits of this nature were commonplace for the Storks as they had been created from the outset as a

Rapidly earning a reputation as the elite fighter group of the French air service, the Storks were able to recruit a high proportion of the nation's top aviators. Among them were (from right) Lieutenant Alfred Hertaux, Lieutenant René Dorme and Captain Felix Brocard, the commander of the group. Above right: Captain Georges Guynemer, France's most popular air ace of the war, describes the advantages of his prototype-model Spad S-VII to General Franchet d'Esperey on 11 June 1917. He was awarded the Croix d'Officer de la Legion d'Honneur on this day. Far right: Pilots of the Storks' Escadrille N. No.3, with Georges Guynemer third from left.

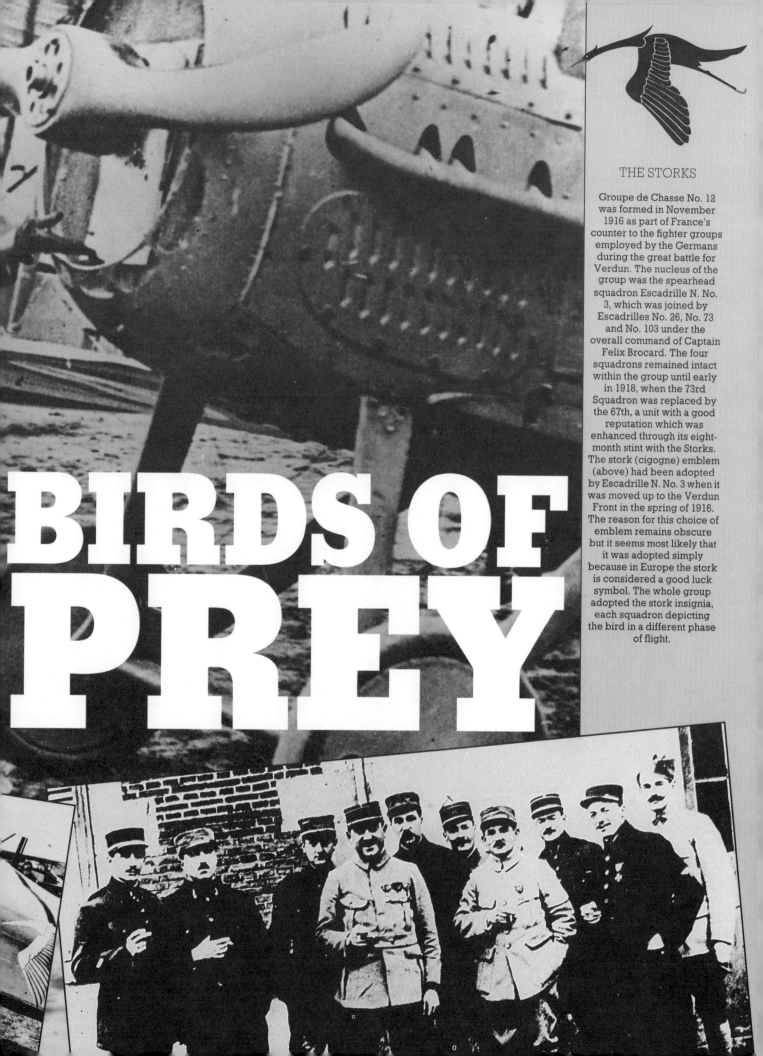

BIRDS OF PREY

Lieutenant Deullin, Escadrille N. No.3, Groupe de Chasse No.12, France 1916

Lieutenant Deullin is wearing the uniform of the French Aviation Militaire, incorporating a horizon blue tunic and dark blue breeches. His dark blue kepi bears the two gold bars of a lieutenant, and these are repeated in chevron form on his sleeves. His tunic bears the stork insignia of Groupe de Chasse No.12 with the ribbons of two decorations, and the pilot's badge of the French air service is on his right breast. The uniform is completed by the distinctive high laced leather boots of Aviation Militaire aircrew.

Groupe de Chasse No. 12
The Western Front, 1916-1918

Formed to take on the cream of the German air arm over the Western Front during World War I, the ranks of Groupe de Chasse No. 12 were filled with some of the finest French aces. In air combat they proved to be deadly opponents.

Key
— Front line, June 1916
--- Armistice Line, November 1918
✈ Major Stork bases

Ostend
Nieuport
Dunkirk
Bruges
Ghent
Schelde
St Pol
Ypres
Lys
Messines
BELGIUM
Brussels
Tournai
Lille
Mons
Meuse
Vimy
Douai
Maubeuge
Arras
Cambrai
Le Cateau
Somme
Albert
Peronne
Amiens
St Quentin
Mésières
Sedan
Longwy
Metz
Laon
FRANCE
Fismes
GERMANY
Oise
Aisne
Vesle
Verdun
Marne
Rheims
Epernay
Meaux
Château-Thierry
Noblette
Nancy
Paris
Châlons

CAPTAIN GEORGES GUYNEMER

Repeatedly rejected for military service through frail health, George Guynemer went on to become the best-loved of France's fighter aces, shooting down 53 enemy aircraft. Born in Compiègne in 1894, he managed to gain entrance to the military as an apprentice aircraft mechanic and, once in, he successfully persuaded his commanding officer to let him train as a pilot. After gaining his wings he was posted to Escadrille M.S. No.3 in June 1915, whose inspired commander, Felix Brocard, taught him the basic elements of combat flying. He gained his first victory within a month of his arrival at the front and for the remainder of the year gained combat experience under the guidance of the unit's veteran pilots. After converting to Nieuports, Guynemer's tally began to rise rapidly, and during the battles of Verdun and the Somme, he shot down 21 enemy aircraft, bringing his score to 29 victories by the end of 1916. By now he was France's top-scoring ace and a war-weary public's demand for national heroes turned Guynemer into an overnight sensation. His pale good looks and easy charm, combined with his aerial prowess, guaranteed him universal popularity. During 1917 his score continued to rise but a number of near-fatal crashes and the weight of the public's expectations bore down heavily on him. Despite failing health, Guynemer refused to take a rest from active service, and shortly after assuming command of his squadron, he set off on a morning patrol on 11 September, never to be seen again. His death was an occasion for national mourning and, although his final tally of 53 victories was overtaken by Captain René Fonck, he remained France's favourite ace.

fighting elite. Their formation had been a response to the air superiority gained by the Germans during the great assault against Verdun in the spring of 1916. The Germans had stolen a lead over the Allies with their specialised fighter units equipped with the then devastating Fokker monoplane. Having attained aerial control over Verdun, the Germans denied the French the aerial intelligence so vital in the long-range artillery duels that characterised this battle. In desperation, the French copied the German lead to form dedicated fighter groups (groupes de chasse), their sole purpose being to find, engage and destroy the enemy. Luckily for the French, improved versions of the Nieuport biplane (superior to the Fokker monoplane) were used to equip these new units, so that by the middle of 1916 the balance was swinging in favour of the Allies.

The success of the new fighter units led to the formation of Groupe de Chasse No.12. Its commander, Felix Brocard, was determined that his squadrons would be the best and he immediately set about 'poaching' top combat fliers from other units. The reputation of Escadrille N. No.3 was normally sufficient to attract ambitious young pilots, following an invitation from Brocard. Protests from the commanding officers of those units about to lose their best fliers counted for little, and Brocard usually got his men. To balance the influx of new pilots, the timid, incompetent or just mediocre found themselves transferred out.

Part of the appeal of the Storks lay outside the strict confines of combat glory; life in the unit was lived at a furious pace. Grants and other payments from aviation and armament companies (including endorsement fees and even straight bribes) provided the necessary cash for hard living. The French people idolised the aces and when in public they were treated as celebrities. Society hostesses would despatch their chauffeur-driven limousines to the airfields, so that when a squadron returned from an afternoon mission certain favourites could be

whisked back to Paris for a night's entertainment. Their existence a far cry from the misery of the trenches, the Stork pilots lived in a schizophrenic world of short flashes of aerial combat of the utmost violence alternating with spells of comfort well behind the lines.

The fêting of the Storks did not make them soft, however, and they kept up a fearsome level of aggression against the Germans. Between 19 March and 19 August 1916, 36 aircraft and three balloons were shot down and 36 other badly damaged aircraft were forced to land.

From their privileged position as the air service's top unit, the Stork pilots were able to assess the new Spad S-VII fighter. Two machines went to Heurtaux and Guynemer for trials during September 1916, and although less manoeuvrable than the Nieuport, the Spad S-VII was superior in all other aspects. Accordingly, a replacement order was issued and by February 1917 the whole group had been equipped with the Spad S-VII. It suited the veterans of the renamed Escadrille Spa. No.3 who, in the six months after the aircraft's introduction, accounted for more than 200 enemy aircraft – an extraordinary record never bettered during World War I.

Five or six visits were usually sufficient to bring the Germans out from their trenches and dug-outs

A fighter pilot is by his very nature an individualist and the Storks had a full quota of colourful characters. One such was Lieutenant H. Noel de Rochemont of Escadrille Spa. No.26, who possessed a particularly black sense of humour. One of his favourite ploys during quiet periods was to dive down on a German position, and instead of opening fire, drop a provocative note that promised the holder the charms of a renowned beauty, if only he would meet her in Paris that night. This would be followed up several times by further messages and even erotic photographs which could not fail to intrigue the men below, trench-bound and far from such comforts. Five or six visits were usually sufficient to bring the Germans out from their trenches and dug-outs, waving to the pilot above. Now in a completely vulnerable position, the Germans were easy meat for Rochemont, who would then casually mow them down with accurate machine-gun fire.

Rochemont was a cunning fighter in air-to-air

Above left: Georges Guynemer (on left) with his mechanic and the Morane-Saulnier L monoplane in which he gained his first kill. Above: Guynemer tries the controls of another type of fast machine while fellow officers look on. Above right: Guynemer's prototype Spad S-VII 'Vieux Charles' with stork on the fuselage.

battles as well, but his career as an up-and-coming ace was cut short on 15 September 1916 when his legs were badly shattered by German machine-gun fire. Crashing behind enemy lines, he later died on the operating table as surgeons were attempting to amputate his smashed limbs.

No matter how good the pilot was, life expectancy was always short in the brutal world of dogfights over the Western Front. Few fliers survived the war unscathed. One of the more 'fortunate' aces was the commander of Spa. No.3, Alfred Heurtaux, who made his last patrol on 3 September 1917. While testing one of the latest Spad-XIIIs, he spotted a slow-moving German two-seater below him, and although his aircraft was not battle-prepared, he could not resist the challenge and swooped down for the kill. Unfortunately for Heurtaux, his guns failed to fire properly and during his flying pass the German back-seat gunner caught the Spad with a few-placed shots. The Spad shuddered under the impact and Heurtaux looked down to see blood pouring from a wound in his thigh. Managing to land behind Allied lines, he was rushed to a military hospital where his thigh was found to have been shot through by two incendiary bullets. Despite being officially banned, the incendiary bullets saved his life. During their passage through his leg, they had severed a major artery and vein, but the burning phosphorus which coated the bullets had cauterised the wounds, stopping him from bleeding to death. The damage was sufficient, however, to prevent him flying again, and a successor to lead Spa. No. 3 was called for.

As the Storks' leading scorer, Guynemer was given the job, but like many top aces he was essentially a loner, ill-suited to the burdens of leadership. The new responsibility hung heavily on him and fellow pilots noted how the strains of aerial combat were affecting him. On 11 September he failed to return from a patrol and a short while later the Germans claimed he had been shot down by a Lieutenant Kurt Wissemann.

The aircraft flipped over onto its back and the bodies of the crew dropped out

Guynemer's death came as a profound shock to the airmen of the Storks and his loss was mourned throughout France. His death did, however, spur his former colleagues on to exact revenge, and the sortie rate increased as the Stork pilots roamed the skies for Germans to shoot down. Guynemer's death was avenged within a couple of weeks by a rising young star from Spa. No.103 called René Fonck. On a routine patrol Fonck spotted a German two-seater in the distance. Diving beneath its tail, Fonck hit both crew members with a single burst; the aircraft flipped over onto its back and the bodies of the crew dropped out. On later examination the dead pilot was found to be Wissemann. Fonck became a national hero and took the place of Guynemer in the public's affections. The high command began to promote Fonck as the standard-bearer of French aviation, a trust which was repaid with his ever-increasing score rate. A textbook airman, carefully weighing up the risks before committing himself, he survived the war. His final tally of 75 kills made him the top scorer on the Allied side.

Multiple kills were a notable feature of Fonck's progress. On 9 May 1918 Fonck encountered a German reconnaissance aircraft escorted by two fighters. An initial touch of the trigger raked the

two-seater from end to end; a second burst of fire sent one of the fighters earthward in flames. The third German plane broke up as it raced for safety, victim of Fonck's deadly accuracy at long range. Returning to base to refuel and rearm, he was soon airborne again and after a long search he spotted and stealthily trailed a two-seater which he subsequently despatched without the crew realising what had hit them. The destruction of the two-seater brought nine German fighters onto the scene, but throwing caution to the wind, Fonck set about shooting two down before escaping westward to safety. Although not an unparalleled achievement – three British airmen also attained similar scores in a day – it was a remarkable feat. The final months of the war were a highly productive period for Fonck and he repeated his six-in-a-day victory in September, providing further proof (if any were needed) of his incredible

Below right and below: Captain René Fonck proved himself the 'ace of aces' on the Allied side and his final tally of 75 aircraft shot down greatly exceeded the scores of Guynemer (53 kills) and his arch-rival of Escadrille N. No.65, Captain Charles Nungesser (45 kills). A superb pilot, he achieved his total through cool professionalism rather than the hot-headed bravado of his more charismatic and better-loved rivals. Bottom: Part of Fonck's success lay in an uncanny mastery of shooting. Here he is seen practising with a carbine.

skill as an airborne assassin.

Although many fine pilots were killed during the course of the war, the Storks always managed to maintain the high standard set at their formation in 1916. Most of France's leading aces served with the group and, like Richthofen's Circus on the opposing side, they struck fear into the enemy units facing them. Their contribution to French aviation in World War I cannot be underestimated. Besides the enormous material losses inflicted on the enemy, the Storks were also a vital element in the maintenance of French morale, both civilian and military. France was the battleground over which the war in the west was fought and the loss of a considerable portion of her major industrial centres to German occupation was a grievous blow. Added to this, the grinding attrition that characterised the war lay heavily on France and during 1917 morale faltered: defeatist talk was widespread and a full-scale army mutiny was only just quelled in time. Set against the relentless horror of trench warfare, the marvellous exploits of the Storks were especially important to the French. In the air, at least, France was seen to be successful, and during the lean period from the failure of the Nivelle offensive in the spring of 1917 to the great Allied offensive of the summer of 1918, the Storks gave the soldier in the trenches, the peasant in the fields and the worker in the munitions factory a feeling of hope for a final victory.

THE AUTHOR Adrian Gilbert has edited and contributed to a number of military and naval publications. His book *World War I in Photographs* covers all aspects of the Great War.

75 Victoires.

Above: Powered by an 180hp engine, the Spad S-VII offered high performance and synchronised fire.

The pilots of the 332nd Fighter Group, the USAAF's sole all-black unit in World War II, became renowned for their precision dive-bombing and deadly gunnery

DURING THE YEARS between December 1942 and August 1945, over 35,000 day-fighter pilots were trained by the United States Army Air Force (USAAF). Since each man was the product of a highly professional training programme, this was, and remains, an impressive figure. Equally impressive was the emergence of 966 black aviators from this labyrinthine training system. Despite the prevailing racial attitudes, 450 of these men were able to overcome significant hardships during their training and establish reputations as excellent fighter pilots. Proving their combat skills in the skies over the Mediterranean, the Tuskegee Airmen earned the respect of their fellow white pilots through example, despite little or no press coverage.

The combat statistics of the Tuskegee Airmen speak for themselves. The pilots destroyed 409 enemy aircraft, including the last four kills registered by the US air forces in the Mediterranean theatre. The men flew over 15,000 sorties during the course of 1578 missions, 200 of which were as bomber escorts deep into the heart of enemy territory. The latter were completed without the loss of a single bomber. In addition, the Tuskegee Airmen claimed four of the eight Messerschmitt Me 262 jet fighters shot down by the US 15th Army Air Force (AAF). Incredibly, these superb achievements had been

TUSKEGEE AIRMEN

Commanded by one of the pioneers of black aviation, Colonel Benjamin Davis (far left), the 332nd Fighter Group was given its first combat assignment in June 1944 with the 15th Army Air Force (badge shown bottom left). Right: While a Mustang P-51 is prepared for a dive-bombing sortie, the 'Black Birdmen' of the 332nd pose for the camera (below).

made possible by a training programme that lacked both public support and 'state-of-the-art' equipment.

The primary base for training was the Tuskegee Army Air Base (AAB), situated close to the Tuskegee Institute in Alabama, and the first flying cadets were inducted into the Army Flying School on 19 July 1941. The original plan was for one unit, the 99th Pursuit Squadron, to be formed from this original cadre of 400 enlisted men and officers. The aircraft initially assigned to the squadron were six Boeing PT-13s (primary trainers), four Vultee BT-13s and four North American AT-6 Texans (basic trainers). When these aircraft were passed down to the 99th, they were old and in dire need of repair.

On 19 February 1942, a second squadron was approved. This was designated the 100th Fighter Squadron. Eight months later, this unit would form the basis for the 332nd Fighter Group – the first all-black group in the history of the US air forces. Meanwhile, however, the 99th Pursuit Squadron continued to shape up for combat. Progress was rapid, and when the US Secretary of War, Henry Stimson, visited the Tuskegee facility in late February 1942 he was impressed with what he saw. He left with the words: 'This unit is absolutely outstanding by

any standards!' Six weeks later, on 15 April, the squadron received orders to proceed to Camp Shanks, New York. At last, the opportunity for action had arrived – the squadron was bound for Casablanca, Morocco.

Morale soared when the unit learned that it was to be equipped with Curtiss P-40L Warhawks, a considerable improvement on the basic and primary trainers that the pilots had previously flown. The squadron was attached to the 27th Fighter Group (FG), an experienced outfit well versed in the techniques of dive-bombing. The group quickly developed a good team spirit, with the 99th Pursuit Squadron frequently challenging the North American A-36 Invaders of the 27th FG in mock dogfights.

On 31 May 1943 the squadron arrived at Fordjouna, in North Africa, to complete the final phase of pre-combat training. It was here that the pilots met the famous Colonel Philip Cochran, whose daring exploits in the skies over North Africa had become legendary in the space of a few months. After flying with the 99th Pursuit Squadron on several occasions, Cochran paid the Tuskegee Airmen the following tribute: 'These guys are a collection of natural born dive bombers.' The squadron's first sorties into combat were flown by two P-40s, accompanied by six A-36s from the 27th FG. This combination was designed to provide the 99th with excellent instruction from some of the best pilots in the US air forces. To have thrown the squadron into combat en masse, would have proved disastrous.

When the Allies began to concentrate their efforts on Sicily, the 99th was re-assigned to the 324th FG. The group's primary mission was to escort medium bombers to the western sector of Sicily. Operating out of El Haouria, in North Africa, the Tuskegee Airmen found themselves in the thick of the action. On 2 July 1943, the squadron scored its first kill. Lieutenant Charles Hall later recalled:

'It was my eighth mission and we were escorting some B-25s on a bombing run. Right after the bombers had dropped their bombs, I spotted two Fw 190s following them. I headed for the space between the fighters and their targets, managing to turn inside the '190s. I fired a long burst and saw my tracers hitting the second fighter. He was turning to the left, but suddenly turned off and headed straight down into the ground.'

Shortly after this 'first', General Dwight D. Eisenhower paid a visit to the squadron's base. He congratulated Hall personally on his victory and praised the 99th Pursuit Squadron for its fine performance.

The invasion of Sicily took place on 10 July 1943, and the 99th Pursuit Squadron flew countless strafing and dive-bombing sorties as part of the 324th FG. After a hectic 11 days and 175 sorties with the 324th, the squadron was assigned to the British Eighth Army under General Bernard Montgomery. This brief association lasted only eight days and was followed by a move to Licata, Sicily, as part of the 33rd FG. It was a miracle that their mail ever caught up with them!

Although the 99th Pursuit Squadron had received praise from every quarter, the unit was still regarded

Right: While Captain Andrew 'Jug' Turner waits for the order to take off, his crew chief carries out a last-minute check on the Mustang. Below: Having returned from a mission over the Allied beaches at Anzio, south of Rome, a group of pilots from the 99th Pursuit Squadron trade stories of their encounter with the Luftwaffe. The mission had been an unqualified success, with the Tuskegee Airmen claiming eight of the 28 enemy aircraft destroyed.

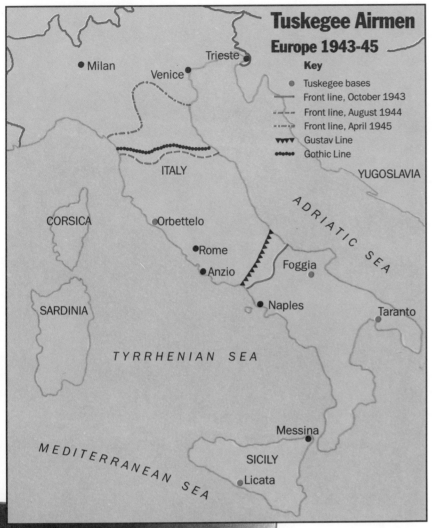

Tuskegee Airmen
Europe 1943-45

Key
- Tuskegee bases
- Front line, October 1943
- Front line, August 1944
- Front line, April 1945
- Gustav Line
- Gothic Line

Milan · Trieste · Venice · ITALY · YUGOSLAVIA · ADRIATIC SEA · CORSICA · Orbettelo · Rome · Anzio · Foggia · Naples · Taranto · SARDINIA · TYRRHENIAN SEA · MEDITERRANEAN SEA · Messina · SICILY · Licata

Far left: A pre-flight briefing for the Tuskegees of the 15th Army Air Force. Lieutenant Edward C. Gleed identifies the day's target, prior to a bombing raid against German military installations. Left: Staff-Sergeant Alfred Morris helps Captain William Mattison into the cockpit of his P-51 Mustang.

through to the squadron from military and civilian sources, and the men started to believe that their situation was a case of 'damned if you do, and damned if you don't.' Several members of the press even suggested that future black outfits should not be allowed to leave the United States. If they were given duties pertaining to defence command, it was argued, this would free a white fighter group for combat.

One man saved the day, and brought a second black outfit to the arena of combat. The commanding officer of the 99th Pursuit Squadron, Colonel Benjamin Davis, was called back to the US on 7 October 1943, having been given command of the fledgling 332nd Fighter Group. The unit had been activated on 13 October 1942, and by the end of April 1943 it had expanded into three fully equipped squadrons: the 100th, 301st and 302nd. Originally, a white colonel had been selected to command the group, but was later passed over in favour of Colonel Davis. It was the latter's determination and convincing manner that eventually ensured a combat assignment for both the 332nd FG and his former unit.

By the end of January 1944, with 17 victories to its credit, the squadron had flown 2548 sorties

When Davis had relinquished command of the 99th, his place as commanding officer had been taken by Captain George S. Roberts. Now, with Davis promoting the cause of the Tuskegee Airmen, the 99th was at last assigned the role of a combat squadron. On 7 October the unit joined the 79th FG at Foggia, Italy, as part of the 12th AAF. When the battle for Anzio began on 22 January 1944, the 12th AAF's assignment was to isolate the battle area and prevent any enemy reinforcements from reaching the front. Five days into the offensive, Captain Clarence Jamison spotted a large gaggle of German fighters over the beachhead. Numerically, the enemy held a two to one advantage. The pilots of the 99th were undeterred by the strength of the opposition, however, and they throttled forward into the attack. A swirling, tangled dogfight quickly developed in which the experience and tenacity of the 99th proved the deciding factor. Five German fighters were shot down within the space of four minutes. Later that same afternoon, a flight led by Lieutenant James T. Wiley shot down a further three aircraft, bringing the day's total to eight. Four more enemy aircraft were destroyed the following day, with Captain Charles Hall claiming two of them.

By the end of January 1944, with 17 victories to its credit, the squadron had flown 2548 sorties during the course of 390 missions. General Henry Arnold, commanding general of the US Army Air Forces, had previously been a sceptic concerning the capabilities of the 99th. However, the unit's prolific success over Anzio now led Arnold to comment: 'The results produced by the 99th Pursuit Squadron over the last two weeks have been very commendable. My best wishes for their continued success.'

Meanwhile, not far away, the 332nd Fighter Group was getting its feet wet. The unit had left Camp Henry, Virginia, on 3 January 1944, arriving in Taranto, Italy, at the beginning of February. Initially, it seemed certain that the unit would be flying the Potez P-63 King Cobra. Due to problems on the production line, however, the group was equipped with Republic P-47 Thunderbolts. These were the D model 'Razorback' aircraft, inherited from the

as the air force's step child'. The pilots were in the air virtually every day and fatigue was beginning to show through. The squadron's complement of 26 pilots was well short of the 30 to 35 average in the Mediterranean theatre, and replacements were desperately needed. These finally arrived on 22 July. However, the squadron was still denied the forward base it desired. At this stage of the war, the Luftwaffe was operating far behind the German lines; a squadron had to be in a forward position if it was to engage enemy aircraft. Adverse publicity was filtering

chequer-tailed 325th FG. The tails were quickly painted over in favour of the red colour scheme that would soon become the 332nd's trademark. The bomber crews that the Tuskegee Airmen protected referred to them as the 'Black Red-Tailed Angels'. To the Luftwaffe, they were known as the 'Schwartze Vogelmenschen' – the 'Black Birdmen'.

Attached to the 306th Fighter Wing, 15th AAF, Colonel Davis' 332nd Fighter Group reached combat status on 9 June 1944. Two days later, the pilots demonstrated their aerial prowess when five enemy fighters fell to their guns over northern Italy. Lieutenant Wendell O. Pruitt of the 302nd Squadron later recounted his part in the action:

'We were assigned to fly top cover for the B-24s. On approaching the Udine area, several Me 109s came out of the clouds and began attacking the bombers. Each enemy fighter made a pass at the bombers, then fell off into a rolling turn. I rolled over, shoved everything forward and closed in on a '109 at about 475 miles per hour. I waited until he shallowed out of a turn and gave him a couple of two-second bursts and watched him explode.'

One of the most spectacular of Allied achievements in the Mediterranean theatre was credited to the 332nd FG. On 25 June 1944, Captain Joseph Elsberry was leading a patrol when he spotted a German destroyer in Trieste Harbour. Despite a heavy anti-aircraft barrage, the Thunderbolts swept in on a firing pass. Lieutenant Pruitt started the show by scoring a series of direct hits that resulted in a small fire. Lieutenant Gwynne Pierson then screamed in, guiding his machine-gun fire onto the ship's magazine. There was a huge explosion and minutes later the destroyer sank to the bottom of the harbour. At first, the 15th AAF refused to believe that such a feat could have been accomplished without the use of bombs. After viewing Pierson's gun-camera film, however, the issue was put beyond doubt. The remarkable accuracy of the Thunderbolt's 0.5in fire was there for all to see.

Meanwhile, the 99th Pursuit Squadron continued to move around from group to group. After leaving the 79th, they flew with the 324th and 86th FGs. On 29 June 1944 the squadron moved to Orbetello, Italy, and joined the 332nd FG. This was an historic occasion – the first all-black four-squadron group in the US air forces. Initially, the merger was resented by the men of the 99th, who felt that their separate identity was threatened. These feelings soon subsided when the group received news of its imminent conversion to P-51C Mustangs. On 12 July, the 332nd FG had cause for celebration when Captain Joseph Elsberry scored a 'triple', only the second achieved by a black pilot. The group had been tasked to hook up with B-17 Flying Fortresses from the 5th Bomb Wing, but had been forced to execute a slow 360-degree turn when the bombers failed to show up on time. As the Mustangs were circling, about 30 Fw 190s intercepted the bombers. The German pilots thought they were going to have a field day. Once the Tuskegee Airmen spotted the enemy fighters, however, they throttled their Mustangs forward into a high-speed dive. The enemy pilots suddenly realised their predicament and broke off the engagement. The P-51s swarmed in with a crucial airspeed advantage and started to pick off the German fighters. Elsberry later recounted his memorable part in the action:

'I picked out a '190 within range and began firing. He absorbed numerous hits, had a mild explosion, rolled over and headed straight down. A second fighter crossed my path at about a 70-degree angle and I turned inside of him. He began to smoke and fell into a dive towards the ground. I followed the third '190 through a series of 'split-S' manoeuvres as he tried to lose me. Initial contact began at 11,000ft and ended up below 2000ft. He continued his dive and, misjudging his pull up, hit the ground.'

The 332nd FG had proved itself a well organised combat machine. The men had no press to speak for them, so they let their actions and accomplishments do the talking.

Colonel Davis' unit had its finest day on 24 March 1945 when it took part in the longest mission in the history of the 15th AAF – a 1600-mile round trip to Berlin. The Mustangs were to fly cover for B-17 bombers. When another of the three fighter groups involved was late at its release point, the 332nd was ordered to continue on to the target with the Flying Fortresses. However, German Me 262 jet fighters were up in force over Berlin. Up until this time, only two jets had been shot down by the 15th AAF.

Several well-placed bursts of machine-gun fire sent the jet fighter spinning out of control

The first kill went to Lieutenant Roscoe Browne. Glancing behind, Browne found an Me 262 locked onto the rear of his Mustang. By weaving from side to side, he caused the enemy pilot to overshoot and then manoeuvred his Mustang into position behind the Messerschmitt. Several well-placed bursts of machine-gun fire sent the jet fighter spinning out of control. That same day, three more Me 262s fell to the guns of the Tuskegee Airmen.

On 31 March, the 'Red Tails' continued their winning streak during an encounter with 17 German fighters over Linz, Austria. When the dust finally settled, 13 of the enemy had been downed without loss. The group added a further 12 kills to its victory tally the following day. Finally, on 26 April, the 332nd FG claimed the last four enemy aircraft to be shot down in the Mediterranean theatre.

As the war in Europe came to a close, the 332nd returned to the US where it was de-activated at Camp Kilmer, New Jersey. The men were sent back to Tuskegee AAB and Godman Field, Kentucky, only to discover that racial conditions had not changed during their absence. The officers were assigned jobs that offered very little opportunity for advancement. When Tuskegee AAB was finally closed down in January 1946, the primary bases for black airmen shifted to Godman Field and Lockbourne AAB, Ohio.

On 1 June 1949, the US Congress passed legislation that integrated the armed forces. The Tuskegee Airmen were now provided with the opportunities that they had deserved for so long. Many black servicemen were later to achieve a high status in all branches of the armed forces. It is clear that the original Tuskegee Airmen were true pioneers... in time of war and in time of peace.

THE AUTHOR Warren E. Thompson is a freelance historian and writer whose speciality is World War II nightfighters and all aspects of military aviation in World War II, Korea and Vietnam.

Left, main picture: B-17 Flying Fortresses of the 15th Army Air Force drop their payload on a Messerschmitt factory in Austria. Left, top: Lieutenant Westmoreland of the 332nd Fighter Group. Left, centre: Lieutenant Samuel Curtis. Right: Captain Charles McGee (left of picture). McGee's remarkable service career spanned three wars. In Korea, he served as a forward air controller (below) and went on to see combat during the Vietnam War (bottom). In Vietnam, he was the commanding officer of the 16th Tactical Reconnaissance Squadron. He is sitting in the cockpit of an RF-4C Phantom.

NO.249 (GOLD COAST) SQUADRON

Formed in 1917 as Royal Naval Air Squadron, Killingholme, it was not until 18 August 1918 that the unit became No.249 Squadron, Royal Air Force. No.249 operated from Dundee until being disbanded on 8 October 1919. Brought out of retirement on 16 May 1940, No.249 was re-formed as a gift fighter squadron from the Gold Coast at Church Fenton. After flying Spitfires for only a month, the squadron was equipped with Hurricanes, and on 3 July became operational, moving to Boscombe Down in August in time for the Battle of Britain. On 16 August 1940, Flight Lieutenant James B. Nicolson of No.249 won the only Victoria Cross ever awarded to Fighter Command when, although wounded and with his Hurricane ablaze, he proceeded to destroy his attacker, a Bf 110. On 21 May 1941, the squadron was transferred by aircraft carrier to Malta where it played a decisive role in the air battles there. No.249 converted back to Vickers-Supermarine Spitfires in March 1942, and in October 1943 moved to Italy, carrying out sweeps over Albania and Yugoslavia. In September 1944 No.249 converted to Mustangs. Following a short spell in Yugoslavia, the squadron returned to Italy and was disbanded on 16 August 1945, having destroyed 244 enemy aircraft.
Above: The badge of No.249 Squadron: the motto translates as 'With fists and heels'.

BATTLE FOR MALTA

In the defence of Malta during World War II the pilots of No. 249 Squadron made a heroic stand against the might of the Axis air forces

BETWEEN MARCH and late June 1940, the air defence of Malta relied solely upon four Gladiator biplanes. On 21 June some Hurricanes arrived and were used to bolster Malta's defences against the Italian Regia Aeronautica's bombing raids. Six weeks later 12 Hurricanes of No. 148 Flight landed at Luqa. These and Malta's surviving fighters were formed into No. 261 Squadron.

In May 1941, following heavy engagements with both the Aeronautica and the Luftwaffe, the squadron's remaining Hurricanes were quickly incorporated into the newly-formed No. 185 Squadron. On 28 June, No. 126 Squadron was also reformed, operating from Ta'Qali airfield. A third squadron, No. 249, arrived from Britain when the aircraft carriers *Ark Royal* and *Furious* delivered several Fleet Air Arm Fulmars and 46 Hurricanes during Operation Splice on 21 May 1941.

During its service in Malta, No. 249 Squadron was to become a highly cosmopolitan unit. It came to lose its British identity, becoming an informal, if not casual, mixture of nationalities. Yet, as was often the case with such units, No. 249 continued to do its job, and to do it very effectively indeed. From May 1941 until it left Malta at the end of October 1943, No. 249 Squadron built up an impressive tally of Axis aircraft destroyed. Out of Malta's 10 top-scoring fighter pilots, five flew with the squadron, and between

them these pilots, hailing from Australia, New Zealand, Rhodesia and Canada, notched up a total of 62 confirmed 'kills'.

In his papers, Field Marshal Rommel was prompted to write of Malta that the island 'has the lives of many thousands of German and Italian soldiers on its conscience.' Both Britain and the Axis powers knew that control of Malta would have a crucial bearing on the campaigns in North Africa. Consequently, from 1940, Malta and the convoys which served her were subjected to relentless aerial attacks by German and Italian bombers based in Sicily. The Axis objectives were to sever the garrison's supply lines, thereby ensuring safe delivery of fuel and ammunition to Rommel in North Africa, and to destroy the Allied defences prior to an invasion of the island.

The heroic defence of Malta lasted three years, and the aerial warfare above her shores during 1941-42 must rank as the most vicious and uncompromising of the entire war. For the RAF, heavily out-numbered and short of supplies, it was a desperate fight for survival. Between March and May 1942 there were 803 air-raid alerts. According to II Fliegerkorps, 345 reconnaissance and 11,474 bomber/fighter sorties were flown against the island during the period 20 March to 28 April 1942. For a time the RAF could barely muster more than six fighters to counter the onslaught. In the face of such adversity the tenacity of No. 249 Squadron was to become almost legendary. With the anti-aircraft defences, the RAF exacted a heavy toll of enemy machines. As an indication of Malta's incredible fighting spirit it is known that Field Marshal Kesselring confided to Maresciallo Ugo Cavallero, Chief of the Italian General Staff, that Luftwaffe aircrew who were engaged in daily sorties over Malta invariably developed a state of extreme tension, known to the Germans as 'Maltese sickness'.

On the RAF side, the veteran No. 249 pilot Squadron Leader Johnny Plagis is quoted as saying that he did not believe '… the Battle of Britain had anything over Malta!' No. 249 found itself fighting a ruthless battle, and one unpleasant aspect of it was the occasional practice on both sides of finishing off aircrew who had abandoned their aircraft. Wing Commander P.B. 'Laddie' Lucas, DSC, DFC, CBE, witnessed one such incident involving a Rhodesian pilot officer, Douglas Leggo:

'Bounced out of the sun by the German ace Neuhoff, whom 249 then shot down, Leggo rolled his Spitfire onto its back and parted company. His parachute opened immediately. As he descended earthwards, a lone Messerschmitt, appearing seemingly from nowhere, sprayed the canopy with tracer bullets in a callous gesture of murder. It was over in seconds…'

Less than a week later, Leggo's death was avenged by a Canadian pilot of No. 249. Laddie Lucas recalled:

'A Junkers 88 had been shot down southwest of the island. The aircraft had ditched in the sea, and now the crew of three were in a dinghy 10 miles or so from Delimara Point… as we headed home for Takali, my eye caught sight of a single Spitfire away to my left, at the bottom of a shallow, fast dive, heading straight for the dinghy. A sustained burst of fire sent geysers of sea water creeping up on the tiny inflated boat. Not content with one run, the pilot pulled up into a tight climbing turn to the left and dived again…'

Background: Takali airbase on Malta is pounded by Ju 88s operating from Sicily. The Regia Aeronautica and the Luftwaffe never succeeded in grounding Malta's air defence, however, even when it numbered only a handful of fighters. Far left: Flight Lieutenant Johnny Plagis, veteran pilot of No. 249 Squadron. Below: Although it was believed that Pilot Officer 'Screwball' Beurling had shot down the 1000th Axis aircraft over Malta, that distinction was finally accredited to Squadron Leader John Lynch, also of No. 249 Squadron, on 28 April 1943. Right: Pilots of the squadron's A Flight with a Hurricane.

MALTA

By virtue of its proximity to Sicily (60 miles), the European mainland (140 miles), and Africa (180 miles), the island of Malta provided a crucial air and naval base for British control of the Mediterranean during World War II. Malta-based aircraft, submarines and ships took a vast toll of Axis convoys to Rommel's Afrika Korps. The cost, however, was high.

Only 18 miles long and nine miles wide, Malta was subjected to 3340 air raids in which 1540 civilians lost their lives and nearly 4000 more were injured. Over 14,000 tons of bombs rained down upon the island's population, airfields and dockyards. In the capital, Valletta, 75 per cent of the houses were destroyed or damaged. A total of 1252 Axis and 707 RAF aircraft were reported lost, and hundreds more were damaged.

Supplies had to be brought in by sea, through the Axis blockade. The Royal and Merchant Navies made 17 convoy runs between August 1940 and December 1942, delivering over 395,000 tons of essential provisions. Of the ships on convoy duty, 37 were sunk and a further 37 rendered unserviceable.

At the height of the campaign, Malta's anti-aircraft guns were firing 13,000 rounds per day, and during the 283 alerts in April 1942, her formidable box barrage shot down 102 Axis aircraft. Ammunition supplies ran desperately short and anti-aircraft guns had to be rationed to six rounds a day, but Malta held out.

On 15 April 1942 the islanders were awarded the Commonwealth's highest civilian honour; the George Cross. Their ordeal continued for another seven months; then, on 20 November 1942, the siege was finally lifted.

Pilot Officer George 'Screwball' Beurling (top right) was shot down during an intense aerial dogfight on 14 October 1942. He had just succeeded in disrupting a force of eight Bf 109s which had been in hot pursuit of a Spitfire flown by Pilot Officer Eric Hetherington (above right).

Ditched aircrew were not entirely safe even when fortunate enough to be picked up by one of the marine craft and Air Sea Rescue launches. In fact, High Speed Launch 129 had had to be written off following a vicious attack in February 1942 when German fighters shot up the vessel, killing several of the crew.

By 1942, fighter pilots on both sides were using extreme measures in the air. Some pilots would go to any length in order to destroy an enemy, even at the risk of sacrificing themselves. One such incident involving a No. 249 pilot occurred when Raoul Daddo-Langlois attacked a Bf 109 head-on. Neither pilot broke, and the two aircraft struck each other in mid-air, breaking a wing off the German fighter and leaving the Spitfire without a wing-tip. Daddo-Langlois crash-landed on Malta and, with enemy fighters attempting to finish him off, leapt from his machine and ran for the nearest available cover.

Shortly after, Johnny Plagis found himself involved in a similar close shave off the coast of Sicily. At sea level and separated from the rest of his squadron, he became surrounded by 10 or so Italian fighters. Not surprisingly, Plagis thought his last moment had come. So, determined to sell his life as dearly as possible, he flew straight at the nearest machine, fully intending to ram it. The pilot of the Macchi was obviously horrified and desperately took violent evasive action, only to stall and crash into the Mediterranean. Plagis survived to escape back to Malta where, five days later on 16 May 1942, No. 249 celebrated its hundredth Axis aircraft destroyed

Above: The Spitfire VC in which Pilot Officer 'Screwball' Beurling was shot down off Malta in October 1942.

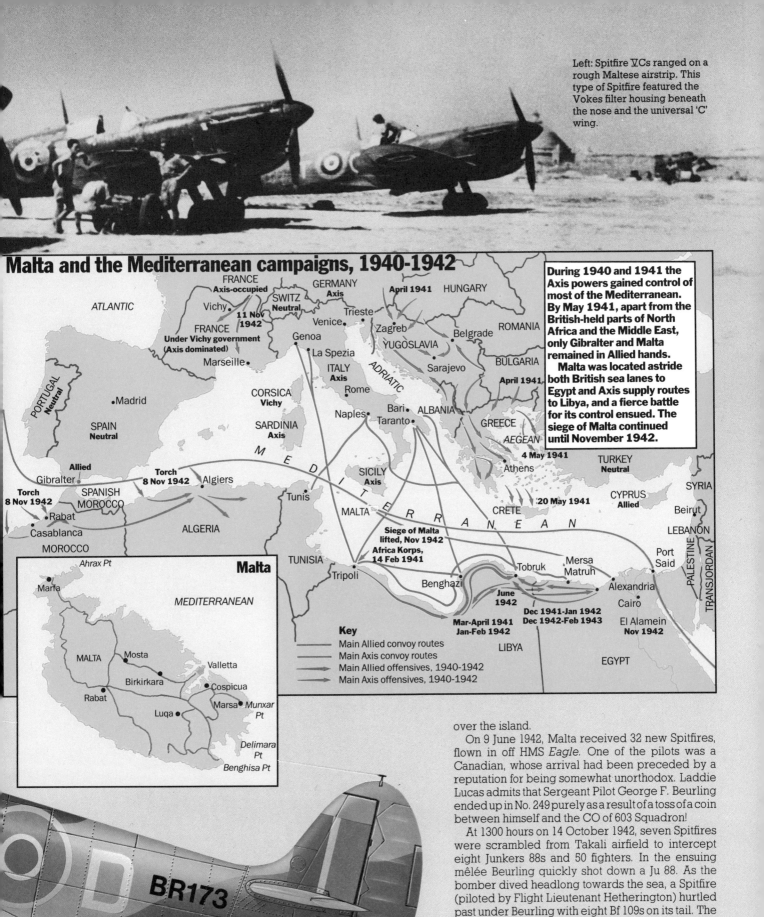

Left: Spitfire VCs ranged on a rough Maltese airstrip. This type of Spitfire featured the Vokes filter housing beneath the nose and the universal 'C' wing.

Malta and the Mediterranean campaigns, 1940-1942

During 1940 and 1941 the Axis powers gained control of most of the Mediterranean. By May 1941, apart from the British-held parts of North Africa and the Middle East, only Gibralter and Malta remained in Allied hands.
Malta was located astride both British sea lanes to Egypt and Axis supply routes to Libya, and a fierce battle for its control ensued. The siege of Malta continued until November 1942.

ATLANTIC

FRANCE Axis-occupied
Vichy
FRANCE Under Vichy government (Axis dominated)
11 Nov 1942
Marseille

SWITZ Neutral

GERMANY Axis

April 1941 **HUNGARY**
Trieste
Venice
Genoa
La Spezia
Zagreb
Belgrade **ROMANIA**
YUGOSLAVIA
Sarajevo
BULGARIA
April 1941

PORTUGAL Neutral
•Madrid
SPAIN Neutral

CORSICA Vichy
ITALY Axis
Rome
Naples
Bari
Taranto
ALBANIA
GREECE
AEGEAN
4 May 1941
Athens

SARDINIA Axis

ADRIATIC

TURKEY Neutral

Allied Gibralter
Torch 8 Nov 1942
Algiers
Tunis
SICILY Axis
MALTA
CRETE
20 May 1941
CYPRUS Allied
SYRIA
Beirut

Torch 8 Nov 1942
•Rabat
Casablanca
SPANISH MOROCCO
MOROCCO

ALGERIA

TUNISIA
Tripoli
Siege of Malta lifted, Nov 1942
Africa Korps, 14 Feb 1941
Benghazi
Mar-April 1941 Jan-Feb 1942
June 1942
Tobruk
Mersa Matruh
Dec 1941-Jan 1942
Dec 1942-Feb 1943
Alexandria
Cairo
El Alamein Nov 1942
LIBYA
EGYPT

MEDITERRANEAN

LEBANON
Port Said
PALESTINE
TRANSJORDAN

Malta

Ahrax Pt
Marfa
MEDITERRANEAN
MALTA
Mosta
Valletta
Birkirkara
Cospicua
Rabat
Marsa •Munxar Pt
Luqa
Delimara Pt
Benghisa Pt

Key
— Main Allied convoy routes
— Main Axis convoy routes
→ Main Allied offensives, 1940-1942
→ Main Axis offensives, 1940-1942

BR173

over the island.

On 9 June 1942, Malta received 32 new Spitfires, flown in off HMS *Eagle*. One of the pilots was a Canadian, whose arrival had been preceded by a reputation for being somewhat unorthodox. Laddie Lucas admits that Sergeant Pilot George F. Beurling ended up in No. 249 purely as a result of a toss of a coin between himself and the CO of 603 Squadron!

At 1300 hours on 14 October 1942, seven Spitfires were scrambled from Takali airfield to intercept eight Junkers 88s and 50 fighters. In the ensuing mêlée Beurling quickly shot down a Ju 88. As the bomber dived headlong towards the sea, a Spitfire (piloted by Flight Lieutenant Hetherington) hurtled past under Beurling with eight Bf 109s on its tail. The Canadian flung his machine towards the leading German fighter and in doing so passed the burning Junkers he had just shot up. The resolute rear gunner of the doomed aircraft was quick to take this last opportunity to shoot at Beurling's Spitfire. One round nicked the middle finger of the Canadian's throttle hand, and another pierced his left forearm. Beurling

Above: The pilot of this downed Ju 88, trapped alive in the burning wreckage, was mercifully shot after it proved impossible to save him.
Above right: Aircrew at Takili airbase. On the right is Raoul Daddo-Langlois, who survived a head-on crash with a Bf 109. Right: Wing Commander P.B. 'Laddie' Lucas, one of No. 249's commanding officers. Far right: A German photograph showing a tanker blazing after a strike on Valletta in the summer of 1942.

afterwards recounted:

'What was more important and inconvenient at the moment, however, was that I'd picked up two Messerschmitts on my own tail and still had Hether to worry about. I had to shoot in one hell of a hurry to clean Hether up and salvage my own neck, so I took a chance and tried for a long shot, from about 450 yds from above and to port. I got the bastard in the engine and he dove into the sea, streaming smoke and shedding pieces…'

But while Beurling was intent on shooting down this second aircraft, one Messerschmitt on his tail had riddled his port wing:

'…like a sieve, and put a couple of bullets through the perspex hood, right over my head, while the other Schmitt blasted my starboard wing full of holes…Well, Hether was out in the clear again…'

Moments later Beurling answered a call for assist-

ance. In characteristic fashion he dived from 24,000ft straight into the action below:

'I went down vertically, hitting almost 600mph in my riddled crate, and at 14,000ft pulled up under a Messerschmitt, just as he was all set to pot Willie the Kid (Pilot Officer Williams)...just as I pulled up from the dive and was going up vertically I gave the [Bf 109] a two-second burst and blew his whole left wing off at the root...Willie's ship...was just about able to cart him home...'

With its controls shattered and the throttle jammed wide open, the Spitfire went into a full-power spin

But in rescuing Williams, Beurling had made the cardinal error of failing to look behind before going in to attack. (Perhaps he had good cause for his mistake. Not only had he been wounded, he was weakened by the island's poor diet and by the bouts of dysentery that the British called 'Malta Dog', and had lost close to 50lb in weight.) He was now wounded again as a Bf 109 sent a burst of cannon fire into the belly of his Spitfire. This time he was hit in the right heel, left elbow, ribs and left leg. With its controls shattered and the throttle jammed wide open, the Spitfire went into a full-power spin. Desperately Beurling threw back the cockpit hood, but when he tried to climb out he found himself pinned to the seat by centrifugal force With the Merlin engine streaming flame the Canadian fought to escape his doomed machine:

'Somehow I managed to wriggle my way out of the cockpit and out onto the port wing, from which I could bale into the inside of the spin. By the time I got out onto the wing I was down to 2000ft. At about 1000 I managed to slip off. Before I dared pull the ripcord I must have been around 500.'

Beurling landed in the Mediterranean several miles south of Malta. As a pair of Bf 109s hovered nearby, Pilot Officer Robert Seed circled around the Canadian until he climbed into his dinghy. Twenty minutes later Beurling was rescued by High Speed Launch 128. The following day the *Times of Malta* reported that:

'It was disclosed by the Air Ministry on Wednesday (13 October 1942) that the Axis lost its 1000th aircraft over or near Malta soon after dawn on Tuesday to 20-year-old Canadian ace fighter pilot Pilot Officer Beurling... The Air Ministry says his sense of positioning is instinctive and he must be one of the best marksmen in the RAF...'

Before leaving Malta at the end of October, 'Screwball' Beurling was awarded the DSO, DFC, DFM and Bar, and he became the highest scoring RAF ace in the entire Mediterranean theatre of war. He destroyed 26⅓ aircraft, probably destroyed another, and damaged seven. That he did not account for more than he did can be attributed to the fact that for a month after his arrival in Malta there was an unusual lull in aerial activity. There followed three hectic weeks with Beurling in his element, shooting down 16 aircraft over six separate days. Then for six weeks there was another lull. Thereafter Beurling, now a pilot officer, enjoyed only a few more days of activity. In all, he flew 27 sorties that resulted in contacts with the enemy. Nineteen of these, spread over 14 separate days, led to the impressive tally run up by this unique fighter pilot.

August 1942 had witnessed the arrival of the famous Pedestal convoy, bringing sufficient rations to the island to ward off starvation. The first three merchant vessels arrived in Grand Harbour on 13 August, followed on the 14th by another, and on the next day by a battered tanker, lashed between two destroyers and with her decks almost awash. Loaded with oil and aviation fuel essential to the maintenance of Malta's air defence, the tanker, *Ohio*, had arrived at a most critical period of the siege. With the arrival of Pedestal, and with Malta now fairly brimming with fighters, the Germans were reluctant to risk losing more bombers. The Luftwaffe, therefore, took to sending over 100 fighters as escort for only 14 bombers, preferring to use the Bf 109 in a fighter-bomber role. No. 249 Squadron, always in the forefront of battle, often succeeded in intercepting the enemy before they could even reach Malta.

A new concept of warfare was initiated in August, when Spitfires were fitted with improvised bomb racks and used for the first time on bombing missions from Malta. Modified to carry two 250lb GP bombs slung directly underneath their two outboard cannon, Spitfires of No. 249 Squadron were soon carrying out offensive sorties against Sicily.

On 27 August the whole Spitfire force on Malta attacked the airfields of Comiso, Biscari and Gela. Contemporary wartime accounts claim that between 22 and 39 Axis aircraft were destroyed on the ground and in the air. There were two RAF casualties; one pilot who crash-landed and was captured, and the Takali station commander Group Captain Churchill who was hit by anti-aircraft fire and killed over Biscari.

The battle over Malta reached a climax when, for 10 days in October 1942, the enemy flew 2400 sorties against the island. But gone were the days when Malta could muster only a handful of worn-out Hurricanes in its defence. July and August had seen the arrival of 125 Spitfires, and whereas Malta had often received inexperienced fighter pilots in the past, this time the quality of the new pilots was of a satisfactorily high standard.

Suddenly, unbelievably, it was over: the battle for Malta had been won

On 20 October the Axis air offensive came to an abrupt halt when nearly all of its aircraft were transferred from Sicily to North Africa. Suddenly, unbelievably, it was over: the battle for Malta had been won. Enemy attacks did continue, but never with the same tenacity as before. The Regia Aeronautica carried out its last raid on 26 February 1943, and intermittent raids were carried out by the Luftwaffe even after the surrender in May of the Afrika Korps in Tunisia.

On 10 July 1943 the Allies landed in Sicily. The Spitfires of No. 249 Squadron left Hal-Far airfield the following month, flying north to their new base in Italy in order to resume operations with fighter sweeps and bomber escorts on the east coast. Behind them they left many comrades, lost in the depths of the Mediterranean, or buried in military cemeteries on the islands over which No. 249 had flown and fought during two-and-a-half years of operations.

THE AUTHOR Anton Sammut has researched aspects of the history of Malta for many years, and has a particular interest in the island's defences during World War II.

FLYING TIGERS

Main picture: Shark-nosed P-40s stand ready to meet the mighty Japanese Air Force. Inset left: One of the many badges worn by the Flying Tigers. Right: AVG Pilots, including Bill Reed (sitting, far right) and Ken Jernstedt (sitting, second from left), pose for the camera.

Helping China against the invading Japanese armies, the men of Claire Chennault's American Volunteer Group, the 'Flying Tigers', became a legendary flying unit

DURING the early months of the war in the Pacific, American and Allied fighter pilots found themselves completely outclassed by the exceptionally man-oeuvrable and well-flown fighters of the Japanese Army Air Force (JAAF) and Japanese Navy Air Force (JNAF). As a consequence, they suffered serious defeats, and the myth of Japanese invincibility in the air was established. One of the first Allied fighter units to demonstrate that the Japanese fighters had weaknesses that could be exploited by skilful tactics were the pilots of the American Volunteer Group (AVG), nicknamed the 'Flying Tigers', who flew with the Chinese Nationalist Air Force (CNAF). During some 30 weeks of combat in 1941 and 1942, the AVG was credited with 297 confirmed victories for the loss of 80 fighters and 25 pilots killed or made prisoner of war. These considerable successes were largely due to the effective leadership and tactical skills of Colonel Claire L. Chennault, the AVG's commander.

Shortly after leaving the United States Army Air Corps in 1937, Chennault was invited to China as air adviser to the Nationalist government of Chiang Kai-shek. On arriving, he found the CNAF in a poor state, with fewer than 100 effective combat aircraft out of a nominal strength of 500, and an inadequate number of trained pilots. Therefore, when the Japanese-engineered Marco Polo Bridge Incident precipitated a full-scale Sino-Japanese War in July 1937, the CNAF was unable to put up anything more than a token defence against the invaders.

In the short term, China was able to negotiate a Non-Aggression Pact with the Soviet Union in August 1937, which resulted in an infusion of Soviet combat aircraft and 'volunteer' airmen. For the following three years this was sufficient to stave off the complete collapse of Chinese air power, but by the end of 1940 Soviet aid had dried up and the Japanese air

Left: Colonel Claire Chennault, a dynamic and inspirational leader, commanded the Flying Tigers throughout their short but brilliant campaign against the Japanese.

forces were operating virtually at will over China. It was under these circumstances that Chennault accompanied a CNAF mission to the United States in order to acquire a force of modern fighters and recruit American pilots to fly them.

Operating under the cover of the Central Aircraft Manufacturing Co. (CAMCO), Chennault succeeded in obtaining 100 Curtiss Tomahawk Mk II fighters (generally referred to as P-40s by the AVG). These Tomahawks had been ordered by the RAF before the Battle of Britain, but, as the pressure on the British air defences had eased by early 1941, the fighters were released to China. Recruiting suitably-qualified pilots was a more difficult matter and it was necessary to obtain President Roosevelt's permission to seek volunteers from the US armed forces.

Eventually, a total of 109 pilots was signed up by CAMCO, about half of them coming from the US Navy and Marine Corps, a third from the Army Air Corps and the remainder from civilian flying organisations. Their one-year contracts provided a monthly pay of 600 US dollars for pilots, 675 dollars for flight leaders and 750 dollars for squadron commanders. A further incentive to recruitment was the Chinese government's offer of a 500 dollar bonus for every Japanese aircraft confirmed as destroyed. The groundcrews, numbering about 150 men, were mostly recruited from the United States forces and were paid between 150 and 400 dollars a month. Pay was an important factor in attracting personnel to the AVG, but the spirit of adventure – a wish to see active military service and to escape from the constraints of a peacetime routine – was an equally strong attraction.

The aircraft and their pilots were despatched by sea to Rangoon in Burma, where they assembled in late July 1941. After the P-40s had been uncrated and assembled, training began at the airfield at Kyedaw, near Toungoo. This had been made available to the AVG by the RAF authorities, as the Flying Tigers' main base at Kunming in western China was still under construction.

Eastern Asia

In December 1941, as the Japanese launched their attacks against the Allies in eastern Asia, the American Volunteer Group reached a state of combat readiness and went into action alongside the Chinese Nationalist Air Force against the Japanese. Until the end of the war, the 'Flying Tigers' remained in the fore-front of the air battles over China and Burma.

Key
Extent of Japanese empire, July 1942

Far left: Bob Neale of the 1st Squadron chalked up 16 victories to become the Tigers' leading ace. Left.: Ed Rector, a pilot with the Panda Bears, sits in the cockpit of a P-40 modified to carry out photo-reconnaissance work. Below: Dwarfed by the bulk of his P-40, Eric Shilling, the flight leader of the 3rd Squadron, strikes a nonchalant pose. Below right: 1st Squadron pilots, including Greg Boyington (revolver in hand), stand outside their makeshift billet.

Chennault set to work training AVG pilots according to his tactical doctrines. A network of ground observers had already been established in China at his suggestion and so the chances of receiving sufficient early warning of an incoming raid were good. However, Chennault realised from his study of Japanese aircraft and tactics that special procedures would be needed to deal with the enemy's fighters. The manoeuvrable Japanese aircraft would win a traditional turning dogfight every time and Chennault stressed that this type of combat had to be avoided at all costs. He proposed that the P-40's high diving speed and comparatively heavy firepower should be exploited:

'You must use your superior speed to climb above them before you commit yourselves. And you then can use your greater diving speed to make a pass at them. Get in short bursts and get away. Break off and climb back for the advantage of altitude after you have gotten away safely. In such combat, and

only in that kind, you have the edge.

Once the AVG fighters had achieved an advantageous firing position, accurate gunnery was sure to achieve good results. The Japanese aircraft were both lightly constructed and poorly armoured, and tended to burn or break up easily.

By the time that the Flying Tigers had completed their training in December 1941, the United States was at war with Japan. Nonetheless, the AVG retained its volunteer status. The group was organised into three squadrons, each made up of three flights of six fighters. The 1st Pursuit Squadron adopted an 'Adam and Eve' insignia as a pun on their designation. The squadron was commanded by Robert J. Sandell until he was killed in a flying accident on 7 February 1942, and then Robert H. Neale took over. The 2nd Pursuit Squadron, the 'Panda Bears', was led by John V. Newkirk and the 3rd Pursuit Squadron, the 'Hell's Angels', by Arvid Olsen. Apart from their individual squadron insignia, the AVG P-40s were painted with a distinctive shark-mouth marking, copied from No. 112 Squadron RAF which flew similarly-decorated Tomahawks in North Africa, and this embellishment became as much the group's identifying marking as the Chinese national insignia on the wings. Some aircraft also carried the Flying

Tiger emblem designed for the AVG by the Walt Disney studios.

By the second week of December the Flying Tigers were deploying for combat. The 1st and 2nd Squadrons deployed to Kunming, while the Hell's Angels moved to Mingaladon, joining the Brewster Buffaloes of No. 67 Squadron RAF in the air defence of Burma. The Kunming squadrons were the first to see action. On 20 December an unescorted formation of 10 JAAF Mitsubishi Ki-21 Sally bombers was picked up by the raid-reporting network en route from Hanoi to Kunming. Chennault scrambled four P-40s of the Panda Bear Squadron, led by Newkirk, to intercept. A further six of the squadron's fighters were reserved to cover Kunming, while Sandell's 1st Pursuit Squadron flew to an auxiliary airfield to the southeast, from where they later scrambled to cut off the bombers' retreat.

Newkirk's section met the Japanese bombers some 30 miles short of Kunming, and in their initial attack Ed Rector gained his first victory. However, Newkirk's P-40 then suffered a gun and radio failure and was forced to break off the combat. He was followed by the other three pilots, who in the absence of any instructions from their leader, were reluctant to contravene the AVG's strict formation discipline. The Adam and Eve Squadron then intervened, forcing the Ki-21s to jettison their bombs and turn away from their target. The most successful pilot during this combat was former US Navy dive-bomber pilot Fritz Wolf, who reported:

'I attacked the outside bomber in the Vee. Diving down below him, I came up underneath, guns ready for the minute I could get in range. At 500yds I let go with a quick burst from all my guns. I could see my bullets rip into the rear gunner. My plane bore in closer. At 100yds I let go with a long burst that tore into the bomber's gas tanks and engine. A wing folded and the motor tore loose. Then the bomber exploded. I yanked back on the stick to get out of the way and went upstairs.

'There, I went after the inside man of the Japanese bomber formation. I came out of a dive and pulled up level with the bomber, just behind his tail. I could see the rear-gunner blazing away at me, but none of his bullets were hitting my plane. At 50yds I let go with a long burst, concentrating on one motor. The same thing happened and I got number two. The bomber burned and then blew up.'

In all, six bombers were confirmed as destroyed and the Flying Tigers lost only Ed Rector's P-40, which force-landed after running out of fuel.

The focus of action then shifted to Burma, where the Hell's Angels were operating in defence of Rangoon. On 23 December a force of some 70 JAAF aircraft, Ki-21 bombers escorted by Nakajima Ki-27 Nate and Nakajima Ki-43 Oscar fighters, raided Rangoon from their bases in Thailand. The AVG P-40s scrambled with the RAF's Buffaloes to intercept, but were too late to prevent the bombing. However, the AVG pilots claimed six bombers and four fighters destroyed (although only six of these could be confirmed), in return for the loss of three P-40s and two pilots. Charles Older, a former Marine Corps pilot, claimed two victories in this fight.

Two days later the JAAF returned in even greater force, and 12 AVG P-40s and 18 RAF Buffaloes were scrambled to meet a force of over 100 enemy aircraft. The Allied fighters made their interception over the Gulf of Martaban and, with the advantage of superior altitude, tore into the Japanese formation. The out-

Top left: Alerted by the early-warning system created by Chennault, pilots scramble to meet a formation of enemy bombers. Top right: A Tomahawk from the 3rd Squadron patrols the skies over northern Burma. Centre right: Returning to base after a successful combat mission. Right: The Curtiss Tomahawk flown by Charles Older, a pilot with the 'Hell's Angels'.

The Curtis-Wright P-40 was by no means one of the truly great fighters to see action in World War II, yet nearly 14,000 had been built when production ceased in late 1944. Because of its rugged dependability and firepower, the P-40 remained a firm favourite with the Flying Tigers. Development of the aircraft began in 1937, and after several modifications of the basic design, the P-40 was selected to serve with the US Army Air Corps in May 1939. At the same time, the British government had ordered 100 P-40Bs, known as the Tomahawk II, but decided to wait for the improved E Model. Already assembled and ready for shipment, the Tomahawks were despatched to China. The Tomahawk had self-sealing fuel tanks, armour, and carried two wing-mounted .303in machine guns and a pair of synchronised 0.5in guns that fired through the aircraft's propeller.

The Flying Tigers soon discovered that the Tomahawk could take a lot of damage and keep flying. However, it was also clear that despite the P-40 being able to outdistance any enemy fighter in a dive, it was far slower and much less agile than the Japanese Zero in a conventional dogfight. Unable to replace losses, Chennault ordered his pilots to follow strict operational procedures and concentrate on the enemy's bombers.

Pilot, Flying Tigers, China 1941

Dressed in lightweight kit, this pilot of the 3rd Pursuit Squadron, the 'Hell's Angels', carries the unit insignia on his leather flying jacket. Light khaki trousers, short flying boots and cloth helmet complete the outfit.

51

come was a complete vindication of Chennault's tactical theories. For the loss of two P-40s, the Flying Tigers had downed 28 enemy aircraft. Japanese tactics were equal to the challenge, however. On 28 December the Hell's Angels were decoyed into pursuing a small formation of JAAF aircraft and, when on the ground refuelling after this mission, were attacked by a second JAAF formation. Only four P-40s were scrambled to meet the attack and they were unable to prevent Mingaladon from being heavily bombed.

Relief for the hard-pressed Hell's Angels came on 30 December, when Newkirk's Panda Bears flew in from Kunming to relieve them. The new unit soon took the fight to the enemy's camp. On 3 January 1942 Newkirk led a strafing attack by three P-40s on the Japanese airfield at Meshod in Thailand, claiming five enemy aircraft destroyed on the ground and a further three in air combat. Japanese retribution was swift: on 4 January six P-40s on patrol were bounced by about 30 Ki-27s and became ensnared in just such a turning dogfight which Chennault had counselled his pilots to avoid. Three kills were claimed, but for the loss of three AVG P-40s, and the combat led one pilot, Gregory Boyington, wryly to reflect that the peacetime training which the Marine Corps gave its fighter pilots was completely worthless as a preparation for fighting the Japanese.

Bill Reed and Ken Jernstedt destroyed 15 Japanese fighters in a series of firing passes

Heavy fighting in January took its toll of the AVG's P-40s, and early in February the 1st Pursuit Squadron relieved the Panda Bears in Burma. By the end of that month, the Japanese advance forced the evacuation of Mingaladon. During 10 weeks of combat in defence of Rangoon, the AVG and RAF fighters had claimed a total of 291 enemy aircraft destroyed.

The fight was continued from Magwe, 200 miles to the north of Mingaladon. Before Japanese air attacks forced this base to be evacuated late in March, two AVG pilots carried out a highly successful strafing attack on a newly occupied Japanese airstrip near Moulmein. Bill Reed and Ken Jernstedt were flying an armed reconnaissance mission in the area on 19 March, when they spotted a line-up of Japanese Ki-27 fighters on the ground and destroyed 15 of them in a series of firing passes.

The AVG then withdrew to Loiwing across the Chinese border, but remained within range of Japanese forces. On 24 March Robert Neale led a six-aircraft strafing mission against the JAAF airfield at Chieng-mai in Thailand, leaving more than two score Ki-27 and Ki-43 fighters as blazing wrecks. Yet whatever successes were gained in the air, the advance of the Japanese armies was inexorable and on 1 May the AVG was forced to evacuate Loiwing, destroying 22 unserviceable P-40s.

With the approach of the monsoon season on the Burma front, Chennault's attention shifted to the defence of the cities of western China from bombing attack. This necessitated the dispersal of his slender resources, the depleted Hell's Angels providing cover for the AVG's main base at Kunming, the Panda Bears defending Chunking and Hengyang, and the Adam and Eves protecting Kweilin. The latter squadron was first to see action, intercepting a force of 20 JAAF aircraft over Kweilin on 13 June, accounting for 11 of them for the loss of only two P-40s, and no pilot casualties.

Poor weather then enforced a lull in operations, and during this period the AVG was transformed from a volunteer unit of the CNAF into the 23rd Fighter Group of the United States Army Air Force (USAAF). However, the transition was mishandled by the regular USAAF officers responsible, with the result that only five pilots agreed to transfer to the new unit. Urgent entreaties from Chennault, who had been given command of the USAAF's new China Air Task Force with the rank of brigadier-general, persuaded a further 19 pilots to stay on for a further two weeks after the AVG's official disbandment. This led to the curious anomaly that ex-US Navy pilot Bob

Far left: When tigers meet.
Pilots from the American
Volunteer Group survey
the mangled wreckage
of a Japanese photo-
reconnaissance aircraft shot
down over China in 1941. Left:
Part of its tailplane smashed
beyond repair, an enemy
fighter dives to destruction.
By the end of their first tour of
duty, the heavily
outnumbered Flying Tigers
had accounted for nearly 300
enemy aircraft and lost fewer
than 30 pilots. Renamed the
23rd Fighter Group in mid-
1942, the Tigers continued to
inflict heavy casualties on the
Japanese. Main picture: As
the scale of American
involvement in Asia
escalated, the group was
increasingly involved in flying
escort missions for USAAF
bombers.

Neale (the AVG's top-scoring pilot), who was then
technically a civilian, often led the USAAF's 23rd
Fighter Group during its first two weeks of existence.

It would be wrong, however, to suggest that the
23rd Fighter Group was but a poor shadow of its
predecessor. Indeed, the new unit's pilots were able
to carry on the traditions of the Flying Tigers with
distinction. Foremost among them was the group's
new CO, Colonel Robert L. Scott, who led his new
command in the interception of JAAF raiders over
Kweilin. With the advantage of superior altitude, the
P-40s dived onto the enemy formation. Scott recalled:

'Their formation was so perfect and so close we
couldn't miss. Even the new kids remembered not
to shoot at the whole formation but to concentrate
on one ship at a time, with short bursts, then skid to
another. Hang on, aim, then fire – always short
bursts. They didn't see us until it was too late.
Twenty or more of them were already going down
and those we didn't burn on the first pass broke
and ran in all directions. After the first dive, when
we'd climbed back into the sun for altitude, we
broke, too, and took out after the stragglers. I
followed one with my wingman all the way to
Canton, 200 miles southeastward, and shot it down

when the pilot lowered his landing gear prepara-
tory to landing.'

After the results of this combat had been properly
assessed, the American pilots were credited with 13
enemy aircraft destroyed, for no loss to themselves.
It was an auspicious start for the new Flying Tigers of
the 23rd Fighter Group.

A particularly noteworthy combat was fought later
that month, when, early in the morning of 30 July,
Major John R. Alison and Major A. J. 'Ajax' Baumler
intercepted six JAAF night-bombers over Hengyang and destroyed four of them. Alison ended the
war with 10 victories and Baumler, who had gained
eight kills flying with the Republicans during the
Spanish Civil War, added a further five to his score in
China. Another distinguished newcomer to the
Flying Tigers was Scott's successor as commanding
officer, Colonel Bruce K. Holloway, who finished the
war with 13 victories and went on to become general
commanding the USAF's Strategic Air Command.
Three of the original Flying Tigers later returned to
the 23rd Fighter Group, Colonel David L. 'Tex' Hill
and Colonel Edward F. Rector as commanding
officers, and Lieutenant-Colonel Charles Older as a
squadron commander.

The 23rd Fighter Group remained in China until
the end of the war against Japan, latterly replacing its
P-40s with North American P-51 Mustangs. From its
formation on 4 July 1942 until the end of the fighting,
the group was credited with 621 enemy aircraft shot
down, plus a further 320 destroyed on the ground.

THE AUTHOR Anthony Robinson was formerly on the
staff of the RAF Museum, Hendon, and is now a
freelance military aviation writer. His books include
American Air Power and *Aerial Warfare*.

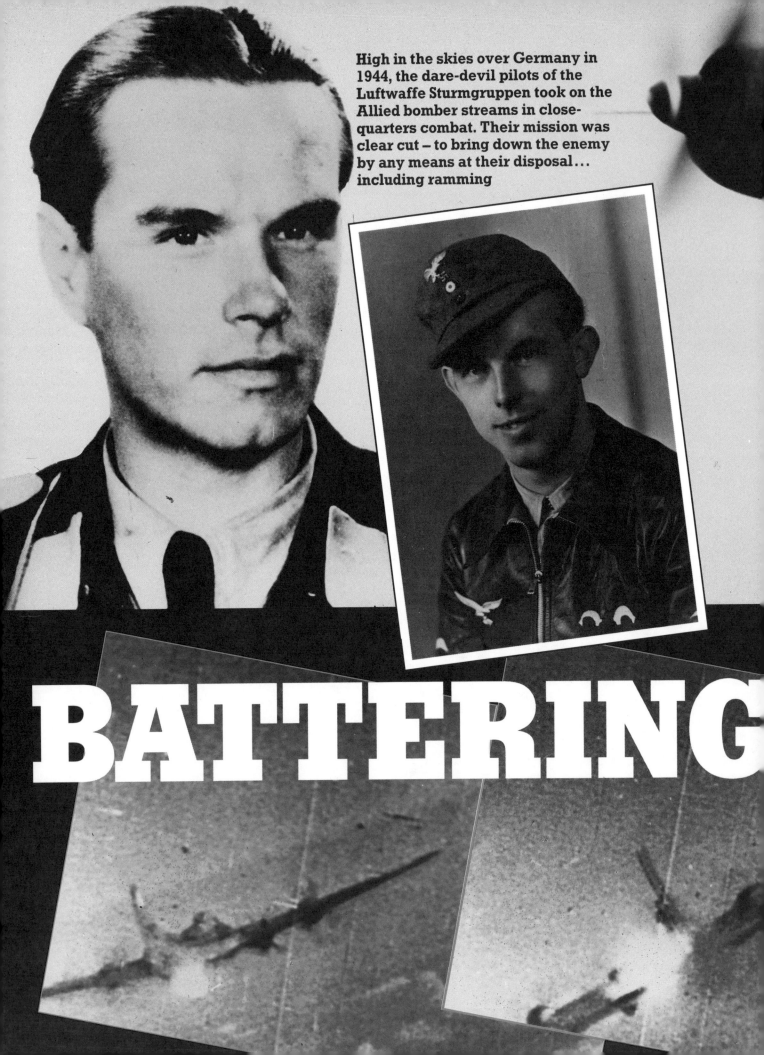

High in the skies over Germany in 1944, the dare-devil pilots of the Luftwaffe Sturmgruppen took on the Allied bomber streams in close-quarters combat. Their mission was clear cut – to bring down the enemy by any means at their disposal... including ramming

BATTERING

DURING THE EARLY months of 1944, the US Army Air Force's bombing offensive against Germany entered a new and more devastating phase. Formations of several hundred heavy bombers, now protected by large numbers of Mustang, Thunderbolt and Lightning fighters, were able to reach any part of the Reich from their bases in England and Italy. Quite apart from the severe damage they caused to targets, these raids, carried out in broad daylight, demonstrated clearly to the German population that the Luftwaffe was unable to defeat such incursions.

The introduction of the American long-range escort fighters posed an almost insoluble problem for the Luftwaffe, for it was not long before the escorts outnumbered the defending fighters by a wide margin. During the hard-fought battle on the occasion of the first all-out American attack on Berlin on 6 March 1944, for example, 814 Fortresses and Liberators were sent against the capital, supported by 644 escorting fighters which flew a total of 943 sorties. In reply, the Luftwaffe flew 528 fighter sorties, but of these, only about 370 made contact with the enemy.

For the German fighter force, being heavily outnumbered was not the only problem. Its heavy fighters – the twin-engined Messerschmitt Bf 110s and Me 410s, which had the firepower necessary to knock down the bombers – were extremely vulnerable to attacks from the American fighters. On the other hand, its single-engined Messerschmitt Bf 109s and Focke-Wulf Fw 190s, which had the performance to dog-fight with the American escorts, were short on firepower with which to engage the heavy bombers.

By the beginning of 1944, the standard German procedure when engaging American daylight attacks was to assemble formations of up to 100 fighters, which were then directed by ground control into position for a head-on attack on part of the American bomber force. Such head-on attacks were made at a combined closing speed of about 500mph, however, which meant that a German pilot had time

Above: The heavily armoured, upgunned 'Sturmbock' version of the Fw 190, created for relentless close-quarters combat with the huge Allied bomber formations of 1944. **Far left:** Ace Sturmbock pilot Leutnant Walther Hagenah, and (near left) Feldwebel Hans Schaefer, with the 'whites of the eyes' insignia of the Sturmgruppen painted on his leather flying jacket. **Below:** A B-17 is photographed from an Fw 190 as it weaves under the bomber's guard to deliver its lethal 30mm rounds.

RAMS

only for a single half-second burst before he had to pull up to avoid colliding with the bomber he was engaging. To be successful, these tactics required considerable skill, and they were beyond all but a few ace Luftwaffe pilots.

Generalmajor (Major-General) Adolf Galland, at the time General der Jagdflieger (Inspecting General for Fighters), received many suggestions of ways to destroy greater numbers of American bombers and thus halt their debilitating attacks. One such proposal came from Major Günther von Kornatzki, who asked to be allowed to lead a special fighter unit, manned by volunteer pilots who would be willing to ram the American bombers and then hope to escape from their wrecked fighters by parachute. Galland later commented to the author:

'I did not think it a good idea. To get into position to ram, pilots had first to break through the screen of escorts and then close with the bombers. But if they could get that close a short burst with ordinary cannon would be lethal anyway and the fighter pilot would have a much greater chance of escaping with his life.'

Although it was not taken up in its original form, Kornatzki's idea spawned one that did find favour: to use volunteer pilots to fly an especially heavily armed and armoured version of the Focke-Wulf Fw 190 fighter in the close-in fighting or 'Sturm' (shock) role. This fighter, nicknamed the 'Sturmbock' (battering ram), was to engage the American formations not from the front, but from the rear where, although the bombers' defensive fire would be at its most powerful, the German pilot could engage with greatest effect. The ramming option was retained as a last resort, in cases where the bomber being engaged survived the attack with cannon.

'Failure ... would render us liable to trial by court martial on a charge of cowardice in the face of the enemy'

Early in 1944 Sturmstaffel (shock squadron) 1 was formed to test the feasibility of the new tactics. Its fighters were not to fly in pairs to engage enemy bombers as other units did; instead they were to engage as a Staffel of about a dozen aircraft flying wing-tip to wing-tip in a broad arrow formation, concentrating their attack on one part of the enemy bomber force to achieve the greatest possible shock effect. Operational trials of the new tactics showed considerable promise and, thus encouraged, Generalmajor Galland introduced the concept of using Sturmbock fighters in Gruppe strength (three Staffeln, about 36 aircraft) accompanied by Messerschmitt Bf 109 fighters to protect them from the American escorts. Three of the Jagdgeschwader engaged in Reich Air Defence operations, JG 3, JG 4 and JG 300, were reorganised, each with one Gruppe of Fw 190 Sturmbock aircraft, and three other Gruppen equipped with Bf 109s with reduced armament and special uprated engines to make them more effective against American fighters. Galland's plan was to assemble mighty Gefechtsverbande (battle formations), each comprising one Gruppe of Sturmbock aircraft and two or three Gruppen of escorting fighters – a total of 100 or more aircraft – and send these in to make a concentrated attack against a single formation of American bombers.

The hazardous nature of Sturmgruppe operations decreed that only volunteers would be suitable; and before a pilot was accepted he had to sign an affidavit which stated:

'I ... do solemnly undertake that on each occasion on which I make contact with an enemy four-engined bomber I shall press home my attack to the shortest range and will, if my firing pass is not successful, destroy the enemy aircraft by ramming.'

Leutnant (Second Lieutenant) Walther Hagenah was one of the volunteers who signed the affidavit on joining IV (Sturm) Gruppe of Jagdgeschwader 3 when it formed in July 1944. He explained its terms:

'It was made clear to us that, having signed the affidavit, failure to carry out its conditions would render us liable to trial by court martial on a charge of cowardice in the face of the enemy. No man was forced to sign, however, and there were no recriminations against those who did not wish to do so; they simply did not join the ranks of the Sturmgruppen.'

The first large-scale use of the new Gefechtsverband tactics was on 7 July 1944, when a force of 1129 Fortresses and Liberators of the US Eighth Army Air Force set out from England to bomb aircraft factories and synthetic oil plants near Leipzig. As the bombers headed deep into Germany, the Luftwaffe fighter controller for the area was passing intercept vectors to Major Walther Dahl leading a formation comprising IV.(Sturm) Gruppe of JG 3 escorted by two Gruppen of Bf 109s from JG 300 – a total of about 100 aircraft. Just west of the target, Dahl caught sight of his quarry: box after box of bombers streaming eastwards. Dahl swung his force in behind a formation of Liberators of the 492nd Bombardment Group which, as luck would have it, was temporarily without fighter cover. The attack fell on the group's Low Squadron. Led by Hauptmann (Captain) Wilhelm Möritz, the Sturmgruppe closed to short range then opened a withering fire on its victims: bomber after bomber tumbled out of the formation until none was left. The 11-aircraft squadron was wiped out. Those Sturmbock aircraft with ammunition remaining attacked another part of the American force, then broke away and dived for home. The US 2nd Air Division lost 28 Liberators from all causes that day, the majority to Möritz's fighters. Walther Hagenah

Above: Three famous pilots of Jagdgeschwader 3; from the left, Walther Dahl, Wilhelm Möritz and Oskar Romm. Below: Sturmbock aircraft lined up at their base near Leipzig.

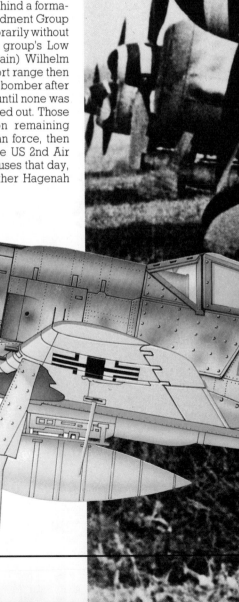

was credited with the destruction of one of them. The Sturmgruppe lost nine fighters shot down and three more were forced to crash-land; five of the unit's pilots were killed. By the standards of the time, it had been a highly successful operation for the Luftwaffe.

During the months that followed, Gefechtsverband tactics were frequently employed and there were occasions when they inflicted severe losses on bomber formations. On 2 November, for example, two Sturmgruppen were able to obtain firing positions behind separate American bomber formations attacking targets in the Leipzig area. During the first such engagement, IV.(Sturm) JG 3 attacked the 91st Bomb Group and knocked down 13 Fortresses, including two by ramming; then II.(Sturm) JG 4 attacked the 457th Bomb Group and destroyed nine Fortresses. The losses were not all on one side, however, and on the arrival of a strong force of Mustangs the slaughter of the heavy bombers ended and it was the Sturmgruppen that suffered heavily.

THE FOCKE-WULF BATTERING RAMS

The Focke-Wulf Fw 190, converted in 1944 for Sturmbock (battering ram) operations, was one of the Luftwaffe's most feared fighter types. Introduced into combat against the Spitfire Mk V in September 1941, it had proved itself more than a match for its adversary. Powered by the big BMW 801C 14-cylinder air-cooled radial engine, its top speed of 388mph enabled it to out-run the Spitfire, and it could out-fly its rival on almost every count except the British plane's superb turning circle. Even the replacement of its original MG 17 wing-stub machine guns with much heavier 20mm MG FF cannon could not impair its overall performance.

Germany, unlike the Allies, did not introduce significant new types of fighter as the war progressed. Instead, existing successful aircraft such as the Bf 109 and the Fw 190 were subjected to a bewildering array of modifications and improvements as new roles suggested themselves. When, in 1944, the urgent necessity of close-range attacks on bombers became obvious, the current Fw 190 models were adapted, and only one version, the Fw 190 A-9, was produced specifically for ramming tactics: it featured a 2000hp BMW 801F engine and an armoured wing leading edge.

Most of the Sturmbock aircraft, however, were older Fw 190s with their 20mm cannon replaced by two 30mm Mk 108 cannon supplied with explosive rounds. To improve protection against the bombers' close-range defensive fire they were given additional steel plating around the cockpit and ammunition boxes. The 400lb of extra weight imposed by these additions did reduce the performance and manoeuvrability of the aircraft, but it was now far better equipped for its potentially suicidal missions.

THE GEFECHTSVERBAND

Late in 1943, the US Army Air Force began to deploy the North American P-51 Mustang in the long-range fighter escort role. Other types, including the Republic Thunderbolt, were modified to increase their range, and by early 1944 US Army Air Force daylight bombing raids were accompanied by large numbers of escort fighters able to engage and destroy the Luftwaffe's Messerschmitt Bf 109s and Focke-Wulf Fw 190s. In addition to providing close escort, the Mustang squadrons ranged up and down the bomber stream searching for German fighter formations and engaging them. As German losses mounted, the Luftwaffe tacticians sought a better way of deploying their fighters.

The solution they adopted was the 'Gefechtsverband', or battle formation, which consisted of a Sturmgruppe of heavily armed and armoured 'Sturmbock' Fw 190s escorted by two 'Beleitgruppen' (light groups) of escort fighters – normally Messerschmitt Bf 109s. While the Bf 109s engaged the American Mustangs and Thunderbolts, the Sturmgruppe Fw 190s were free to close on the bombers and hit them at point-blank range.

Although the giant battle formations were difficult to assemble, and could on occasion be broken up by enemy fighters before reaching the bomber stream, the Sturmgruppen were able to inflict devastating losses when they succeeded in getting close to their targets.

Altogether the day's fighting cost JG 3 15 out of 39 Sturmbock aircraft committed, while JG 4 lost 16 out of 22. During these actions the two Sturmgruppen suffered heavy losses in pilots killed and wounded.

Walther Hagenah described the tactics employed during a typical Sturm attack. As the Gruppe approached an American bomber formation from behind it would split into its three Staffeln, each of which would go after a different squadron within the enemy formation:

'Once a Sturmstaffel was in position about 1000yds behind "its" squadron of bombers, the Staffel leader would order his aircraft into line abreast

and, still in close formation, they would advance on the bombers. At this stage our tactics were governed by the performance of our wing-mounted 30mm cannon. Although the hexogen high-explosive ammunition fired by this weapon was devastatingly effective, the gun's relatively low muzzle velocity meant that its accuracy fell off rapidly with range. And since we carried only 55 rounds per gun, sufficient for about five seconds' firing, we could not afford to waste ammunition in wild shooting from long range. To be sure of bringing down a bomber it was essential we held our fire until we were right up close against the bombers. We were to advance like Frederick the Great's infantrymen, holding our fire until we could see "the whites of the enemy's eyes".

'During the advance each man picked a bomber and closed in on it. As our formation moved forwards, the American bombers would, of course, let fly at us with everything they had. I can remember the sky being almost alive with tracer. With strict orders to withhold our fire until the leader gave the order, we could only grit our teeth and press on ahead. In fact, however, with the extra armour, surprisingly few of our aircraft were knocked down by the return fire; like the armoured knights in the middle ages, we were well protected. A Staffel might lose one or two aircraft during the advance, but the rest continued relentlessly on. In my Gruppe we positioned ourselves about 100yds behind the bombers before opening fire. Then our chance came and we made the most of it. From such a range we could hardly miss and as the 30mm explosive

rounds struck home we could see the structure of the enemy bombers literally falling apart in front of us. On average, three hits with 30mm ammunition would be sufficient to knock down a four-engined bomber, and the shortest burst was usually sufficient to achieve that.'

As a mark of pride, in recognition of the short-range engagements which characterised their operations, pilots flying with Sturm units had a 'whites of the eyes' insignia painted on their leather flying jackets.

It was, nevertheless, rare for a Sturm pilot to ram a bomber; Walther Hagenah never had to, and he never saw anyone else do so:

'If we held our formation, ran the gauntlet of the bombers' defensive fire and reached a firing position 100yds behind a bomber, with our powerful cannon it was a relatively simple matter to get a kill. There were a few occasions when people reached a firing position and found, for example, that their weapons had jammed. They then opened their throttle, pulled up a little, dived down and rammed. By and large, however, our weapons were very reliable and that was rarely necessary.

'We received no detailed instructions from our High Command on how best to ram the enemy bombers though the matter was, of course, the subject of several discussions in our crewroom. Of the pilots who made ramming attacks, about half escaped without serious injury.'

Although the Sturmgruppen were able to achieve occasional successes against heavy bombers during the autumn and winter of 1944, the hoards of American fighters sweeping ahead and on the flanks of the bombers made such operations increasingly costly and finally put a stop to them altogether. German

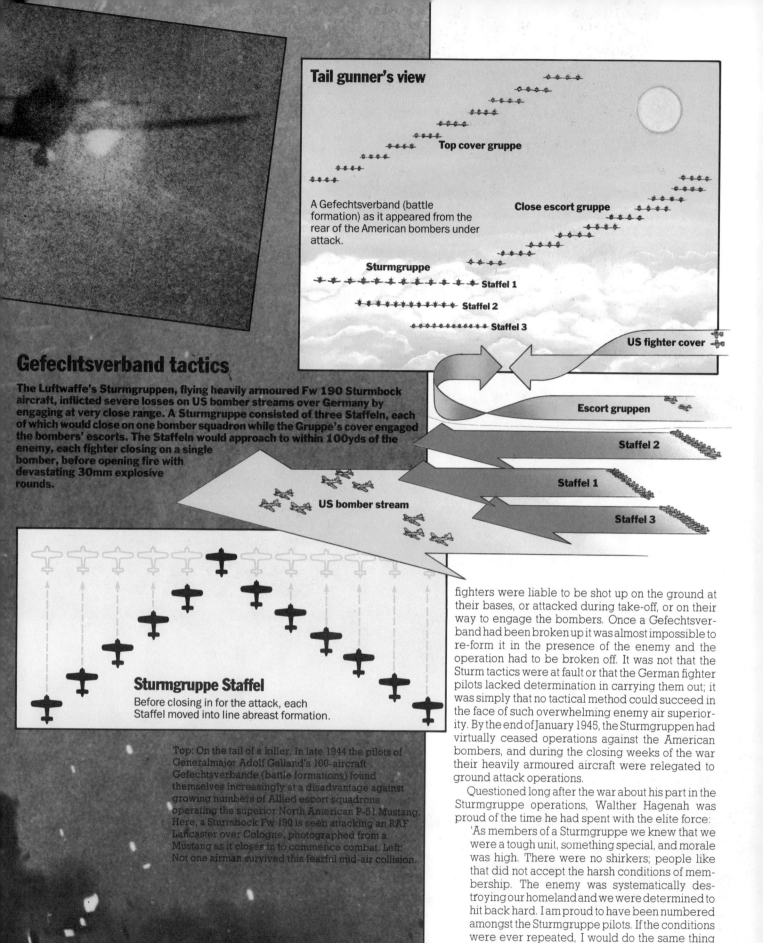

Tail gunner's view

Top cover gruppe

Close escort gruppe

A Gefechtsverband (battle formation) as it appeared from the rear of the American bombers under attack.

Sturmgruppe

Staffel 1

Staffel 2

Staffel 3

US fighter cover

Escort gruppen

Staffel 2

Staffel 1

Staffel 3

US bomber stream

Gefechtsverband tactics

The Luftwaffe's Sturmgruppen, flying heavily armoured Fw 190 Sturmbock aircraft, inflicted severe losses on US bomber streams over Germany by engaging at very close range. A Sturmgruppe consisted of three Staffeln, each of which would close on one bomber squadron while the Gruppe's cover engaged the bombers' escorts. The Staffeln would approach to within 100yds of the enemy, each fighter closing on a single bomber, before opening fire with devastating 30mm explosive rounds.

Sturmgruppe Staffel

Before closing in for the attack, each Staffel moved into line abreast formation.

Top: On the tail of a killer. In late 1944 the pilots of Generalmajor Adolf Galland's 100-aircraft Gefechtsverbande (battle formations) found themselves increasingly at a disadvantage against growing numbers of Allied escort squadrons operating the superior North American P-51 Mustang. Here, a Sturmbock Fw 190 is seen attacking an RAF Lancaster over Cologne, photographed from a Mustang as it closes in to commence combat. Left: Not one airman survived this fearful mid-air collision.

fighters were liable to be shot up on the ground at their bases, or attacked during take-off, or on their way to engage the bombers. Once a Gefechtsverband had been broken up it was almost impossible to re-form it in the presence of the enemy and the operation had to be broken off. It was not that the Sturm tactics were at fault or that the German fighter pilots lacked determination in carrying them out; it was simply that no tactical method could succeed in the face of such overwhelming enemy air superiority. By the end of January 1945, the Sturmgruppen had virtually ceased operations against the American bombers, and during the closing weeks of the war their heavily armoured aircraft were relegated to ground attack operations.

Questioned long after the war about his part in the Sturmgruppe operations, Walther Hagenah was proud of the time he had spent with the elite force:

'As members of a Sturmgruppe we knew that we were a tough unit, something special, and morale was high. There were no shirkers; people like that did not accept the harsh conditions of membership. The enemy was systematically destroying our homeland and we were determined to hit back hard. I am proud to have been numbered amongst the Sturmgruppe pilots. If the conditions were ever repeated, I would do the same thing again.'

THE AUTHOR Alfred Price served as an aircrew officer in the RAF for 15 years, specialising in electronic warfare, aircraft weapons and air-fighting tactics.

PHANTOM
ATTACK

8th TFW

The 8th TFW can trace its descent from the 8th Pursuit Group, which was activated at Langley Field, Virginia, in 1931. When the United States entered World War II in December 1941, the 8th Pursuit Group was operating P-40s from Mitchell Field, New York, but in the following March it moved to Australia where it was redesignated the 8th Fighter Group.

In late 1944 the Group moved forward to the Philippines and in the last days of the war, operating from Ie Shima, attacked airfield and railway targets in Japan. By VJ-Day the 8th Fighter Group had been credited with destroying 443 enemy aircraft in air combat and its leading pilot, Major Jay T. Robbins. had a personal score of 22 victories.

In June 1950 it was one of the first USAF groups to see action in Korea, flying Lockheed F-80 Shooting Stars for most of the conflict.

In the Spring of 1953, the 8th Fighter Bomber Wing converted onto the North American F-86 Sabre and in 1958 it was redesignated as the 8th Tactical Fighter Wing. After 22 years service in the Pacific, the 8th TFW returned to the United States in 1964, converting to the F-4C Phantom at George AFB, California.

Left, top to bottom: Fully armed Phantoms of the 8th TFW roar towards a rendezvous with North Vietnamese MiGs; Colonel Robin Olds (with characteristic cigar). the commander of the 'Wolfpack'; an enemy MiG-17 takes evasive action to avoid a Phantom's missiles.

THE F-4D PHANTOM II

The Phantom II multi-role combat aircraft was designed by the McDonnell Aircraft Corporation to fulfil the US Navy's need for a fleet defence fighter. The success of early models attracted the attention of the Department of Defense. In 1962, after a comparison of the Phantom II's capabilities with those of US Air Force fighters then in service, Tactical Air Command received authorisation to acquire F-4s for its squadrons.

The F-4D, which equipped the 8th Tactical Fighter Wing, first flew in December 1965. It is a heavy aeroplane with a high wing-loading, which leaves it with poor manoeuvrability for a dogfight. Its large size makes it easy to spot, a problem made worse by the high smoke emissions of the General Electric J79 engines. All in all, the F-4D was at a disadvantage in close-in combat with the agile Soviet-designed fighters of the North Vietnamese Air Force. The strength of the Phantom II lies in its avionics and missiles. The F-4D's search and track radar, the APQ-109, has a range of over 40 miles. It provides the lock-on for the aeroplane's AIM-7 Sparrow radar-homing missiles, whose range approaches 30 miles. The F-4D also carries heat-seeking missiles to complement the Sparrows. These can be either four AIM-4 Falcons, four AIM-9 Sidewinders, or a mix of the two. Their ranges are six and 11 miles, respectively. This combination of missiles and radar gave the F-4D a decided advantage in combat over longer ranges.

The pilots of the US 8th Tactical Fighter Wing worked out a deadly plot, codenamed Operation Bolo, to lure North Vietnamese MiGs into combat in January 1967.

IN DECEMBER 1965 the McDonnell F-4C Phantoms of the 8th Tactical Fighter Wing, the 'Wolfpack', arrived at Ubon Royal Thai Air Base at the start of a seven-year tour of combat duty in Southeast Asia. The wing's primary missions were to carry out tactical bombing sorties over North Vietnam and to provide fighter escort for the strike forces, as part of

COLONEL ROBIN OLDS

Robin Olds was born in Honolulu, Hawaii, on 14 July 1922, the son of Robert C. Olds, a US Army Air Corps pilot who rose to the rank of brigadier-general before his untimely death in 1943. Robin entered West Point in 1940, and then trained as a pilot. In May 1944 he went overseas with the 479th Fighter Group, which was the last fighter unit to be assigned to the US Eighth Army Air Force in Britain. The group's P-38 Lightnings began to operate from Wattisham in Suffolk. By the time that the unit converted to the P-51D Mustang in September 1944, Olds had gained nine victories. In January 1944 he took command of the 479th FG's 434th Fighter Squadron and by VE-Day had completed 107 combat missions. Old's personal score of 24½ victories made him the 479th FG's top-scoring pilot. After World War II he was a co-founder of the USAF's first jet aerobatic team, which flew P-80 Shooting Stars, and, in 1949, when on an exchange posting with the RAF, Olds was given command of No.1 Squadron flying Gloster Meteors from Tangmere in Sussex. In 1951 Olds was promoted to Lieutenant Colonel and became a full Colonel two years later, returning to Britain to command the USAF's 81st TFW.

the USAF's Rolling Thunder campaign. American air attacks against North Vietnam had begun in August 1964, in the aftermath of the Tonkin Gulf Incident, and at that time the enemy's air defences consisted of some 1400 anti-aircraft weapons, with associated early-warning and fire-control radars. Yet, as the USAF built up its strength in Thailand, so too did the

North Vietnamese air defense systems increase their effectiveness.

MiG-17 fighters first appeared in action during April 1965 and three months later the SA-2 Guideline surface-to-air missiles around Hanoi and Haiphong claimed their first victim. The highly manoeuvrable MiG-17s proved to be dangerous opponents to the heavily bomb-laden Republic F-105 fighter-bombers, but they could be countered by providing the strike force with an escort of F-4 Phantoms.

It was not until April 1966 that the air war over the North intensified and by that time the Wolfpack was in the thick of the action. The 8th TFW's first year in combat was to be an eventful one, with a total of some 14,000 missions flown. On 23 April 1966, the Wing's 555th 'Triple Nickel' Tactical Fighter Squadron reopened the USAF's air combat score against the Vietnam People's (North Vietnamese) Army Air Force (VPAAF). A flight of four F-4Cs was providing a fighter screen to cover an F-105 strike 25 miles northeast of Hanoi, when four MiG-17s were picked up on radar. The two formations met in a head-on pass and then a hard-turning dogfight developed at heights ranging from 10,000ft to 18,000ft. Captain Max F. Cameron, with First Lieutenant Robert E. Evans in the back seat, accounted for one enemy fighter with an infra-red guided AIM-9 Sidewinder air-to-air missile (AAM). 'As the MiG went down, it was falling apart and trailing thick, whitish-gray smoke,' Evans reported. A second kill went to the F-4C crewed by Captain Robert E. Blake and First Lieutenant S.W. George, who caught their victim with two radar-guided AIM-7 Sparrow AAMs.

During the following week a further three MiG-17s were destroyed in combat by the Wolfpack. Two of these were accounted for by AIM-9 Sidewinder AAMs, but Captain Larry M. Keith, with First Lieutenant Robert A. Bleakley in the back seat, manoeuvred his opponent into the ground. The MiG pilot 'either lost control of the aircraft, or attempted a split-S [a diving half-roll] with insufficient altitude,' reported Keith.

Above: An F-4D Phantom of the 8th TFW flown by Colonel Robin Olds. Below: General (then Colonel) Daniel 'Chappie' James who led Ford Flight on Operation Bolo in January 1967. At this time, James was the 8th TFW's deputy commander of operations and was one of the few black pilots to achieve a high rank in the US air force.

On 16 September the wing lost an F-4C during combat with MiG-17s, but this was avenged by First Lieutenant Jerry W. Jameson and First Lieutenant Douglas B. Rose during the same fight. After manoeuvring into a MiG-17's 12 o'clock position, Jameson 'fired two missiles. Then I turned hard to the left and back to the right again to get away from another MiG that had begun firing on me. When I straightened out again, I saw a man in the air.'

On 30 September 1966 Colonel Joseph G. Wilson was relieved by Colonel Robin Olds as commander of the 8th TFW. Olds, then aged 44 years, was one of the USAF's most experienced and skilful fighter leaders, having fought over Normandy during the D-day landings in World War II and gaining a high level of expertise, flying jets in the USAF's first jet aerobatic team. One of the pilots who served under Olds in Thailand, First Lieutenant Norman E. Wells, recalled that 'the esprit de corps of the 8th was exceptional. Olds was an inspirational leader.'

The MiG threat could only be met in the air and Olds was summoned to HQ to discuss the problem

Enemy fighter activity proved to be particularly high in late 1966, with Atoll-AAM-carrying MiG-21s (first encountered in April 1966) representing a more serious threat than the cannon-armed MiG-17s. The principal MiG airfields in the Hanoi/Haiphong region – Phuc Yen, Kep, Gia Lam, Kien An and Cat Bi – were off limits to American bombing attacks and this immunity continued until the spring of 1967. Consequently, the MiG threat could only be met in the air. Colonel Olds was summoned to Headquarters, Seventh Air Force, in December 1966 to discuss the problem. The outcome of this meeting was Operation Bolo, an offensive fighter sweep intended to bring the North Vietnamese fighters into action under conditions which favoured the Americans. This was to be achieved by luring the enemy into intercepting a force of F-4 Phantom fighters, which would simulate bomb-laden F-105 'Thuds' during their flight into North Vietnam.

If the ruse was to succeed, the F-4s would have to use the same tanker rendezvous points and refuelling heights over Laos as the F-105s, and also follow the Thuds' usual approach routes, speeds and altitudes when penetrating enemy airspace. Thus, the

Phantom formation would appear indistinguishable from a normal strike force on enemy radars. The deception was extended to adopting the communications procedures and callsigns normally used by the F-105s and by fitting the F-4s with ECM jamming pods, which only the Thuds had carried up until then.

Once the North Vietnamese MiGs had been drawn into combat by the bogus strike formation, known as the West Force, their escape route into the People's Republic of China (which was of course another sanctuary area off limits to American airmen) would be cut off by a second fighter formation known as East Force. Each F-4 flight's 'time on target' was separated by a five-minute interval, which would give the Phantoms a total of 55 minutes over the enemy airfields – a time which coincided with the MiGs' estimated endurance in combat. The F-4s of the Wolfpack provided West Force, while those of the 366th TFW made up East Force. The F-105s of the 355th TFW and 388th TFW were to carry out 'Iron Hand' flak and SAM suppression sorties, as they would for a normal strike force. Further support came from Boeing KC-135A tankers, Douglas EB-66 ECM aircraft, Lockheed RC-121 Big Eye radar-warning aircraft and Lockheed F-104 Starfighters, which flew combat air patrols over Laos.

After a one-hour delay in the hope of better weather conditions, the operation was launched

Three days of intensive aircrew briefings preceded Operation Bolo, which was scheduled for 2 January 1967, and a 24-hour stand-down prior to the mission was needed to ensure that all participating aircraft were serviceable. Consequently, when heavy cloud was forecast over the target area on the morning of the 2nd, the USAF commanders were reluctant to cancel the mission and have all the disruption to normal operations, which its preparations had entailed, go to waste. Therefore, after a one-hour delay in the hope of better weather conditions, the operation was launched as planned. The poor visibility over enemy territory would undoubtedly hamper the mission, firstly because it prevented the Phantoms from covering the North Vietnamese fighter airfields, in order to engage the MiGs as they took off or approached to land. Secondly, it would give the enemy fighters a good means of escape by diving into the overcast for cover. Only the Wolfpack's leading flight, headed by Olds, would be able to launch AIM-7 Sparrow radar-guided AAMs at beyond visual range, because once a second USAF flight had entered the area there would be too great a danger of shooting down a friendly aircraft by mistake. In the event, because the VPAAF was slow to react to the American incursion, all the Phantoms' missiles had to be launched after positive visual identification of the target as hostile.

The four aircraft of Olds Flight (rather unusually the commander's name was used as its callsign) entered the target area at 1500hrs and began to fly a search pattern in the vicinity of Phuc Yen airfield. As the flight turned for a second sweep past the North Vietnamese base, one of the F-4s picked up a radar contact, which was then lost as the target aircraft passed beneath Olds Flight on an opposite heading. The enemy fighter was flying in or beneath the cloud cover and so could not be seen by the Phantom crews. However, shortly afterwards, as Ford Flight led by Colonel Daniel 'Chappie' James entered the

area, the air battle started in earnest. Colonel Olds, flying with First Lieutenant Charles C. Clifton in his back seat, remembered that:

'At the onset of this battle, the MiGs popped up out of the clouds. Unfortunately, the first one to pop through came up at my 6 o'clock position. I think this was more by chance than design. As it turned out, within the next few moments, many others popped out of the clouds in varying positions around the clock.

'This one was just lucky. He was called out by the second flight that had entered the area; they were looking down on my flight and saw the MiG-21 appear. I broke left, turning just hard enough to throw off his deflection, waiting for my three and four men to slice in on him. At the same time I saw another MiG pop out of the clouds in a wide turn about my 11 o'clock position, a mile and a half away. I went after him and ignored the one behind me. I fired missiles at him just as he disappeared into the clouds.

'I'd seen another pop out in my 10 o'clock position, going from my right to left, in other words, just about across the circle from me. When the first MiG fired at disappeared, I slammed full afterburner and pulled in hard to gain position on this second MiG. I pulled the nose up high about 45 degrees, inside his circle. Mind you, he was turning around to the left so I pulled the nose up high and rolled to the right. This is known as a vector roll. I got up on top of him and half upside down, hung there, and waited for him to complete more of his turn and timed it so that as I continued to roll down behind him, I'd be about 20 degrees angle off and about 4500 to 5000ft behind him. That's exactly what happened. I am not sure he ever saw me. When I got down low and behind, I let him have two Sidewinders..'

'The first missile went slightly down, then arced gracefully up, heading for impact. Suddenly the MiG-21 erupted in a brilliant flash of orange flame. A complete wing separated and flew back in the airstream, together with a mass of smaller debris. The MiG swapped ends immediately and tumbled forward for a few instants. It then fell, twisting, corkscrewing, tumbling lazily towards the top of the clouds. No pilot ejection occurred above the overcast.'

Meanwhile, Olds 02, crewed by First Lieutenant Ralph Wetterhahn and First Lieutenant Jerry K. Sharp had accounted for another MiG-21 with a radar-guided AIM-7 Sparrow. A further successful combat was fought by Olds 03, Captain Walter S. Radeker III and First Lieutenant James E. Murray III, who launched an AIM-9 Sidewinder at their victim. As Radeker watched his MiG-21 tumbling uncontrollably into the overcast, Olds and Wetterhahn were just completing their attacks.

By that time Ford Flight was also engaged. Their leader, Colonel James, the 8th TFW's deputy commander for operations (and one of the few black pilots to reach high rank in the USAF) reported that: 'my flight was attacked by three MiG-21s, two from the ten o'clock high and one, simultaneously, from 6 o'clock low.' James failed to spot the enemy aircraft closing in on the rear of his flight, until his backseater, First Lieutenant Bob C. Evans, called an urgent warning. James and his formation broke away sharply to the right, while the MiG pilot miscalculated and

Above: A bombed-up F-4 prepares to emerge from the cover of its hangar. Below: An ordnance team re-arms an F-4 Phantom of the 8th TFW at Ubon air base in Thailand, prior to a mission over North Vietnam.

pulled round to the left. This gave James the opportunity for a missile shot. His Sidewinder missed its target, but forced the enemy aircraft to break into the flightpath of his wingman, Captain Everett T. Raspberry Jr. Raspberry seized the opportunity and his Sidewinder sent the MiG falling into 'a slow spiral, falling towards the undercast.'

Olds and Ford Flights were then forced to break off their engagement, because they had reached their fuel limits. The fight was continued by the four Phantoms of Rambler Flight, led by Captain John B. Stone, which arrived in the Phuc Yen area at 1510 hrs. They spotted a loose formation of four MiG-21s at the 2 o'clock low position, with a further two in trail about a mile behind. Breaking into his attack, Rambler 04 (Major Philip P. Combies, with First Lieutenant Lee R. Dutton) launched an AIM-7 Sparrow which impacted on its target's tailpipe, 'followed by a large orange ball of fire and a chute sighting.' Stone and his wingman picked out the leading two MiGs for attack, but were forced to break away as two more MiGs came in to attack them.

Stone then reversed his course and launched a salvo of three AIM-7 Sparrows at the leading MiG. The second AAM found its target and detonated near the enemy aircraft's wing root. Stone's wingman, First Lieutenant Lawrence J. Glynn, with First Lieutenant Lawrence E. Cary in the backseat, then managed to get into firing position behind another enemy aircraft and dispatched it with an AIM-7 Sparrow. This left Rambler 03, piloted by Major Herman L. Knapp as the only Phantom in Stone's flight without a victory. Knapp had fired a Sparrow at a MiG which was in pursuit of his flight leader, but apparently it failed to ignite as he saw no trace of its flight path.

Overall Operation Bolo had achieved a notable success, with seven MiG-21s destroyed for no loss to the Wolfpack. Furthermore, if the weather had not been so poor on 2 January, an even greater victory would have been possible, as only three Phantom flights out of the fourteen parti-cipating in the operation had engaged the enemy.

It seemed unlikely that the *ruse de guerre* employed in Operation Bolo could be successfully repeated, although the Wolfpack did gain two further kills using deception tactics on 6 January, when two Phantoms simulated a weather reconnaissance aircraft. Thereafter, however, the USAF had to rely on the standard tactics of escort and combat air patrol to bring the North Vietnamese fighters to battle. Eventually, the MiG threat to American bombing operations became so serious that the restrictions on attacking the North Vietnamese airfields were lifted in April 1967. Nevertheless, when the Rolling Thunder campaign ended with the bombing halt of October 1968, the balance sheet for air-to-air combats was very much in the Americans' favour, with 55 of their own aircraft lost for 116 VPAAF fighters destroyed. The USAF's ascendency over the North Vietnamese pilots, established by the Wolfpack in Operation Bolo, while often contested, was never in serious jeopardy.

Colonel Olds' assignment as commander of the 8th TFW came to an end in September 1967. During the year in which he had led the Wolfpack they had gained a total of 18 victories to add to the six kills achieved under his predecessor. Four of these victories had been scored by Olds himself, who was then promoted to brigadier-general and became Commandant of Cadets at the Air Force Academy, Colorado Springs, before his retirement from the USAF. The 8th TFW ended the Southeast Asia conflict as the most successful fighter wing in the Seventh Air Force, with a total of 38½ victories (the ½ being a victory shared with an F-105F 'Thud' of the 355th TFW. Thereafter it remained in the Pacific theatre, moving to Kunsan Air Base in South Korea in 1974. Today it still operates there, flying the F-16 Fighting Falcon which replaced the F-4 Phantom in 1981.

THE AUTHOR Anthony Robinson was formerly on the staff of the RAF Museum, Hendon and is now a freelance military aviation writer. He has edited the books *Aerial Warfare* and the *Dictionary of Aviation*.

PHANTOM VS MiG

Above the skies of North Vietnam in 1972, the crack pilots of Squadron VF-96 US Navy were faced with the fight of their lives

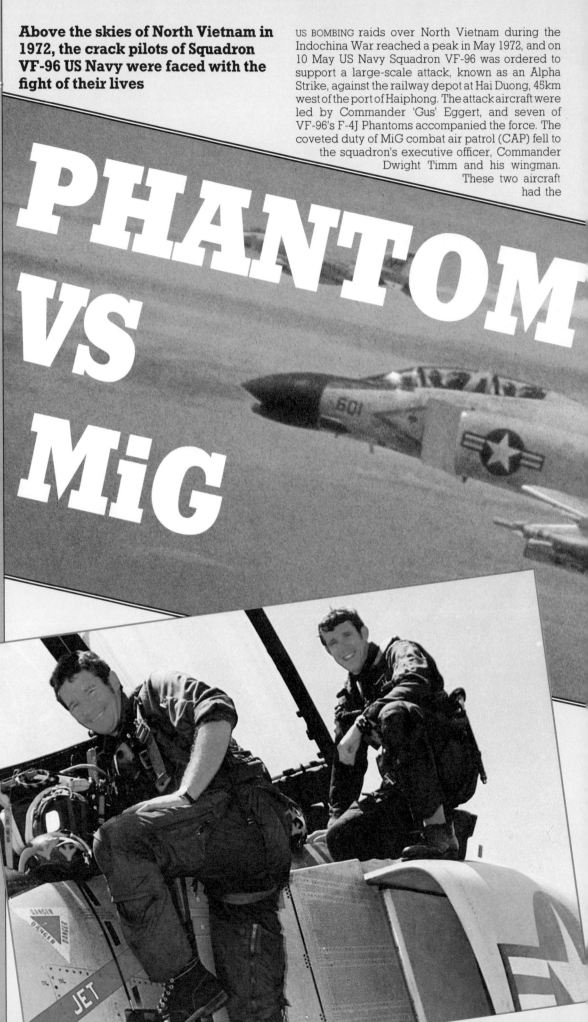

LIEUTENANT RANDALL CUNNINGHAM

Lieutenant Randall Cunningham was born in Los Angeles, California, but grew up in Shelbina, Missouri, and graduated from the State University in 1964. Three years later he was commissioned into the US Navy, and then trained as a pilot, receiving his wings in September 1968. After learning to fly Phantoms with VF-121 at Miramar, California, he was assigned to VF-96 (whose tailplane insignia is shown above). The most valuable part of his training had proved to be the combats against A-4 Skyhawks and F-5E Tigers acting as MiG-17s and MiG-21s.

Cunningham completed his first combat cruise of the Vietnam War aboard USS *America* in 1969-70, and, together with his second combat tour with USS *Constellation*, he amassed a total of 300 missions before the end of hostilities. The pinnacle of his career was the destruction of three North Vietnamese MiG-17s on 10 May 1972. This action, which took his tally to five, earned Cunningham the Navy Cross and elevated him to the status of an ace.

Following his promotion to Lieutenant-Commander, Cunningham undertook duties with the US Navy Fighter Weapons School, VF-154, and was attached to the staff of the Commander, Seventh Fleet. In January 1984 he was appointed executive officer of VF-126, a US Navy 'aggressor squadron' that simulates Soviet fighter tactics to provide air combat training for American pilots.

US BOMBING raids over North Vietnam during the Indochina War reached a peak in May 1972, and on 10 May US Navy Squadron VF-96 was ordered to support a large-scale attack, known as an Alpha Strike, against the railway depot at Hai Duong, 45km west of the port of Haiphong. The attack aircraft were led by Commander 'Gus' Eggert, and seven of VF-96's F-4J Phantoms accompanied the force. The coveted duty of MiG combat air patrol (CAP) fell to the squadron's executive officer, Commander Dwight Timm and his wingman. These two aircraft had the primary mission of attacking any airborne MiGs in the area. The target combat air patrol (TARCAP), which covered the strike force over its objective, was provided by the F-4Js of Lieutenants Matt Connelly and Dave Erickson. Lieutenant Steve Shoemaker was responsible for escorting the A-7 Corsairs attacking the surface-to-air missile (SAM) sites, and Lieutenant Randall Cunningham and his wingman Brian Grant were made responsible for suppressing enemy anti-aircraft fire. Cunningham knew that the attack on Hai Duong would be perilous; it was a heavily defended target and VF-96, although it had scored two kills in recent weeks, was a relatively untried unit.

VF-96, 'The Fighting Falcons', was formed in the 1950s. As reserve squadron VF-791, it was called to active duty during the Korean War and operated F4U

VF-96), three attack squadrons flying A-7 Corsairs and A-6 Intruders, reconnaissance, early warning and electronic warfare squadrons and a helicopter detachment. The Fighting Falcons, under the leadership of Commander 'Al' Newman, had a total of 12 Phantoms, together with their pilots, 'backseaters' (officially known as Radar Intercept Officers or RIOs), and maintenance crews.

About 350 of the ship's crew worked on the flight deck, moving and refuelling aircraft and manning the catapults and arrester gear. Their work was arduous, dirty and often hazardous, amid the noise and blast of aircraft launches and recoveries.

Yet, despite the difficulties, VF-96 ace 'Duke' Cunningham remembered that these young men, many of them just out of high school, 'never complained, never slacked in their work. Often these enlisted guys lifted my spirits by their dedication and relentless effort. I was proud to be part of such a team.'

As the air battle over North Vietnam increased in intensity during the early months of

Below left: Three F-4B Phantoms of VF-96 fly in close formation over South Vietnam in May 1966. Excellent pre-combat training gave US pilots an invaluable edge in most air battles with the North Vietnamese and by 1972 the Americans' kill-to-loss ratio had soared to 12 to 1. Navy air ace Randall 'Duke' Cunningham had over 200 mock dogfights behind him before he ever met an enemy MiG in combat. Bottom left: A devastatingly effective team. Cunningham and his RIO, William 'Irish' Driscoll, pose with the F-4J Phantom they flew in VF-96's most famous engagement on 10 May 1972. Both men received the Navy Cross following the action.

Corsairs from the carrier USS *Boxer*. By the mid-1960s the squadron had converted to two-seat F-4B Phantoms. These first saw action in April 1965, when the Fighting Falcons engaged Chinese Communist MiG-17s south of Hainan during their first combat cruise to Vietnam. One of the enemy fighters was recorded as a probable victory, but an F-4B also failed to return. Three years later, a second probable victory was scored, when one of VF-96's F-4Bs engaged a MiG-21 on 9 May 1968.

By October 1971, when VF-96 began its seventh tour of duty in Vietnam, the Squadron had re-equipped with improved F-4J Phantoms. It formed part of Commander Eggert's Air Wing 9 and was embarked on the carrier USS *Constellation*. The Wing comprised two F-4 squadrons (VF-92 and

1972, VF-96 pilots scored the first of many victories. On 19 January, Cunningham and his RIO, Lieutenant William 'Irish' Driscoll, shot down a MiG-21. The same redoubtable team had an easy kill on 8 May, and Cunningham recalled that 'the MiG driver must have been last in his class in aerial gunnery'. These combats, however, were only a curtain-raiser to the epic air battle of 10 May, that was to put the US Navy fighter pilots' ascendency over the North Vietnamese Air Force (NVAF) beyond doubt.

On the afternoon of 10 May 1972 the plan was that

after Cunningham and Grant's flak-suppression aircraft had unloaded their payload of Rockeye cluster bombs, they could engage enemy fighters with a reduced missile armament of two AIM-7 Sparrow (the F-4J usually carried four) and four AIM-9 Sidewinder air-to-air missiles (AAMs). As the A-7 and A-6 attack aircraft dived onto their target, North Vietnamese fighter aircraft made their appearance. Hai Duong was ringed by enemy airfields, and about 20 MiGs from Kep, Phuc Yen, Yen Bai and Bai Thuong engaged the American aircraft. Matt Connelly and his RIO, Lieutenant Tom Blonski, pounced on a MiG-17, which was attacking one of the A-7s. Connelly launched a heat-seeking Sidewinder which locked-on the MiG's jet exhaust and exploded. The North Vietnamese pilot ejected, as the blazing fighter spun to the ground. Moments later, Connelly spotted a second MiG-17 on the tail of an A-7 and this aircraft was also despatched with a Sidewinder missile. A third North Vietnamese fighter proved to be more alert, and pitched up into a vertical climb to shake off the American fighter. Both fighters slowed to a speed of 175 knots in the climb, before the MiG broke away and escaped. At one point, the two aircraft were so close that Connelly claimed he would recognise the North Vietnamese pilot if they ever met! Lieutenant Shoemaker and his RIO, Keith Crenshaw, were also in the thick of the combat. Spotting a MiG-17 on the tail of a Phantom, Shoemaker fired a Sidewinder at too great an angle from the enemy's tail for it to guide onto the MiG's jet exhaust, although it did force the MiG to break away from his intended victim. Shoemaker's Phantom then came

Right: The menacing array of weapons carried by the Phantom is clearly visible in this picture taken on the flight deck of the *USS Constellation* in April 1972. Although the Phantom was capable of a wide range of combat roles, most of VF-96's F-4Js were deployed as interceptors in the 10 May battles. In their contest with the MiGs of the NVAF, the Phantoms were generally superior in performance, although the MiGs were more manoeuvrable.

Below right: Crewmen grimace as they manhandle an AIM-9L Sidewinder air-to-air missile into position. The Sidewinder was the most effective weapon carried by the Phantoms of VF-96 during the Vietnam War. The AIM-9L had a range of 11 miles and carried a 25lb warhead.

under attack, but he made his escape at high speed and low level. This manoeuvre, however, brought him to the outskirts of Hanoi, the heavily-defended North Vietnamese capital, where an SA-2 SAM was fired at his aircraft. Waiting until the missile was nearly in range, Shoemaker executed a 'high-G' break, which the SA-2 was unable to follow. He was then able to take his revenge on a nearby MiG-17, which he shot down with a Sidewinder missile.

Cunningham and Grant were directed by Eggert to drop their bombs on a supply dump, as there were no flak emplacements, their primary targets, in the area. As they were pulling away from the target, a pair of MiG-17s flashed past Grant's F-4 and opened fire on Cunningham. Turning his Phantom into the attack, Cunningham forced the leading MiG-17 to overshoot. He then turned in behind it and launched a Sidewinder.

'The enemy fighter was well within minimum range, but by the time the missile got to him he was about 2500 feet out in front of me...that's how fast he was going. The 'winder blew him to pieces. That engagement lasted about 15 seconds.'

As the MiG-17's wingman pulled in towards Cunningham's tail, Brian Grant's Phantom came under attack from a second pair of North Vietnamese fighters. Exploiting the vastly superior speed of their aircraft, the two American pilots pulled away and accelerated to a speed of 600 knots.

Then, after pulling up into a vertical climb, Cunningham executed an Immelmann turn (a roll off the top of a loop, named after the World War I ace) and dived back into the fight. He remembered:

'The scene below was straight out of "The Dawn Patrol". There were eight MiG-17s in a defensive wheel with three F-4s mixed in! Our guys should never have been in there...they were down to 350 knots, a good place to die. I called for Brian to cover and rolled in.'

As Cunningham dived, Timm's F-4 broke from the circle, missing him by inches. Timm was hard pressed by a pair of MiG-17s and a MiG-21, but Cunningham could not fire a missile at the enemy fighters

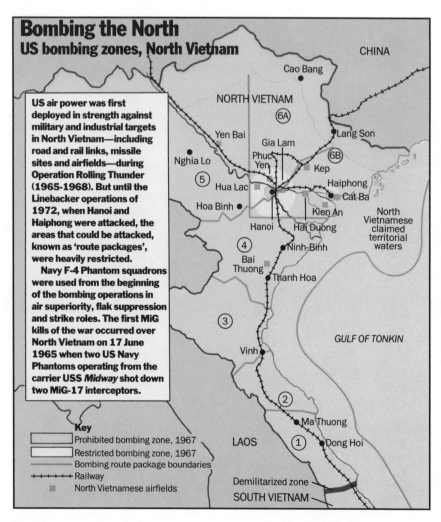

Bombing the North
US bombing zones, North Vietnam

US air power was first deployed in strength against military and industrial targets in North Vietnam—including road and rail links, missile sites and airfields—during Operation Rolling Thunder (1965-1968). But until the Linebacker operations of 1972, when Hanoi and Haiphong were attacked, the areas that could be attacked, known as 'route packages', were heavily restricted.

Navy F-4 Phantom squadrons were used from the beginning of the bombing operations in air superiority, flak suppression and strike roles. The first MiG kills of the war occurred over North Vietnam on 17 June 1965 when two US Navy Phantoms operating from the carrier USS *Midway* shot down two MiG-17 interceptors.

Key
- Prohibited bombing zone, 1967
- Restricted bombing zone, 1967
- Bombing route package boundaries
- +++ Railway
- ■ North Vietnamese airfields

CHINA
Cao Bang
NORTH VIETNAM
(6A)
Yen Bai
Gia Lam
Lang Son
Nghia Lo
Phuc Yen
(6B)
(5)
Kep
Hua Lac
Haiphong
Hoa Binh
Cat Ba
Kien An
North Vietnamese claimed territorial waters
Hanoi
Hai Duong
(4)
Ninh-Binh
Bai Thuong
Thanh Hoa
GULF OF TONKIN
(3)
Vinh
(2)
Ma Thuong
LAOS
(1)
Dong Hoi
Demilitarized zone
SOUTH VIETNAM

without endangering Timm's aircraft. As Cunningham called for Timm to break from the fight, to give him a clear field of fire, four more MiG-17s turned in behind, and a pair of MiG-19s, with cannon blazing, dived into the combat.

'I was still screaming for Timm to break starboard when Irish called out, "Duke, look up at nine o'clock". There, 4000 feet above us, I saw four MiG-21s just cruising along, content to keep an eye on the fight below.'

Finally Timm broke away, allowing Cunningham to fire a Sidewinder which blew a MiG-17 to pieces. The MiG-21s reacted by diving into the attack, but Cunningham evaded them and headed after Timm

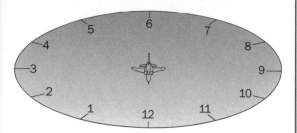

Above: The Clock Code. Aircraft are particularly vulnerable to missiles launched from the six o'clock position.

Left: The Vertical Rolling Scissors.
① Phantom breaks and MiG-21 overshoots.
② Phantom reverses with barrel roll.
③ Phantom in firing position.

F-4

MiG-21

THE PHANTOM AT WAR

Although the twin-engined McDonnell Douglas F-4 Phantom became the premier 'MiG killer' of the Vietnam War, it began its service life as a single-seat attack aircraft. By the time the prototype made its debut on 27 May 1958, however, the aircraft's role had changed to that of a missile-equipped, long-range, high-altitude interceptor.

Lieutenant Cunningham, with over 2000 hours and 500 carrier landings in F-4s to his credit, described the Phantom's qualities: 'it is one of the most honest aeroplanes in the world and will almost "talk" to a pilot. She will tell you every move she's going to make.'

The Phantom is capable of carrying up to 16,000lb of external armaments. These can be made up of a combination of bombs, rocket launchers, cluster bombs, napalm and either 20mm Vulpod or 7.62mm Minipod gun packs. For the action of 10 May, however, Cunningham's F-4J carried 2000lb of Rockeye cluster bombs, two AIM-7 Sparrow and four AIM-9 Sidewinder air-to-air missiles.

The Phantom's speed, sophisticated electronics and potent weapon's load made it more than a match for the enemy's MiGs.

③

Left: The High-G Barrel Roll.
① Phantom breaks.
② MiG-21 overshoots.
③ Phantom in firing position.

MiG-21

F-4

Achtung Bier Über Alles Luftwaffe

Dies Wird Geprüfen Dass

Baron Randy Von Cunningham

1st Ein Privilegiert Mitglied
Von Bier Trinken Staffel

Staffel Baron Von Bullock

Ein Prosit

towards the east.

Flying at 10,000ft, Cunningham spotted a MiG-17 slightly below him and heading straight for Timm's F-4. He decided to pass the MiG as closely as possible. This tactic had worked well against A-4s during training as it increased the radius of the turn needed to get onto the Phantom's tail.

'This proved to be my first near-fatal mistake,' Cunningham recalled, 'because A-4s [against which US pilots fought in combat training] don't have guns in the nose.' As the MiG-17 opened fire, its 'nose lit up like a Christmas tree' and Cunningham realised his error. He pulled up into a vertical climb and then looked down to see if he could pick up the MiG, which he felt sure would have gone into a horizontal turn or just run from the fight. This was the way that MiG-17s had acted in the past – their pilots were reluctant to fight in the vertical plane. 'As I looked back over my ejection seat I got the surprise of my life. There was the MiG, canopy to canopy with me, barely 300 feet away.' Cunningham lit his afterburners and climbed away from his opponent. This gave the MiG another opportunity to open fire, before Cunningham pulled out of his climb. However, he completed the manoeuvre and began to dive away without being hit.

The MiG-17 rolled after the F-4 and, as its nose came down to follow the F-4's dive, Cunningham attempted to gain the advantage. He pulled up towards the North Vietnamese fighter and executed a roll off the top. This action put the F-4 at the MiG's five o'clock position, but at too short a range and at too high an angle to be able to fire a missile. The MiG pilot countered immediately, attempting the same tactic against Cunningham in order to reverse their positions. The fight then developed into the classic 'rolling scissors' manoeuvre, with each aircraft rolling around the other in an attempt to reach the opponent's vulnerable six o'clock position. Cunningham realised that in such a situation the MiG-17's superior manoeuvrability would eventually give the enemy pilot the advantage. Consequently, he waited for an opportunity to disengage, and then

executed a tactic practised during air combat training in the United States. As the MiG pilot pulled up, Cunningham snapped the nose of his aircraft down and then accelerated away from the MiG's six o'clock position. By the time that the MiG had turned to follow, the F-4 was out of missile range and flying away at a speed of 600 knots.

With his speed advantage regained, Cunningham pulled back towards his opponent. The second engagement followed the same pattern as the first, with the fight developing into a rolling scissors and the F-4 being forced to disengage. For a third time Cunningham pulled towards the MiG:

'Once again I met the MiG-17 head-on, this time with an offset so that he couldn't use his guns. As I pulled up into the pure vertical, I could again see this determined pilot a few feet away. Winston Churchill once wrote, "In war, if you are not able to beat your enemy at his own game, it is nearly always better to adopt some striking variant." My mind simply came up with a last ditch idea. I pulled hard towards his aircraft and yanked the throttles back to idle, popping the speed brakes at the same time.

'The MiG shot out in front of me for the first time. The Phantom's nose was 60 degrees above the horizon and the airspeed was down to 150 knots in no time. I had to go full burner to hold my position. The surprised enemy pilot attempted to roll up on his back above me. Using only rudder to avoid stalling the F-4 with the spoilers [control surfaces] on the wings, I rolled to the MiG's blind side. He attempted to reverse his roll, but as his wings banked sharply he must have stalled the aircraft momentarily, and his nose fell through, placing me at his six but still too close for a shot. This is no place to be with a MiG-17, I thought, at 150 knots…this slow he can take it away from you.

'But he had stayed too long. We later found out that this superb fighter pilot (identified as Colonel

"Tomb" or "Toon", a 13-victory ace of the NVAF) had refused to disengage when his controller ordered him to return to base. After the war we found out that "Tomb"…had to run for it if he was going to get down before flaming out.

'He pitched over the top and started straight down. I pulled hard over and followed. Though I didn't think a Sidewinder would guide straight down, with the heat of the ground to look at, I…squeezed one off. The missile came off the rail and went straight to the MiG. There was just a little flash and I thought it had missed him. As I started to fire my last Sidewinder, there was an abrupt burst of flame. Black smoke erupted from the 17. He didn't seem to go out of control…the fighter simply kept descending, crashing into the ground at about a 45 degree angle.'

'They looked like fleas evacuating a dog, splitting off in every direction to get out of the way'

Cunningham's troubles were far from over, however. Two MiG-17s, intent on avenging their six comrades, dived down on his Phantom from the ten o'clock position. As he pulled the F-4's nose up and around to meet their attack head-on, he received warning of another danger. Matt Connelly, who had been watching the fight, radioed, 'Duke, get the hell out of there. There are four 17s at your seven o'clock.' Connelly then launched a Sparrow missile at the enemy formation, 'they looked like fleas evacuating a dog, splitting off in every direction to get out of the way.' Then, the two Phantoms headed for the coast, flashing past three enemy fighters at close range. 'If I'd had a gun I might have made three more kills,' recalled Cunningham. As it was, the targets were too close for a missile to guide onto them.

Nearing the coast, an SA-2 SAM streaked up towards the F-4 and exploded, before Cunningham could take evasive action. It knocked out the aircraft's hydraulic system, leaving the pilot with only his rudder and throttles available to control the F-4. Yet amazingly, Cunningham was able to roll his disabled aircraft for 20 miles, before he and Driscoll ejected from the now-blazing Phantom over the Red River estuary. They were quickly rescued by the destroyer-tender USS *Samuel Gompers* and, later, a Marine CH-46 helicopter returned the two men to a hero's welcome aboard *Constellation*.

Cunningham and Driscoll's triumph was doubly remarkable; not only were they the first American aircrew to qualify as aces during the Vietnam War, but they were also the Navy's only ace crew of the conflict. Their remarkable achievement should not, however, overshadow the three victories of their comrades, Connelly and Shoemaker. Thanks to these efforts, the Fighting Falcons lived up to their name in Vietnam – with eight confirmed and two probable victories to their credit they ended the war as the top-scoring Navy fighter squadron.

THE AUTHOR Anthony Robinson was formerly on the staff of the RAF Museum, Hendon, and is now a freelance military aviation writer. He has edited the books *Aerial Warfare* and the *Dictionary of Aviation*.

Above: Cunningham poses for the cameras after receiving the Navy Cross. Above left: Back on the *Constellation*, the 'Duke' relives his three kills with fellow pilots. Left: A facetious certificate presented by the US Air Force to commemorate his victories. Below: An F-4J returns to its carrier after a combat air patrol.

THE 81ST TACTICAL FIGHTER WING

The 81st Tactical Fighter Wing (badge shown above) traces its descent from the 81st Pursuit Group, which was activated at Morris Field, North Carolina, in February 1942. After training with the Bell P-39 Airacobra, the unit moved to North Africa in the wake of the Torch landings in November 1942. Its first combat mission, a low-level sweep over Tunisia, was flown on 22 January 1943. In April 1943 the group received P-38 Lightnings and operated over southern Italy during the winter of 1943 and early 1944. The 81st then moved to India in March 1944 and converted to the P-47 Thunderbolt. It became part of the Fourteenth Army Air Force in China two months later, and operated in that theatre until the end of World War II. It was deactivated in Huhsien, China, on 27 December 1945.

The new 81st Fighter Group was formed at Wheeler Field, Hawaii, in October 1946. Initially equipped with the P-51 Mustang, it later converted onto the P-47N Thunderbolt. After moving to Kirtland Air Force Base, New Mexico, in 1949, the unit began flying Lockheed F-80 Shooting Star jet fighters. In the following year it was redesignated the 81st Fighter Interceptor Group, flying North American F-86A Sabres. In August 1951, the unit moved to the United Kingdom and has remained there ever since.

The unit was redesignated the 81st Tactical Fighter Wing in 1958, and flew a number of aircraft including the Republic F-84F Thunderstreak and the McDonnell F-101 Voodoo and F-4 Phantom. The wing began to convert to the A-10 during 1979.

The A-10A 'Warthogs' of the USAF will play a crucial anti-armour role in any future land battle

THE A-10A 'WARTHOGS' of the United States Air Force's 81st Tactical Fighter Wing (TFW) play a key role in the defence of NATO's Central European theatre. In the event of war, their mission is to provide the ground forces with close air support and their primary target will be Soviet armoured forces. The angular and pugnacious A-10A, officially named the Thunderbolt II after the classic American ground-attack fighter of World War II, was specifically designed as a 'tank buster'. Its massive GAU-8/A seven-barrelled Gatling cannon can pump out 30mm shells at the maximum rate of 4200 rounds per minute, and can 'kill' an enemy tank at a range of one mile. The Thunderbolt's AGM-65 Maverick air-to-surface missiles (ASMs) have an even greater stand-off capability, able to devastate targets over 10 miles away. These factors contribute to the Warthog's own survivability, for the A-10As would have to run the gauntlet of fire from large concentrations of anti-aircraft artillery (AAA) and surface-to-air missiles (SAMs) in order to carry out their mission.

For self-defence, the pilots would rely upon skilled tactical flying at low level, taking advantage of any irregularities in the terrain to mask their approach to the target area, so that the enemy air defences would only be given a fleeting opportunity to engage them. The Warthogs would also make continuous changes in heading and altitude, further complicating any attempt to track them as they wove through the terrain. Additional protection is provided by the aircraft's electronic counter-measures (ECM) equipment, and the design of the aircraft enables the A-10A to absorb battle damage and continue to fly. Yet it is on individual pilot skill, rather than equipment, that the A-10A depends in order to carry out its mission effectively; and the pilots of the 81st TFW are agreed that, whereas the slow-flying Warthog is a very easy aircraft to fly, it is a difficult aircraft to employ properly.

The 81st TFW, which operates from the twin bases of RAF Woodbridge and Bentwaters in Suffolk, is the largest wing in the USAF, with an established strength of 108 A-10As and some 200 pilots. In all, about 5000 USAF personnel are assigned to the wing,

more than half of whom are employed in maintenance work. The wing commander, Colonel William A. Studer, has three vice-commanders, who are responsible to him for Operations, Maintenance and Resources (support functions other than maintenance). Flying operations are carried out by the wing's six tactical fighter squadrons (TFSs), each with a strength of 18 A-10As: the 92nd, 509th, 510th and 511th squadrons operate from Bentwaters, and the 78th and 91st squadrons share Woodbridge, together with the 67th Aerospace Rescue and Recovery Squadron. In addition to its two main operating bases, the wing flies from four Forward Operating Locations (FOLs) in the Federal Republic of Germany, with Detachment 1 at Sembach, Detachment 2 at Leipheim, Detachment 3 at Ahlhorn and Detachment 4 at Norvenich. With the exception of Sembach (which is a USAF Air Base) these airfields belong to the West German Luftwaffe, but support from the host nation is good and the two services work well together. A further two FOLs will be used in wartime and the wing has operated from these during exercises, but their identity remains classified information. With the wing operating from six airfields, strong leadership at lower levels of command is essential. Colonel Studer therefore regards one of his main tasks as choosing the most suitable officers as flight commanders, because they will be out of sight, if not out of mind, for much of the time.

The aircraft's outstanding manoeuvrability can be used to great advantage in combat

The A-10A Warthog is very much a pilot's aircraft, and all who fly it are enthusiastic in its praise – for Lieutenant Scott Purdie of the 510th TFS it is 'the last of the real aeroplanes.' Flying the A-10A means getting back to basics. The aeroplane has few of the sophisticated computer systems fitted to most modern fighter aircraft, and so its pilots have to master thoroughly the fundamental skills of airmanship and gunnery. This grounding is of vital importance for all pilots, since if automatic systems fail they can then fall back on their instinct and basic abilities. For this reason, the A-10A is considered an excellent introduction to the tactical fighter force for a newly-qualified pilot. The most recent winner of the USAF-wide 'Top Gun' fighter weapons competition was a former 81st TFW pilot who learned his tactics on the Warthog. Another pilot of the 510th TFS, Lieutenant

WARTHOGS

Mark Schroer, offered a further reason for the A-10A's popularity: its pilots get more flying time than those of other aircraft. Last year the 81st TFW flew a total of some 50,000 hours (comprising 29,000 sorties) and an individual pilot can expect to fly between 15 and 17 sorties a month.

Operating at low level, below 500ft, and at a speed of between 300 and 330 knots, feels comfortable for an A-10A pilot. Visibility from the cockpit is good, and the layout of the controls and instruments has been well designed, with essential flight information projected onto the pilot's head-up display. However, because of the need to fly tactically – constantly twisting and turning and using every feature of the terrain to mask an approach – piloting the A-10A can be very difficult. Despite the comparatively slow speeds, things can happen very fast and the pilot must always be aware of the danger of flying into the ground. He has to know both the capabilities and the limitations of his aircraft, and in order to survive in a high-threat environment he must be able to fly the A-10A at maximum performance. The aircraft's outstanding manoeuvrability can be used to great advantage in combat, however, and even for a pilot of Colonel Studer's experience 'its capability to turn is fantastic: the angles generated are awesome.' Another problem facing an inexperienced Warthog pilot is communications management. The aircraft carries three radios, which enable him to talk both to other aircraft and to the ground forces. Yet it requires a great deal of skill to cope with this workload effectively, and Lieutenant-Colonel Dennis Domin. the 510th TFS's Operations Officer, wryly remarked

Below: A-10As of the 510th Tactical Fighter Squadron return to RAF Bentwaters following a training sortie. Top right: Captain Susalla of the 510th. Right: During an exercise in West Germany, Warthog pilots come face to face with a Soviet T-62 target tank.

that three radios are probably two too many. Generally though, the A-10A's characteristics are well suited to its mission. In the opinion of Lieutenant Bobby Concannon, 'no other aircraft can do the close air support job so well as the A-10A. It is slow enough to observe, react and attack and not just flash past a potential target.'

The 81st TFW follows a rigorous training programme, with pilots spending on average 90 days each year at the FOLs in West Germany. Generally, each squadron provides an eight-aircraft detachment for this duty, while the remainder of the unit carries out weapons training in Britain. During a rather busier week than usual in June 1986, the 'Buzzards' of the 510th TFS flew more than 100 sorties, including a deployment to the FOL at Leipheim led by the

Above left: An A-10A, silhouetted against the dawn sky, reveals the angular features that have led US pilots to dub it affectionately the 'Warthog'. Left: The Fairchild A-10A Thunderbolt II. Powered by two General Electric TF34-100 turbofans, it has a maximum speed of 423mph and a strike range of 620 miles.

squadron's commanding officer, Lieutenant-Colonel Art Hedlund. Most of the tactical flying training takes place over West Germany, since it offers more military low-flying areas than the United Kingdom, and, more importantly, it allows the Warthog pilots to train in peacetime over the areas where they may have to fight in the event of war. Even the restricted areas near the border zone, which cannot be flown over, are reconnoitred by the A-10A pilots flying in US Army helicopters or on foot.

The majority of sorties flown in Britain are weapons-training missions over the east coast ranges, where the pilots can practise both gunnery and ordnance delivery. The process of learning is continuous. For pilots straight from training (learning to fly the A-10A with the 355th Tactical Training Wing at Davis-Monthan AFB in Arizona), there is the need to adapt to the demanding tactical requirements of the European theatre. After about a year's experience and 400 hours or so flying as wingmen, they

Top left: The pilot's instrument panel, with weapons select and release panels located on the left. Far left: Lieutenant-Colonel Ken Joyce of the 78th Tactical Fighter Squadron. Inset left (left to right): Executing a roll with split-second timing, an A-10A pilot demonstrates the aircraft's remarkable agility. As a flight of two Thunderbolts takes off from Bentwaters, a smoke deflector is clearly visible at the front of the rotary cannon. This prevents smoke from the gun impeding the performance of the aircraft's engines. Above left: An A-10 is doused with water to avoid the hazards of corrosion.

will have gained sufficient experience to qualify as flight leads. 'We educate ourselves,' reflected Lieutenant Bobby Concannon (himself a flight leader); 'learning begins after formal education.'

Air-to-ground gunnery is one of the essential skills to be acquired by the Warthog pilot, and, as the aircraft has no computerised aiming systems, this is not an easy task. However, if used properly, the GAU-8/A Avenger 30mm cannon is an impressive and very effective weapon. Its muzzle velocity is so high that even the solid metal rounds used for practice would be able to destroy a soft-skinned vehicle. The usual ammunition load is a mixture of armour piercing and high explosive incendiary shells, the latter for setting unarmoured vehicles alight. The A-10A's other main anti-armour weapon is the AGM-65 Maverick ASM, with a standard load of either two or four missiles carried by each aircraft. The AGM-65B has an electro-optical guidance system, which the pilot locks onto his target before the missile is launched. He does this using a cockpit-mounted TV screen, on which the scene viewed by the missile's guidance system appears. Employing a throttle-mounted control, the pilot centres the screen's cross-hairs over the target, locks on and fires the missile. Thereafter, guidance is entirely automatic and the pilot is able to switch his attention to a second target, or take evasive action if neces-

Below: Engulfed by smoke, the fearsome seven-barrelled gun of an A-10A delivers a salvo of 2lb shells in full flight. The GAU-8/A Avenger 30mm cannon (bottom) comprises the main armament of the A-10A, and is the most powerful rapid fire weapon ever installed in any aircraft. It is protected by titanium armour (far right), and is mounted at a downward angle of two degrees, offset to the left, so that the barrels come on to the aircraft's centreline as they fire. High-explosive or armour-piercing rounds are fed into the firing chamber from the drum using hydraulics, though the danger of overheating restricts firing to two 10-second bursts separated by a one-minute cooling period. Top right: Loading shells into the Warthog's cannon.

With its 11 external stores pylons, and a maximum weapons load of 16,000lb, the A-10A is also able to carry a wide range of conventional free-fall ordnance. Although these could be accurately delivered by dive bombing, this would involve overflying the target and exposing the aircraft to high risk from Soviet ZSU-23-4 AAA and SAMs. Nonetheless, the 81st TFW does practice with free-fall bombs and is equipped with Rockeye II cluster-bomb units for use against enemy armour.

One aid to accurate bombing is the wind correction data provided to the pilot's head-up display by the Litton inertial navigation system (INS). This equipment was not fitted to the A-10A when it first entered service, but the modification has greatly eased pilot workload. Its primary function is to navigate the pilot into his target area with the minimum waste of time. Yet, although it is a very precise and reliable system (Lieutenant Scott Purdie has only once experienced an INS failure in the A-10A), pilots still need to keep an independent check on their position using maps. Once over the battle area, the problem of locating individual targets for attack can be made easier by use of the Pave Penny laser spot tracker. This can pick up a target illuminated by the forward air controller's (FAC's) laser designator, and then indicate its position to the pilot on his head-up display. Lieutenant-Colonel Domin re-

sary. The 81st TFW is at present receiving the improved AGM-65D IR Maverick, which utilises an imaging infra-red guidance system. Since this relies on heat emitted by the target for its picture, it can be used in poor visibility and will not be deceived by camouflage, unlike the earlier AGM-65B. Lieutenant-Colonel Domin is impressed with the clarity of the IR picture as well as the new missile's longer range.

GAU-8/A rotary cannon

Calibre 30mm
Ammunition heavy armour-piercing
No. of barrels 7
Feed linkless, hydraulic motor-driven
Length 6.71m
Weight 1856kg

firing and extractor assembly

front housing
7-barrel assembly
roller bearing housing
barrel drive shaft

Rate of fire 2100 or 4200rpm
Muzzle velocity 1067mps

membered one exercise with live ordnance over the Otterburn ranges in Northumberland. He was working with a British FAC, who had marked a target and cleared him to attack. Despite hazy weather and the fact that he was flying into the sun – far from ideal conditions for a laser system – the tracker worked perfectly.

The pilot's choice of weapons will largely be dictated by the opposition encountered over the target area. The A-10A's gun would probably be employed on the initial attack and, in the absence of AAA fire, it would continue to be used. However, should the aircraft be shot at, the pilot could decide to stand off and launch an AGM-65 Maverick ASM against the source of fire from longer range. Armour is the Warthog's main enemy, but as AA fire would prevent a pilot from aiming his weapons accurately, it is important that this is dealt with first. The 30mm GAU-8/A can be aimed and fired more quickly than a missile can be locked on and launched; an abundance of cannon ammunition is carried (maximum 1350 rounds), but only a limited number of missiles. The A-10As usually operate in pairs, but, if increased firepower was required, a 'four ship' formation would be used and the 81st TFW spends a great deal of time practising the co-ordination of two flights operating together.

Close co-ordination is also the key to working.

feed track

spent case track

rotating inner drum

barrel drive gear assembly

ammunition drum

THE 'BUZZARDS'

The 510th Tactical Fighter Squadron was originally formed as the 625th Bomb Squadron (Dive) in February 1943, equipped with the Douglas A-24. However, it saw no combat in the dive-bombing role, being redesignated as the 510th Fighter-Bomber Squadron in August 1943 and re-equipping with the Bell P-39 Airacobra.

In March 1944, the squadron moved to the United Kingdom as a component of the Republic P-47 Thunderbolt-equipped 405th Fighter-Bomber Group. The squadron later returned to the United States and was deactivated in October 1945 at Camp Kilmer, New Jersey.

The 510th re-appeared in December 1952 as a fighter-bomber squadron, flying Republic F-84 Thunderjets from Goodman Air Force Base (AFB), Kentucky. It moved to Langley AFB, Virginia, in April 1953 and re-equipped with the North American F-100 Super Sabre. In July 1958, along with its parent unit, the 405th Fighter-Bomber Wing, the squadron was again deactivated.

Nine months later the 510th was re-activated, again flying the F-100, and was based at Clark AFB in the Philippines. It was assigned to the 3rd Tactical Fighter Wing (TFW) at England AFB, Louisiana, in March 1964 and moved to Bien Hoa Air Base in South Vietnam during November the following year. During four years of combat operations in Southeast Asia, the squadron's F-100s flew over 27,200 missions. Deactivated on 15 November 1969, the 510th Tactical Fighter Squadron became the second squadron of the 81st TFW to equip with the A-10A in 1979.

Above: Unit insignia of the 510th TFS.

Right: An A-10A prepares to receive the solid boom of a KC-135 tanker. Although inflight refuelling does not comprise an important element of the A-10A's combat operations, this facility does enable the 81st Tactical Fighter Wing to deploy quickly to any area of contention as part of America's rapid reaction forces. Below: Groundcrew from the 81st TFW monitor the progress of an A-10A as it taxies out of its hardened shelter prior to take off. As part of the wing's operational strategy, its aircraft are dispersed on a rota basis to Forward Operating Locations. Although these are semi-autonomous, they lack the equipment for extensive maintenance, and this is usually the responsibility of groundcrew at RAF Bentwaters and Woodbridge (main picture). Bottom left: Directly behind the ground technician in this picture can be seen the pod containing the A-10A's electronic counter-measures (ECM) equipment.

successfully with United States Army AH-1 Cobra helicopters and artillery. The 81st TFW's Warthogs would operate with these weapons to bring continuous firepower to bear on enemy AAA and armour using Joint Air Attack Team (JAAT) tactics. The aircraft would be in radio contact with both attack and scout helicopters and also with the ground forces. Timing can present a problem with such tactics, especially with regard to the artillery. However, as the latter can be particularly useful in dealing with enemy air defence systems, Lieutenant-Colonel Domin feels that more practice in co-ordinating the Warthogs with artillery would be extremely beneficial. In general, co-operation with the army is good; the 81st TFW has a US Army ground liaison officer and works frequently with FACs from the armies of its NATO allies. There is no problem with operating helicopters and A-10As in the same airspace, as the helicopters fly at tree-top height and below, leaving the airspace above to the Warthogs.

Whereas terrain masking is considered the A-10As' main defence against AAA and SAMs, in areas such as the North German plain they must rely heavily on ECM for protection. Every aircraft carries an ECM jamming pod, which can deal with a threat over a series of pre-selected frequency bands rather than jamming individual enemy radar systems. The A-10A also carries a radar warning receiver to alert the pilot to enemy radar threats, and he can release chaff and flares to decoy radar-guided and infra-red missiles. Moreover, as Lieutenant Scott Purdie pointed out, the A-10A flies so low that it is outside the engagement envelope of the more sophisticated Soviet SAMs.

The pilot's intention will always be to evade enemy groundfire, but should his Warthog be hit it is capable of absorbing a tremendous amount of damage. The pilot sits in a titanium-armoured 'bathtub'

which can withstand direct hits from 23mm cannon shells fired at close range. The fuel system is self-sealing and if hydraulic power is lost the aircraft can be flown using a back-up manual control system. The A-10A is also designed to remain airborne after the loss of one engine, one of the vertical stabilisers or even half a wing. On the ground, the A-10A would be an equally difficult target, as it operates from hardened shelters on its permanent airfields and requires a take-off run of less than 3000ft. Its rough-field capability also allows it to be dispersed to unsurfaced airstrips, and the 81st TFW has flown from sections of the German autobahn on exercises.

Enemy fighter aircraft could present the Warthogs with a few problems, though the pilots of the 81st TFW take the realistic view that there will be many other, more sophisticated, NATO aircraft to occupy their attention and that the A-10A is likely to be low on the list of Soviet fighter pilots' target priorities. Nonetheless, the threat is taken seriously and the 81st TFW practises defensive tactics against the F-5E Tigers of the USAF's 527th Aggressor Squadron and RAF Lightnings and Phantoms. These exercises give the Warthog pilots confidence that their low altitude and camouflage would provide a good defence against enemy fighters. For the air superiority fighter pilot 'speed is life' and he will be most reluctant to slow down and get into a turning fight with an A-10A close to the ground. Furthermore, the 81st TFW's A-10As will soon be armed with AIM-9L Sidewinder air-to-air missiles (AAMs) which will make them even more dangerous opponents. As Lieutenant Bobby Concannon put it, 'the enemy pilot's decision to attack will be a much more serious matter, because someone will die in the fight.'

The AMU is also responsible for re-arming and refuelling aircraft between sorties

Maintenance support for the A-10A squadrons is provided by Aircraft Maintenance Units (AMUs), which are part of the larger Aircraft Generation Squadrons and are ultimately responsible to the wing's vice-commander for maintenance. Each AMU is associated with a flying squadron, the 510th AMU supporting the 510th TFS for example. Commanded by Captain Casebeer, its only officer, the 510th AMU comprises 165 airmen and NCOs who between them have all the skills necessary for aircraft flightline maintenance. This involves the location, removal and replacement of faulty equipment, with subsequent repair work being carried out by a Component Repair Squadron. The AMU is also responsible for re-arming and refuelling aircraft between sorties and a turn-around time of only 15 minutes is usual.

The 81st Tactical Fighter Wing's fighting spirit and the awareness of all personnel of the vital importance of their war mission was perhaps best summed up by an A-10A pilot at the USAF's Fighter Weapons School at Nellis Air Force Base, Nevada, when talking with air superiority fighter pilots: 'You can shoot down every MiG the Soviet employ, but if you return to base and the lead Soviet tank commander is eating breakfast in your snack bar, Jack, you've lost the war.'

THE AUTHOR Anthony Robinson and the publishers would like to thank the 81st TFW's commander, Colonel William A. Studer, Captain Victor L. Warzin and the other members of the Wing for their help in preparing this article.

COLONEL WILLIAM A. STUDER

Colonel Studer (below) began his flying training with the USAF in 1961, and in 1964 he joined the Air Commandos at Hurlburt Field, Florida, later flying on operations with the 311th Air Commando Squadron in South Vietnam.
In 1969 Studer completed a second combat tour in Southeast Asia, with the 469th Tactical Fighter Squadron (TFS) at Korat Royal Thai Air Base. Studer flew a total of 164 combat missions in the Phantom, including 60 as a forward air controller.
From August 1971 to June 1974 Colonel Studer served as air officer commanding the 19th and 34th Cadet Squadrons at the Air Force

Academy, Colorado Springs. He then entered the Air Command and Staff College at Maxwell AFB, Alabama, and after graduating served with the 4th Tactical Fighter Wing's 334th TFS as a flight commander, assistant operations officer and finally as operations officer. Following an assignment to the 86th TFW at Ramstein Air Base, West Germany, as squadron commander and later assistant deputy commander for operations, Colonel Studer studied at the Air War College, before taking up staff appointments in Washington DC and at HQ United States Air Force in Europe. In 1984 he was appointed vice-commander of the 10th Tactical Reconnaissance Wing at Alconbury, taking command of the wing one year later. Colonel Studer became commander of the 81st Tactical Fighter Wing in March 1986.

SQUADRON OF THE ACES

Above: A lone Me 262 heads for a lumbering formation of B-17s. Below left: Two of the Luftwaffe's top aces confer. Gerhard Barkhorn (right) flew with JV 44. Below centre: After a mission, a jet pilot climbs down from his Me 262. Below right: Adolf Galland, the commander of JV 44.

its commander was the recently dismissed General der Jagdflieger, Generalleutnant Adolf Galland, who himself ended the war with 104 victories. Small wonder, then, that Jagdverband 44 (JV 44) came to be known as the 'Squadron of the Aces'. 'Most of them had been in action since the first days of the war,' recalled Galland, 'and all had been wounded, all bore the scars of war and displayed the highest medals. The Ritterkreuz [Knight's Cross] was, so to speak, the badge of our unit.' Yet the fact that JV 44 included officers holding the ranks of Generalleutnant (one), Oberst (two), Oberstleutnant (one) and Major (three) was even more extraordinary. That such a galaxy of senior and experienced airmen should have been allowed to fight as ordinary combat pilots bears eloquent testimony to the 'Alice-in-Wonderland' mentality of the German High Command during the closing months of World War II.

Germany had not been slow to recognise the tremendous military potential of jet propulsion following the flight of the world's first turbojet aircraft, the Heinkel He 177, in August 1939. In the summer of 1942 flight testing on the Me 262 twin-jet fighter began, and when General der Jagdflieger Galland flew it he was favourably impressed with its blistering performance. By the time it entered operational service in 1944, Galland saw in this aircraft the weapon that would defeat the USAAF daylight bombing raids and regain air superiority for the Luftwaffe.

Adolf Hitler, however, had other ideas, and decreed that the Me 262 should be developed only for

IN FEBRUARY 1945, only months before the final collapse of the Third Reich, a most remarkable Luftwaffe unit began to form at the airfield of Brandenburg-Briest, some 60km southwest of Berlin. It was equipped with the twin-jet Messerschmitt Me 262, which was generally acknowledged to be the best fighter aircraft in service anywhere in the world. Among its pilots were many of the Luftwaffe's top aces: men such as Major Gerhard Barkhorn (301 victories), Oberst Johannes Steinhoff (176 victories), Oberst Günther Lützow (108 victories), and Hauptmann Walter Krupinski (197 victories). And

JAGDVERBAND 44

As the most senior Luftwaffe fighter officer, Adolf Galland did not see eye-to-eye with the C-in-C of the Luftwaffe, Reichsmarschall Hermann Göring. Their differences came to a head over the deployment of the revolutionary Me 262 jet. Facing opposition from the most senior bomber officer, Dietrich Peltz, and Adolf Hitler himself, who wanted to use the jet in the fighter-bomber role, Galland still managed to acquire some Me 262s for his fighter units in the latter half of 1944. In January 1945, however, he was dismissed from his post.

Outraged by what they saw as gross mismanagement and injustice, a group of senior fighter officers led by Oberst Gunther Lützow sought to have Göring replaced as C-in-C of the Luftwaffe. In this they failed; Lützow was banished to Italy as Jagdfliegerführer Oberitalien, and his comrade Oberst Johannes Steinhoff was replaced as Kommodore of Jagdgeschwader 7, the first Me 262 fighter unit, and given no further posting. It was Galland's dismissal and the ensuing 'Mutiny of the Aces' that made available the experienced pilots to form the elite JV 44. Galland sent for Steinhoff and Lützow to form the backbone of the new unit, and other aces such as Barkhorn, Krupinski, Hohagen and Schnell soon joined them. When JV 44 commenced operations on 31 March 1945 it was the most illustrious gathering of airborne fighting talent ever assembled.

the fighter-bomber role. This decision sparked off a furious controversy within the Luftwaffe between Galland and his opposite number, General der Kampflieger Dietrich Peltz, who stood to gain from the Me 262 being supplied to his bomber units. Reichsmarschall Hermann Göring, the Luftwaffe's C-in-C – at any rate in name – did little to resolve the dispute. Relations between him and Galland had always been poor, and they continued to worsen, since the Reichsmarschall's only response to the steadily deteriorating air situation was to rant about the cowardice of the Luftwaffe fighter pilots. Nonetheless, Galland made some headway, and, when the Me 262 entered operational service during the latter half of 1944, it was supplied to both fighter and bomber units. In January 1945, however, his battle with Göring reached its climax and he was dismissed from his post as General der Jagdflieger.

FIGHTER TACTICS

German fighter squadrons, such as JV 44, which flew the Me 262 jet, generally operated in small units of six aircraft. They flew in the three aircraft 'Kette' formation, rather than in the traditional fighter 'Schwarm' of four aircraft because, on encountering the enemy, the jets carried out their attacks singly. There was no need for wingmen to stick to their leaders and guard their tails, as was the case with piston-engined fighters: the Me 262's tremendous speed was the only protection it needed in combat.

The speed of the jet also called for special tactics when attacking USAAF bomber formations. The Me 262s began their attack from above and astern the enemy bombers. They then dived through the fighter escort, which they could easily outdistance. At this speed, however, the jets would have closed with the bombers far too fast to allow the pilots to aim and fire their weapons accurately. Therefore, they dived to a point about 2km behind their targets, carried on down beneath their altitude, and then bled off speed in a 'high-G' climb to the bombers' level. This 'Roller Coaster' manoeuvre (shown above) reduced the closing speed to an acceptable 160 km/h. Once through the bomber formation, the jets would accelerate away, gaining height in readiness for a second attack.

Above: one of JV 44's Me 262s. The jet was armed with the potent Mk 108 30mm cannon (below); a single shell was able to inflict severe damage (right). Far right: Each aircraft also carried 24 R4M 55mm rockets on two underwing racks.

Following his fall from grace, and relieved of all responsibilities for administration and high command, Galland set about forming his elite unit, JV 44. The best men were sent for and his friend and associate Johannes Steinhoff was immediately set to work organising the conversion training of pilots onto the new jets. When they had emerged from hospital where they were recovering from wounds, Major Karl-Heinz Schnell (72 victories) and Major Erich Hohagen (55 victories) joined the experienced nucleus of Lützow, Barkhorn and Krupinski. On 31 March 1945, Galland led his unit on the 40-minute flight from Brandenburg to Munich-Riem airfield, where JV 44 was to begin operations.

The formidable combination of the Me 262 and this unprecedented concentration of flying talent was, however, to have little effect. By 1945 it was clear that the war had been lost. The Luftwaffe fighter forces were under strength, short of fuel and their supply organisation was in chaos. As the perimeters of the Reich steadily contracted, the German early-warning system grew less and less efficient and the few remaining airfields in central and southern Germany became congested with fighter aircraft. Large formations of Allied fighters roamed over German territory and kept an especially vigilant watch on the airfields used by the jets. Under such conditions there was little that the small number of operational Me 262s could do to turn the tide, but the pilots of JV 44 were determined to fight to the end.

JV 44's main target was to be the US bombers that streamed over Germany day after day in massed raids. The unit was soon in action and, on 5 April, JV 44 claimed two bombers destroyed at no loss to themselves. Johannes Steinhoff has written a vivid account of just such a bomber attack, which emphasises the problems of the Me 262's high speed and temperamental engines:

'The formation of four-engined bombers was cruising along like a fly-past. They were pulling long vapour trails behind them and the shadows of the trails lay like the lines of an exercise book on the glaring white cloud below...

'I put the Me's nose down and my speed began to increase. I dived through the vapour trails and on for another few hundred metres until, seeing the bombers right above me, I pulled my machine up into their wake. I regarded the American fighters as harmless and ignored them; after all I was flying at nearly twice their speed.

'The inadequacy of our experience of aerial combat at high altitudes came home to me as the pressures on the Me's control stick grew. Warnings flashed through my head – "Fly no faster than 870km/h", "Careful not to touch the throttle", "Don't charge your revs or the engine may blow up" – as I tried to keep the bombers in view. They were like so many spiders drawing their vapour-trail threads across the grey-blue sky. My leading-edge slats sprang out as I pulled up sharply and began to climb... The colossal acceleration carried me right into the vapour trails...and suddenly the tall tail sections of the Fortresses

W. Nr. 110917

THE ME 262

The Me 262 was a revolutionary twin-jet design which outclassed all the Allied fighters of 1945. Its maximum speed was 870km/h in level flight at 6000m, and it was armed with four Mk108 30mm cannon – the heaviest armament of any World War II fighter. To supplement this weaponry, the Me 262 could carry 24 R4M air-to-air rockets on underwing pylons or up to 500kg of bombs underneath the nose. When General der Jagdflieger Galland test-flew the aircraft on 22 April 1943 he reported: 'No engine vibration, no torque and no lashing noise from the airscrew. Accompanied by a whistling sound my jet shot through the air. Later, when asked what it felt like, I said, "It was as though the angels were pushing".'

The aircraft's twin Junkers Jumo 004B turbojets were notoriously unreliable, however. At high altitude the engines were liable to 'flame out' and suffer from compressor stall, a fault which threatened to limit the aircraft to an operating height of 8000m. The engine's running life was only ten hours between overhauls and 25 hours before replacement, and the undercarriage design was faulty, frequently causing structural damage during heavy landings.

The Me 262 was also slow to accelerate or decelerate in comparison to conventional piston-engined fighters, and pilots had to take particular care to avoid exceeding the jet's design limits. The aircraft could accelerate beyond its limiting speed and become uncontrollable even in a shallow dive. It took all the skill of an experienced pilot to fly the Me 262 properly, but in the hands of an ace it was a deadly machine.

filled my windshield like rows of shark fins. When the bomber filled the circle of my luminous reflex gunsight, when its wingtips exactly touched the outer edge of the circle – that was the moment to fire the rockets.'

Whether the Luftwaffe's comparatively few jet fighters were being put to the best use in attacking bombers had been a matter of debate among Luftwaffe tacticians. Some argued that they would have been better employed in dealing with the fighter escorts, thus clearing the way for the Luftwaffe's more numerous piston-engined fighters to deal with the 'Viermots' (as the German airmen called the American four-engined B-17 Fortresses and B-24 Liberators). As it was, the piston-engined fighters were increasingly heavily committed to defending the jets' own airfields from attack. The Munich-Riem airfield was constantly patrolled by American fighters and frequently came under bomber attack. Thousands of civilian workers were needed to fill in the bomb craters on the runway between raids. On landing, the jets had to be immediately towed off the field, and dispersed over the countryside under camouflage. Some jet units were forced to abandon their regular airfields altogether and to fly from suitable stretches of autobahn. Even on Munich-Riem airfield living conditions were quite primitive. 'The squadron's rest area was a masterpiece of improvisation,' remembered Steinhoff, 'consisting basically of a table and a few rickety chairs set up in the middle of a patch of weeds and undergrowth. A field telephone stood on the table. The pilots lounged in deckchairs sipping coffee out of chunky Wehrmacht cups.'

Some of JV 44's Me 262s were fitted with the R4M air-to-air rockets at this time and Galland has recorded his impressions of a successful attack using these weapons:

'Somewhere near Landsberg on the Lech I met a formation of about 16 Marauders. I opened fire into the close-flying formation... from a distance of about 550m with a salvo of 24 rockets. There were two certain hits: one bomber immediately caught fire and exploded, while a second lost large parts of its right tailplane and wing and began to spiral earthwards.'

Problems were experienced with the firing circuits of these weapons, however, and on two occasions Steinhoff's rockets failed to fire after he had reached a good attacking position, and he was forced to switch hastily to his cannon armament. Another pilot, Galland's wingman Unteroffizer Eduard Schallmoser, became so frustrated on one sortie when his rockets failed to fire that he carried out a ramming attack on his opponent. His Me 262 sliced through the B-17's tailfin with its wing and the bomber rolled clumsily on its back before abruptly going into a vertical dive'. Schallmoser managed to parachute to safety and reported back to Riem in the evening 'with his parachute under his arm and a twisted leg'.

Steinhoff remembered one combat sortie by nine R4M-armed Me 262s in defence of their own airfield

Truly the Squadron of the Aces, the ranks of JV 44 were filled with some of the Luftwaffe's most decorated and experienced pilots. Above left: Major Wilhelm Herget, seen here shaking hands with Hitler in May 1944 after receiving the Ritterkreuz with Oakleaves for 63 victories as a nightfighter pilot, flew with JV 44 in the last days of the war. Centre left: Oberleutnant Heinz Bär (second from right) took charge of the squadron after Galland had been wounded on 26 April 1945 and became the top-scoring jet ace with 16 confirmed kills to his credit. Günther Lützow (below, far left) had scored 108 victories before joining JV 44. A close friend of Galland, he led the rebellion against the misuse of the Me 262, and was killed in action on 24 April. Below: A line of Me 262s undergoing routine checks on a grass airstrip.

at Munich-Riem. Galland was leading the formation, with Steinhoff at the head of the second section of three aircraft. The jets reached their combat altitude just as the American bomber formation arrived over Munich. Galland decided to risk the danger of being hit by German flak over the city and dived into the attack, followed by the two other Me 262s in the leading formation. Then it was Steinhoff's turn:

'I concentrated on the task of picking out what would be the best target for my flight coming in behind me. The smoke trails left by the Fortresses that had been shot down hung eerily in the still air. Pulling gently to starboard I was able to get the remains of a flight of bombers framed in my windshield. They had adopted a policy of every man for himself and were trying to flee westwards as fast as they could.... The bombers were now in a state of utter confusion. Although for the second time I had been unable to fire my rockets, the other pilots had scored hits. The escort of Mustangs and Lightnings dived down at us and came at us from ahead and out of wild banking turns – all without beginning to constitute a serious hindrance to us.

'Our tiny formation had "split at the seams" and we each moved independently through the milling turmoil of bombers and fighters, exploiting our far superior speed. The scale of circling, climbing and diving manoeuvres was so vast with the Me 262 that at times they carried us far away from the action and made the bombers and escort fighters appear to hang motionless in the air.

'I decided not to fly a second attack because I wanted to get back to the airfield with sufficient fuel in reserve. The American fighters would undoubtedly take advantage of our vulnerability during landing and keep an eye on the airfield with the object of shooting us down as we came in.'

Towards the end of April 1945, signs of the general disintegration of the Luftwaffe became apparent at Riem airfield. As units which had been equipped with the Me 262 ceased to function, through shor-

Germany, 1945

By the latter stages of the war, supply shortages severely limited the number of sorties flown by JV 44. The Allies had also introduced more effective measures to combat the Me 262. The jets were especially vulnerable when flying at low speed after take-off (right) or just before landing. Allied fighters would pounce at these moments. Above: During their operations in the last months of the war, JV 44 also suffered heavily from the Allied fighter presence over Germany. In this dramatic photograph, taken by a Mustang, an Me 262 is closing in for a kill. Seconds later, the jet was blasted out of the sky. By early May 1945, the lack of fuel, losses and the systematic bombing of airfields, put an end to the remarkable exploits of JV 44. Although the Me 262s had been dogged by technical problems, JV 44's pilots had downed 45 enemy aircraft.

tonnes needed for a fighter pilot. Little wonder that of the six bomber units intended to convert onto the jet within Dietrich Peltz's Fliegerkorps IX(J), only one, Kampfgeschwader 51, ever operated it on any scale.

JV 44's combat successes were not achieved without loss, and operational accidents were as great a danger as enemy action. On Gerhard Barkhorn's second jet mission, one of the engines of his Me 262 failed while he was attacking some American bombers. Skilfully avoiding the P-51 Mustang escort in his crippled jet, Barkhorn brought his aircraft down to a crash landing. The injuries he sustained kept him in hospital for the remaining weeks of the war. Johannes Steinhoff was also a victim of the Me 262's unreliable engines. On 18 April he began a take-off run in his Me 262, heavily laden with fuel and armament. The jet failed to develop full power and crashed in flames at the end of Riem's bomb-scarred runway. Its pilot suffered appalling burns, but he eventually recovered to become a general in the postwar Luftwaffe. His friend Günther Lützow, member of a famous Prussian military family and a veteran of the Condor Legion in Spain, was killed in action on 24 April. Two days later Galland himself was surprised by a P-51 Mustang while attacking a formation of B-26 Marauders and was wounded in the leg. His injury forced him to hand command of JV 44 over to Oberstleutnant Heinz Bär, a 220-victory ace who ended the war as the top-scoring jet pilot with 16 kills gained flying the Me 262.

During little more than a month in combat JV 44 had been credited with the destruction of 45 aircraft

At the end of April 1945 Bär led JV 44 with some 60 Me 262s to a new airfield at Salzburg-Maxglam. A further move to Prague was ordered, but the unit delayed and was overrun at Salzburg by American forces on 3 May. During little more than a month in combat, JV 44 had been credited with the destruction of 45 enemy aircraft. In all, Me 262-equipped fighter units had destroyed some 150 Allied aircraft for the loss of around 100 jets. It was a creditable performance, but it fell far short of what had been expected from the

tages of fuel, spare parts, or pilots, they passed on their aircraft to JV 44, which acquired a total of some 70 jet fighters in this manner. Only III/JG 7 and Galland's unit continued to operate the Me 262 until the final collapse of the Reich. It was a belated vindication of Galland's outspoken criticism of the folly of converting bomber units onto the jet fighter. For, however experienced and gallant the pilots of the bomber force may had been, they lacked the necessary skills to train rapidly on the radical new jet fighter. At a time when fuel was critically short in Germany, it required 65 tonnes of kerosene to train a bomber pilot on the Me 262, compared with only 25

revolutionary new fighter. Yet, in view of the overwhelming superiority of Allied air power in 1944-45 and the technical problems encountered with the Me 262, it is unlikely that more could have been achieved. The pilots of JV 44 must have realised that the outcome of the war was a foregone conclusion when they flew into action on 31 March 1945, but they, nonetheless, fought gallantly on until the last.

THE AUTHOR Anthony Robinson was formerly on the staff of the RAF Museum, Hendon and is now a freelance military aviation writer. He has edited several books including *Aerial Warfare*.

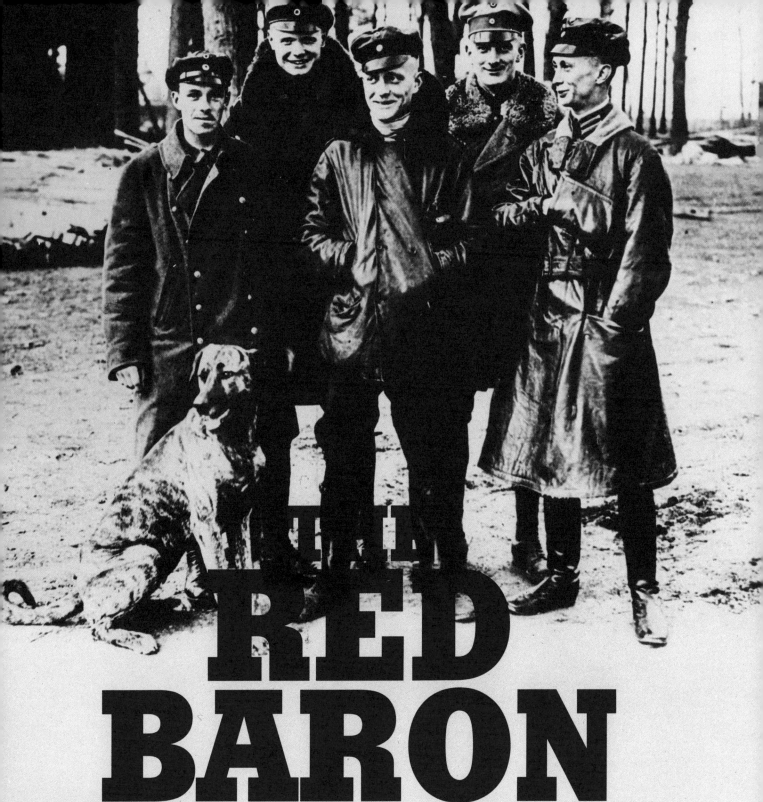

RED BARON

In 'Bloody April' 1917, The Royal Flying Corps lost more than 300 airmen to the guns of Manfred von Richthofen's ace squadron, Jasta 11

I WAS STILL in bed when my orderly ran in exclaiming, "Herr Leutnant, the English are here!" Half asleep, I looked out of the window and saw, circling over the airfield, my "dear friends". Getting out of bed, I dressed quickly: my red bird was all prepared to begin the work of the morning, for my mechanics knew I was not likely to let such a favourable opportunity slip past. Everything was

ready: I got into my flying suit and took off.

'In spite of everything, I was the last to be airborne, and my comrades were already close to the enemy. Suddenly, however, one of the impertinent fellows dropped on me from above, hoping to force me down. Calmly I let him come at me, and then we began a merry dance. My opponent flew on his back, he did this, he did that. He was flying a two-seater, but I was superior to him, and he soon realised that he could not get away from me. I looked around and saw that we were alone: whoever shot the better, remained calmer and held the better position at the moment of danger, would be the victor.

'It didn't take long. I squeezed below him and

Above: The ace pilots of Jagdstaffel 11, flying the superior Albatros D.III, effected an appalling slaughter of Allied airmen in early 1917. Most formidable of all was their commander, Manfred von Richthofen (centre), who eventually achieved 80 confirmed victories. With him (from left to right) are Sebastian Festner, Emil Schaefer, his brother Lothar, and Kurt Wolff. Manfred's beloved Danish hound 'Moritz' is in the foreground.

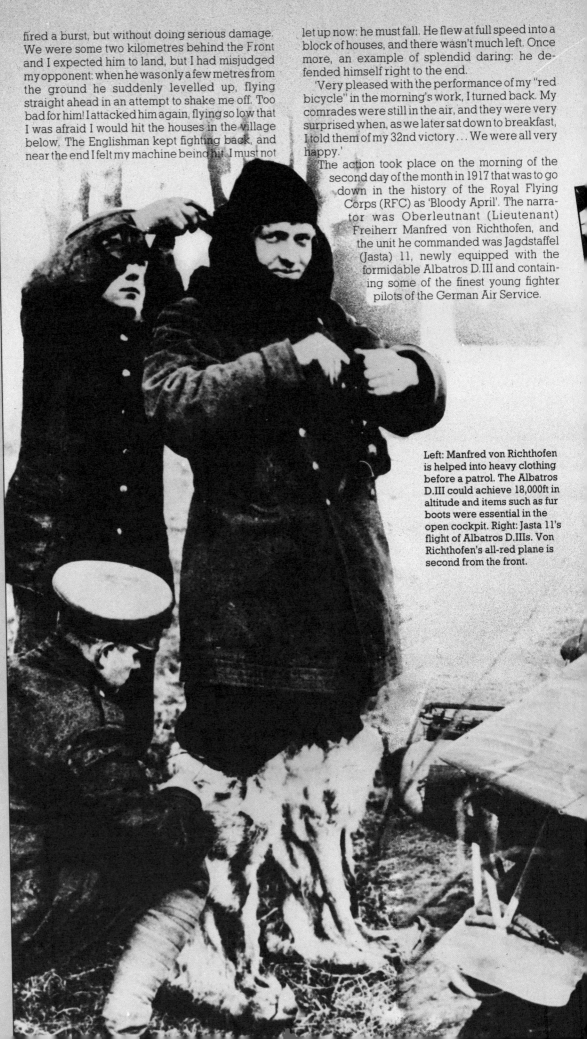

THE ALBATROS JASTAS

When the German Air Service entered World War I it was organised into units of six aircraft known as Fliegabteilungen (flight sections). In 1915 the Bavarian Air Force, encouraged by the great air tactician Oswald Boelcke, experimented with a larger tactical unit called the Kampfeinsitzenkommando (single-seat fighter unit). So successful was it that in 1916 the German Air Service initiated a complete reorganisation of its fighter formations.

The new type of unit was the Jagdstaffel or Jasta (fighter squadron), comprising 14 aircraft. The first to be formed, Jasta 2, became operational in August and it was commanded by Boelcke. When Boelcke was killed in action two months later, the unit was renamed Jasta Boelcke in his honour. Boelcke had taught his pilots well, however, and many left his Jasta to command the new ones that were forming up. Thus Manfred von Richthofen became commander of Jasta 11 in January 1917, and by April there were 37 Jastas in the German Air Service.

During the winter of 1916 Germany produced prodigious quantities of the superior Albatros fighter. With so many aircraft available (305 were operational in March 1917) the Jastas were able to deploy in large, stepped-up formations known as 'circuses'. Enjoying a considerable height advantage over the British bomber and reconnaissance escorts, the well-trained and highly disciplined Jasta pilots steadily gained air superiority throughout the British sector of the Western Front.

fired a burst, but without doing serious damage. We were some two kilometres behind the Front and I expected him to land, but I had misjudged my opponent: when he was only a few metres from the ground he suddenly levelled up, flying straight ahead in an attempt to shake me off. Too bad for him! I attacked him again, flying so low that I was afraid I would hit the houses in the village below. The Englishman kept fighting back, and near the end I felt my machine being hit. I must not let up now: he must fall. He flew at full speed into a block of houses, and there wasn't much left. Once more, an example of splendid daring: he defended himself right to the end.

'Very pleased with the performance of my "red bicycle" in the morning's work, I turned back. My comrades were still in the air, and they were very surprised when, as we later sat down to breakfast, I told them of my 32nd victory... We were all very happy.'

The action took place on the morning of the second day of the month in 1917 that was to go down in the history of the Royal Flying Corps (RFC) as 'Bloody April'. The narrator was Oberleutnant (Lieutenant) Freiherr Manfred von Richthofen, and the unit he commanded was Jagdstaffel (Jasta) 11, newly equipped with the formidable Albatros D.III and containing some of the finest young fighter pilots of the German Air Service.

Left: Manfred von Richthofen is helped into heavy clothing before a patrol. The Albatros D.III could achieve 18,000ft in altitude and items such as fur boots were essential in the open cockpit. Right: Jasta 11's flight of Albatros D.IIIs. Von Richthofen's all-red plane is second from the front.

Von Richthofen's flamboyant and devil-may-care pilots had painted their aircraft in brilliant colours and provocative designs, partly as a gesture of defiance, and partly so that they could easily recognise one another in the air. The principal colour was red, and von Richthofen had all the upper surfaces of his personal planes painted in this colour: for this he became known, first of all as 'le petit rouge', and later as the 'Red Baron'. His brother Lothar's had ailerons

Below: Whenever it was possible, the Red Baron had the serial numbers cut from his victims' aircraft, to hang as trophies in his room.

and elevators in yellow, the colour of his regiment. Karl Allmenröder's plane had a white tail, while Emil Schaefer's had a black tail and elevators.

'Bloody April' had opened, in fact, on 17 March 1917, when the British army before Arras had begun its advance on the Hindenburg Line. An essential part of the British strategy was the use of aircraft in collaboration with the ground forces, dropping messages in bags, identifying targets for the gunners, and pinpointing the German strongpoints (usually by drawing infantry fire from the ground). For these duties, the RFC employed obsolescent FE 2bs, slow but steady two-seater 'pushers' (the engine and propeller were mounted at the rear) protected by a variety of single-seater tractor fighters; few of these craft carried more than a single machine gun, while Jasta 11's Albatros fighters sported pairs of synchronised Spandaus.

Von Richthofen, with 16 kills to his credit, had been appointed to his new command, Jasta 11, early in January; the news came almost as a disappointment to him, for he was transferring from his previous squadron without having been awarded the coveted Pour le Mérite (the 'Blue Max') – even though pilots with no more than four victories had already received it. However, on 16 January he received a telegram to confirm that he, too, had been honoured.

He set off for Jasta 11's base at Douai to take over command, but was depressed by what he found. Even though the Jasta had been in existence for several months, and possessed several pilots with impeccable records, it had no victories in the air to its credit. He determined that this state of affairs would be changed as soon as possible. Of the 12 pilots who made up the squadron, three in particular were to win fame under von Richthofen's command: Karl Allmenröder, Kurt Wolff, and Karl Emil Schaefer.

The triumphant combat career of Jasta 11 began on 23 January, when von Richthofen led seven Albatroses against a flight of single-seater pusher FE 8s of No. 40 Squadron, RFC, and downed one of them with 150 rounds from behind at only 50yds range. The next day, accompanied only by his most junior NCO, he attacked a full formation of FE 2bs. He forced one down, but was then compelled to land himself when the wing of his Albatros cracked up.

'After the first 100 shots, the enemy observer stopped shooting. The plane began to smoke and twist in uncontrolled curves to the right'

During February the weather was bad, and von Richthofen was to score only three additional victories. On St Valentine's Day, for example, von Richthofen was to be found flying back alone from a meeting with his former squadron:

'At this time I was trying to compete with Jasta Boelcke... There were some devilish fellows there, and they were never to be outdone. At best, one could but equal them. They already had the advantage of having downed 100 planes.'

On the way to Douai he scored his 20th kill, a lone BE 2d. The same afternoon, leading his men over very nearly the same spot, he scored again in a fight with five more BEs:

'After the first 100 shots, the enemy observer stopped shooting. The plane began to smoke and twist in uncontrolled curves to the right. As this result was not satisfactory to me, especially over

the enemy's lines, I shot at the falling plane, until the left part of the wings came off. The wind was blowing at a velocity of 20m a second, and I had drifted far over to the enemy side; consequently I could observe that the enemy plane touched the ground southwest of Mazingarbe. I could see a heavy cloud of smoke arising from the place where the plane was lying in the snow…'

For the rest of the month, the weather was so bad that

ALBATROS D. III

Manufactured by Albatros Werke GmbH, the Albatros D series of single-seater fighter biplanes was introduced in 1916.

The first model, the Albatros D.I, appeared in August. Featuring the type's distinctive 'fishtail' and a powerful 160hp straight-six-cylinder engine, it was the first German scout to carry a pair of synchronised 7.92mm LMG 08/15 machine guns without loss of performance. The D.I was superseded by the D.II in October: the upper wing had been moved down, pilot visibility had been improved, and the engine's radiator had been moved from the nose to the interior of the upper wing.

By this time, however, the Albatros designers had been able to examine the highly manoeuvrable Nieuport, and they were not slow to incorporate its features into the Albatros. In January 1917 the first Albatros D.IIIs began service. The chord of the upper wing was lengthened, that of the lower wing shortened, and V-struts had been installed to separate them. The powerplant was uprated to the 175hp Mercedes DIIIa high-compression engine, improving maximum speed to 109mph and ceiling to 18,000ft. It could also stay aloft for two hours, half an hour longer than the D.II. Although it was discovered that the Nieuport's wing configuration prohibited certain types of dive, the D.III maintained Germany's air superiority until the advent of the SE5 and the Sopwith Camel.

no further victories were scored. Then, on 3 March, von Richthofen shot down an old BE 2c, flying in company with Allmenröder, who had so far achieved only one kill. This was von Richthofen's 22nd victory and it marked the opening of two months of triumph: by the end of April von Richthofen was to achieve his 52nd victory, and Jasta

The Western Front 1917

NETHERLANDS

ENGLISH CHANNEL

• Ostend

Dunkirk •

• Ghent

B E L G I U M

Lys

• Lille

• Mons

F R A N C E

• Vimy

Valenciennes

Douai •

Arras •

• Cambrai

Somme   Ancre

Key

✈ von Richthofen's air base
—— Front line, 8 April
▼▼▼ Hindenburg Line

Below: Von Richthofen's all-red Albatros D.III. Bottom: Jasta 11 is inspected at Douai. Von Richthofen and three of his pilots are wearing the Pour le Mérite at the throat. Bottom right: Oswald Boelcke, mastermind of German air tactics. Bottom far right: The German High Command pays Jasta 11 an official visit.

11 would have a total of 88 to its credit.

On the following day, 4 March, two aircraft went down to von Richthofen's guns. His men had taken off without their leader, but:

'I had started out all by myself and was just looking for my squadron when I spotted a BE two-seater, all alone. My first attack was apparently a failure, as my adversary attempted to escape by curves and dives. After I had forced him downward from 3000m to 1000m, he imagined himself safe and began once more to fly in a straight line. I took advantage of this and, putting myself behind him, I fired some 500 shots into him. My adversary dived, but so steeply that I could not follow him. According to our infantry observers, the plane crashed to the ground in front of our trenches.'

This was in the morning; in mid-afternoon, flying with five of his squadron, von Richthofen shot down a Sopwith 1½-Strutter. Five days later, von Richthofen was himself downed after going into an attack:

'About 50m distant I fired some well-aimed shots – but suddenly, when I had fired scarcely 10 shots, I heard a terrific bang, and something hit my machine... At the same moment there was a frightful stench of fuel, and the engine began to slow; the Britisher noticed it too, for he started to shoot even more, and I had to break off the fight.

'I dived straight down, and instinctively I switched off the ignition... I was at an altitude of 3000m and had a long way to go... Soon I was rid of my opponent and had time to look and see what my other four "gentlemen" were doing... Sud-denly a rocket! Was it one of the enemy's Verey flares? No, it is too big – it gets bigger: a machine in flames... thank God, it is one of the enemy ...'Then a second plane falls from the mêlée, and like mine it goes down, spinning and spinning – and then it recovers and flattens out, and as it flies towards me I see it is an Albatros like mine... I find a meadow, not very large, but enough if one is careful, just by the Hénin-Liétard road... My machine has been hit several times, and one shot has gone through both tanks, so that there is not a drop of fuel left in them.'

Two days later, von Richthofen raised his score by one and within a week had added two more. Three or four days after his 27th victory, he received a post-card photograph through the mail. It read:

'Sir: On 17 March 1917 I witnessed your aerial fight, and took this photograph which I send to you with heartfelt congratulations, because you seldom have the opportunity to see your prey. *Vivat sequens!* – With fraternal greetings – Von Riezenstein, Colonel and Commander, 87th Reserve Infantry Regiment.'

The photograph was of the broken body of the English flyer whom von Richthofen had despatched.

'The occupants burnt their machine. It appears to be a new type of plane, ... quick and rather handy'

By this time the British Army had begun its advance, and the German squadrons continued their bloody destruction of observation aircraft and their fighter cover. Von Richthofen was now joined by his brother Lothar, two years younger, who had passed his pilot's exam in March and had been immediately posted to Jasta 11. On 3 April the two brothers, together with Schaefer, attacked three FE 2ds and sent two of them down in flames.

Two days later, Jasta 11 encountered a new British plane, which was making its debut on the Western Front: the Bristol F 2a two-seater fighter. As von Richthofen reported:

'It was foggy and altogether very bad weather when I attacked an enemy flight between Douai and Valenciennes... I personally singled out the last machine, which I forced to land near Lembras after a short fight. The occupants burnt their

91

machine. It appears to be a new type of plane, which we had not known before, and it appears to be quick and rather handy...The Albatros was, both in speed and ability to climb, undoubtedly superior.'

In answer to von Richthofen's criticisms, the new Bristol had been flung into the battle over Arras as a reconnaissance aircraft, and it seems probable that its pilots had not appreciated its capabilities: few of them had much flying experience, as most had

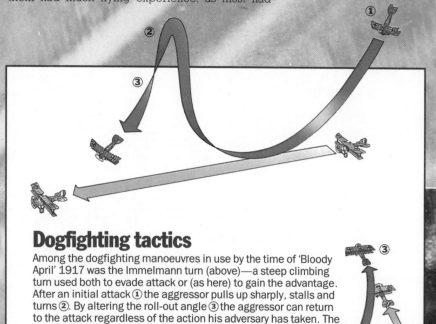

Dogfighting tactics

Among the dogfighting manoeuvres in use by the time of 'Bloody April' 1917 was the Immelmann turn (above)—a steep climbing turn used both to evade attack or (as here) to gain the advantage. After an initial attack ① the aggressor pulls up sharply, stalls and turns ②. By altering the roll-out angle ③ the aggressor can return to the attack regardless of the action his adversary has taken. The Split-S (below) consists of a series of reversing snap turns forcing the attacker to overshoot. As the attacking aircraft ① secures a firing position, the defending aircraft ② performs two or more sharp turns, forcing his opponent to overshoot ③.

DOCTRINE OF AN AIR ACE

On 16 February 1917, Manfred von Richthofen submitted a report to the officer commanding the German Sixth Army air forces:

'The adversary often slips downward over one wing or lets himself fall like a dead leaf in order to shake off an attack. In order to stick to one's adversary, one must on no account follow his tactics, as one has no control over the machine when falling like a dead leaf. Should the adversary, however, attempt to evade attack by such tricks, one must dive with him without losing sight of him.

'Looping the loop is worse than useless in air fighting. Each loop is a great mistake. If one has approached an adversary too close, a loop only offers him a big advantage. Change of speed should be relied upon to maintain the desired position, and this is best effected by adjusting the throttle.

'...Many English airmen try to win advantages by flying tricks while engaged in fighting but, as a rule, it is just these reckless and useless stunts that lead them to their deaths.'

arrived at the Front less than a month before. Once its qualities as a fighting machine were appreciated, however, the Bristol went on to earn a deserved reputation, and it remained in service until 1930.

On the night of 5 April, the RFC hit back:

'As we sat in the officers' mess the telephone rang and it was announced, "The English are coming" ...Everyone dived into the shelters and then we heard, faintly at first, the sound of an aircraft engine...It seemed that the Britishers were flying very high. First they went right round the field – we thought they were seeking another target – then one of them switched off his engine..."This is getting serious," said Wolff. We each had a rifle and we began to shoot at the Britisher...It did not take long for the first and then more bombs to rain down. Our friend put on a wonderful fireworks display, which could only scare a rabbit. I think that bombing at night has an effect only upon morale: if one fills one's pants it is uncomfortable, but it is not often more harmful than that.'

Although 132 bombs were dropped, the damage

they caused seems to have been slight. Four hangars were set on fire, but no aircraft were destroyed. Two mornings later the Jasta was airborne again, and von Richthofen scored another victory. The British bombers came again that night, and caused some further damage, but the men of Jasta 11 had got together a number of captured British machine guns, and gave their visitors a hot reception.

During April, the Albatros proved itself an excellent fighting machine, far superior to anything that the Allies could put up against it. On the day that von Richthofen made his 40th kill, 18 RFC planes were shot down. With 40 victories, von Richthofen had equalled the record of his master, Oswald Boelcke,

Far right: A studio portrait of the Red Baron. Right: The day after he was shot down by a Canadian, Captain A.R. Brown of No.208 Squadron flying a Sopwith Camel, von Richthofen was buried with full military honours at Bertangles cemetery on 22 April 1918. Men of No.3 Squadron, Australian Flying Corps, gave the volley of arms. Above: A lone Albatros patrols above Ypres.

and was on his way to becoming the premier ace in the German Air Service.

He achieved his ambition two days later, bringing down three on 13 April. On that day he was able to report that 'six German machines have destroyed 13 hostile aircraft'. Wolff had downed four, Schaefer, Festner and Lothar von Richthofen had each acccounted for two. April was a cruel month for the RFC: in the first week 75 British planes had been shot down with the loss of 105 crew, and another 56 had crashed and been written off. The average expectation of life for a British airman was 23 days, and no less than 316 airmen were killed in the first week, out of a total of 730 during the month.

On 14 April, Jasta 11 accounted for eight more British aircraft, one of which was credited to von Richthofen. He scored four more victories in the next fortnight, with kills credited also to Wolff and his brother Lothar.

There was a fresh development on 29 April when the 'Anti-Richthofen Squadron' took to the air. Second-Lieutenant W.N. Hamilton later reported: 'While I was in the hangar attending to the guns,

Harvey-Kelly came to me and said that the wing commander had said that von Richthofen had been seen over Douai and he wanted three Spads to go up and deal with them... Harvey-Kelly and myself got off the ground together and waited a moment for Applin... Soon after Applin joined us we sighted the Germans about 1000ft below us. There were 18 planes flying more or less on a line ahead slightly echelon... Harvey-Kelly had already turned and dived at the tail Hun, and I was turning to attack the centre machine, so as to break up the formation and prevent the leading machine getting above us.

'Applin was following me, when I saw him stall on his tail and then go down in a spin and burst into flames. I looked up and saw that von Richthofen in his all-red plane had been cruising about 2000ft above, which incidentally was his usual position, and had evidently shot Applin down...'

Soon afterwards, Hamilton was forced down by Lothar, and Harvey-Kelly, the first British pilot to have landed in France with the British Expeditionary Force, was killed by Wolff.

Applin was von Richthofen's 49th kill. Before the sun had set he had added three more to his score, making 52 in all. On 1 May he went on leave and Bloody April was over.

THE AUTHOR Brian Innes has written a number of books of popular history and two novels, *The Red Baron Lives!* and *The Red, Red Baron*.

MANFRED VON RICHTHOFEN

The man who was destined to become Germany's top air ace in World War I, with 80 confirmed victories to his credit, was born on 2 May 1892 near Breslau in Silesia. His father, Major Albrecht Freiherr von Richthofen, had been the first of his distinguished family to pursue a military career, and both Manfred and his brother Lothar were sent to military school. Commissioned in 1912, Manfred von Richthofen entered the 1st Uhlan Regiment when war began in 1914. He applied for transfer to the Fliegetruppe (flying service) and in August 1915 he was posted as observer to a unit codenamed Brieftaube Abteilung Ostend (Carrier Pigeon Unit, Ostend) to serve on AEG G1 bombers. Following an abortive attempt to bring down a British flier from a reconnaissance plane, von Richthofen met Oswald Boelcke and was encouraged to become a fighter pilot. On 10 October 1915 he made his first solo flight: he then transferred to Kampfstaffel 2 and shot down his first victim (uncredited) on 26 April 1916.

After a posting to the Russian Front, von Richthofen was recruited by Boelcke for his newly-formed Jasta 2. In September 1916 he gained his first official victory, an FE 2b, and on 23 November he claimed the great British air ace Major Lanoe Hawker. Awarded the coveted Pour le Mérite (below) in January 1917, he became commander of Jasta 11 at Douai: when he went on leave at the end of April his score stood at 56 kills. He later added over 20 victories flying Fokker triplanes, and it was in one of these craft that he was shot down and killed on 21 April 1918.

93

NO. 56 SQUADRON

On 8 June 1916 No.56 Squadron was formed around a nucleus supplied by No.28 (Reserve) Squadron at Gosport in Hampshire. In the following month it moved to London Colney in Hertfordshire and began a protracted period of preparation for service in France. In March 1917 it received its first SE5 fighters, becoming the first squadron to be equipped with the type, and in April it flew to France.

On 23 April Captain Albert Ball claimed the squadron's first victim while flying the unit's one Nieuport scout, only to bring down another the same day in an SE5. The other pilots soon followed his example, and they were involved in countless dogfights over the Western Front. Their aircraft were present at the Battle of Messines, the Third Battle of Ypres, and at the tank attack on Cambrai, strafing enemy positions in support of the Allied ground forces. In 1918, now equipped with SE5a scouts, the squadron used 20lb bombs to supplement their machine-gun attacks.

Following the Armistice, No.56 Squadron was disbanded. It was re-formed as a fighter squadron in 1922, and during World War II it operated the Hurricane, the Typhoon, the Spitfire IX and the Tempest. Its many roles included escorting convoys, ground attack, and countering the V1 flying-bomb offensive.

In 1946 No.124 Squadron was renamed No.56, the World War II unit becoming No.16 squadron. The postwar formation flew a succession of fighters in defence of the UK, and now operates Phantom Mark 2 interceptors.

Above: No.56 Squadron's current badge: the phoenix motif refers to the squadron's ability to survive all adversity and rise to fight another day.

PHOENIX SQUADRON

In April 1917, the young pilots of No.56 Squadron flew their SE5 scouts over the Channel to do battle over the Western Front

WHEN CAPTAIN JAMES McCUDDEN, then serving as a flying instructor and destined to become one of the highest-scoring air aces of World War I, was sent to No.56 Squadron in the summer of 1917 for a refresher course in fighter tactics, he thought it the most impressive outfit he had ever seen. Equipped with what was then the latest British aircraft, the SE5a scout (fighter plane), the squadron included a remarkable and innovative team of mechanics, led by Lieutenant H.N. Charles, who, in addition to getting the best out of the machines in their charge, supplied several excellent musicians for the squadron's band, which had become a famous institution within the Royal Flying Corps (RFC). The men of No.56 shared an easy comradeship born of an established tradition of superb flying ability and success in combat. Several of the RFC's most distinguished pilots, in-cluding the legendary Captain Albert Ball, had flown with the squadron, and McCudden became determined to join the unit at the first opportunity.

No.56 Squadron had first moved to France on 7 April 1917, when 13 SE5 scouts flew across the English Channel to an airfield at Vert Galant, south of Doullens. Their aircraft were to provide a welcome reinforcement for the hard-pressed British flying units on the Western Front, whose losses at that time were so severe that the period has become known in aviation history as 'Bloody April'. However, before the SE5s could begin operations, the squadron's mechanics needed to modify a number of unsatisfactory features of the design. Work was needed on the engine and armament, the unpopular 'greenhouse' semi-enclosed cockpit canopy was replaced by a conventional windscreen, and various other changes were made. The first patrol, therefore, was delayed until 22 April. Yet once the SE5's teething troubles had been overcome, it matured into a highly effective aircraft, and many pilots came to think it the finest British fighter of the war.

The commanding officer of No.56 Squadron at this time was Major R.G. Blomfield, and it was he who was

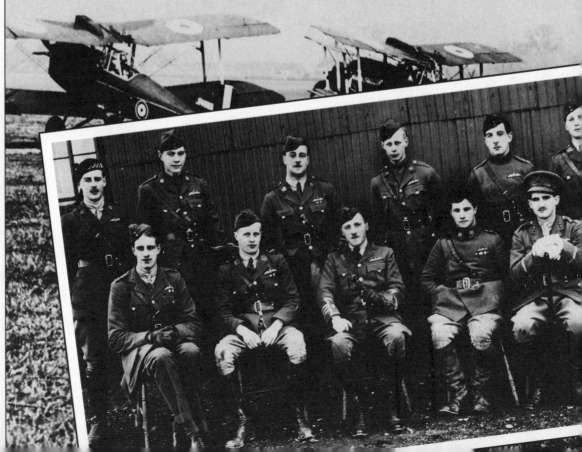

Above: The fine combat record of No.56 Squadron was built up by such aces as Keith Muspratt (top, with his SE5), James McCudden (left) and Albert Ball (right). Below: The aces' aircraft, hard-hitting SE5 biplanes. Inset below left: No.56 Squadron officers, with Major Blomfield (front, centre).

THE ROYAL FLYING CORPS AT WAR

British military aviation began in April 1911 with the formation of the Air Battalion, Royal Engineers. The Royal Flying Corps (RFC) was formed around that battalion in April 1912, and Military and Naval Wings were established. There was no shortage of volunteers, and they were picked from the best men in the army.

The British Army saw its aircraft solely in the role of reconnaissance platforms, reporting on troop dispositions and movements behind enemy lines, and four RFC squadrons flew to France in 1914 for that purpose. Though initially unchallenged by rival aircraft, the vital importance of intelligence gained from the air

was soon realised, and duels were fought between Allied and German aircrews armed only with rifles, pistols and grenades.

The next development was the introduction of armed 'scouts', whose function was to protect the virtually defenceless recce planes. From then on the opposing forces evolved ever more efficient fighters to win control of the air. When No.56 Squadron arrived in France with its SE5s in April 1917, the machines, tactics and piloting skills of both sides had evolved out of all recognition. The chivalrous duels of 1914 had given way to a desperate, no-holds-barred struggle for air supremacy.

CAPTAIN ALBERT BALL

Albert Ball was born on 14 August 1896 at Nottingham, and on the outbreak of World War I he enlisted in the Sherwood Foresters as a private soldier. Later that year he was commissioned and transferred to the North Midland Divisional Cyclist Company. He then determined to become a pilot, and on completion of his flying training he was posted to No.13 Squadron in France, flying BE2c two-seaters.

In May 1916 Ball joined No.11 Squadron, which then operated a mixture of two-seater FE2bs and Bristol Scout and Nieuport single-seaters. It was the latter which especially appealed to the individualistic and aggressive Ball, and during the following two months he had many combats with German aircraft.

In August 1916 Ball was posted to No.60 Squadron, which flew Nieuport scouts, and in the following month he was appointed to command the squadron's 'A' Flight. He returned to Britain in October.

Ball was very much the lone wolf in the air and also tended to prefer his own company when not flying. Yet the combat tactics of this withdrawn and self-sufficient young man were bold to the point of foolhardiness. He would attack any enemy aircraft that he encountered and took no heed of the odds he faced. Ball returned to France with No. 56 Squadron in April 1917, and the following month he was killed in action. His final score was 32 German aircraft shot down, 21 forced to land and two sent down out of control. He was awarded the Victoria Cross posthumously.

to transform it into one of the top RFC scout units. Blomfield had joined the squadron in January 1917 and Lieutenant Cecil Lewis has described him:

'Efficiency was his watchword. In appearance he was shortish and slightly built. He wore leggings, and invariably carried a short, leather-covered cane, with which he directed everything, reminding one irresistibly of a dapper little ringmaster.'

Since squadron COs were forbidden to fly in combat, Blomfield's job was primarily that of an organiser. Tactical leadership of the squadron was exercised by his three flight commanders, whom Blomfield had carefully selected for their experience and skill.

Left: Captain Albert Ball, having downed 32 planes and been awarded the Military Cross, applied for leave in 1916 to rest his strained nerves. The RFC rewarded him with a spell as observer in an unarmed BE2C, which was perhaps the most terrifying task on the Front. Below: The von Richthofen brothers, Lothar and Manfred (right), two of Germany's most dangerous pilots.

96

Foremost amongst them was Captain Albert Ball, commanding 'A' Flight, who then had over 30 victories to his credit. 'B' Flight was led by Captain C.M. 'Billy' Crowe, and 'C' Flight by Captain H. Meintjes. Among the inexperienced squadron pilots fresh from training school were Lieutenants Arthur Rhys Davids, Gerald Constable Maxwell, Leonard Barlow and Keith Muspratt, all of whom were to gain great reputations as air fighters.

Accommodation at Vert Galant airfield was spartan. Most officers and all other ranks were living under canvas during a period of bitterly cold weather with frequent showers of snow and sleet. Yet morale was high and everyone was keen to get into action. The squadron's first success came on 23 April, when Ball shot down an Albatros over Cambrai. On that occasion he was flying a Nieuport 17 scout, which he used for solo patrols. Later the same day he gained his first victories with the SE5, an aircraft which at first he had disliked flying. By the end of the month the squadron had claimed a further five enemy aircraft destroyed and five sent down out of control.

Often, however, No. 56 Squadron found itself outnumbered by the German fighters. Lieutenant Cecil Lewis has described the confusion of a dogfight in which three or more different fighter formations became engaged, 'as if attracted by some mysterious power, as vultures will draw near to a corpse in the desert':

'A pilot, in the second between his own engagements, might see a Hun diving vertically, an SE5 on his tail, on the tail of the SE another Hun, and above him again another British scout. These four, plunging headlong at 200 miles an hour, guns crackling, tracers streaming, suddenly break up. The lowest Hun plunges flaming to his death, if death has not taken him already. His victor seems to stagger, suddenly pulls out in a great leap, as a trout leaps on the end of a line, and then, turning over on his belly, swoops and spins in a dizzy falling spiral with the earth to end it. The third German zooms veering, and the last of that meteoric quartet follows bursting... But such a

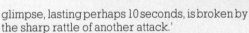

glimpse, lasting perhaps 10 seconds, is broken by the sharp rattle of another attack.'

On the evening of 7 May, 11 of No. 56 Squadron's SE5s set out on patrol, despite poor weather conditions and a mass of cloud building up over the Western Front. The British formation soon broke up into small groups and became heavily engaged, at a serious disadvantage, with German fighters which were out in force. Only five of the SE5s returned to Vert Galant that evening and all three flight commanders were amongst the missing. Rhys Davids had force-landed behind British lines and Crowe had come down at another airfield. Both were unhurt. Lieutenant J.O. Leach and Meintjes were wounded, while Lieutenant R. W. Chaworth-Musters and Ball were missing. It was later discovered that they had been killed. Leutnant Lothar von Richthofen of Jagdstaffel 11, brother of the 'Red Baron', was credited with bringing down Ball, but it has been suggested that he was brought down by a machine gun mounted in the tower of a church. The news of his loss 'cast a gloom through the whole Flying Corps', recorded a staff officer at RFC Headquarters in France.

The loss of both his fellow flight commanders in a single combat threw a tremendous burden onto Captain Crowe, but he was equal to the challenge. During the weeks when Captain Philip Prothero and Captain G.H. 'Beery' Bowman, the new commanders of 'A' and 'C'

THE SE5

Designed by H.P. Folland, whose earlier SE4 aircraft had attained an unofficial world speed record, the first prototype of the SE5 single-seat scout made its maiden flight on 22 November 1916. Powered by a 150hp Hispano-Suiza V-8 engine, the biplane had staggered wings of equal span and featured the first use of tail-trimming gear and the first adjustable seat. The initial production batch of SE5s, manufactured by the Royal Aircraft Factory at Farnborough, began service in March 1917 with No. 56 Squadron. Armament consisted of a .303in Vickers gun firing through the propeller by means of Constantinesco CC synchronising gear, and a .303in Lewis gun on a Foster mounting on the upper wing, which the pilot could angle to fire forward or upward. (The SE5 shown left was that of Captain Albert Ball, who removed the Vickers in order to reduce the aircraft's weight.) The SE5 provided an exceptionally firm gun platform, substantially increasing the range of effective fire in combat. The SE5 had been in production for only three months when the SE5a was introduced. The power plant was uprated to a 200hp Hispano-Suiza engine, later superseded by the Wolseley-made Viper, and by the time of the Armistice about 5000 SE5 and SE5a aircraft had been built.

Flights, were gaining experience after several months away from the Front, Crowe ran all three flights virtually single-handed. Rhys Davids, who was a member of Crowe's 'B' Flight, had a great regard for his abilities. 'He is not afraid of anything and goes after old Huns like a rocket, and yet he is extraordinarily prudent.' At a time when morale in the squadron was low, Crowe helped to restore the pilots' confidence in the SE5, which had come under suspicion as the cause of Ball's death. He also advocated new fighting tactics which made good use of the SE5's speed and steadiness as a gun platform in diving attacks, in preference to the turning fight which was more suited to such nimble scouts as the Nieuport 17 or Sopwith Pup.

At the end of May the squadron moved north to Estrée Blanche in preparation for the Battle of Messines. During its first five weeks in combat, it had been credited with 57 victories for the loss of 10 pilots. However, a welcome respite from the grinding daily routine of offensive patrols over the Front came on 21 June, when No.56 Squadron was withdrawn to Bekesbourne in Kent for two weeks. The move was intended to boost Britain's defences against the German Gotha bombers which had bombed London eight days earlier. 'We do absolutely nothing,' reported Arthur Rhys Davids, 'We spend the whole day playing cards or ragging about and some of us go out every evening on the bust.' On 4 July the Gothas raided the East Coast, but the following day the squadron flew back to France.

During the summer of 1917 the squadron's SE5s were replaced by the improved SE5a, which was fitted with a more powerful engine that gave it a higher rate of climb and increased speed. Yet, as

Below: A German airman takes a bomb aboard. The first bombsights were mounted on the side of the fuselage: the bombardier would lean over, wait, then release the weapon by pulling a trigger.

with its predecessor, early problems with the aircraft's engine and armament had to be resolved by Lieutenant Charles and his mechanics before the SE5a performed entirely satisfactorily. On 21 July, Lieutenant V. P. Cronyn scored No.56 Squadron's one hundredth victory, but its considerable successes had not been gained without loss. Captain Prothero was shot down on 26 July, bringing the unit's casualties up to 23 pilots lost since April. Captain Crowe left the squadron in July, his health suffering from the intense strain of his command and frequent combat (he had gained six victories during his period as 'B' Flight commander). However, by that time Captain Bowman had settled into his stride and during the 10 months that he led 'C' Flight he was credited with 26 personal victories. Maxwell was promoted to captain and took command of 'A' Flight, while the 'B' Flight commander vacancy was filled by Captain James McCudden in mid-August. With three such able and experienced flight commanders, the squadron soon reached a peak of efficiency, especially since many of its other pilots were by then highly skilled air fighters. Lieutenant Richard Maybery was at that time credited with 9½ victories, and during one epic low-level bombing and strafing mission on 31 July, he attacked two enemy airfields, a column of marching troops, two trains and for good measure shot down a two-seater observation aircraft. Rhys Davids brought his score up to 15 victories on 5 September by accounting for three enemy aircraft in that single day. Barlow was credited with six victories and the Canadian Lieutnant R.T.C. Hoidge had no fewer than 13 to his credit.

McCudden's 'B' Flight was especially strong in talent, its pilots comprising Barlow, Rhys Davids, Muspratt, Lieutenant Maxwell Coote and Cronyn. They were 'as splendid a lot of fellows as ever set foot in France,' thought their flight commander. McCudden himself at that time had scored only five victories, but in the following months he was to increase this total more than tenfold. His first successful combat with the squadron came on the morning of 18 August, when he attacked an Albatros DIII over Houthem. 'I attacked it at 50yds range, firing both guns,' he reported. 'Fired about 20 shots from each gun and EA [enemy aircraft] at once went down in a vertical spiral, going down very fast. I last saw it at about 6000ft still going down out of control.'

I heard clack-clack-clack-clack, as his bullets passed close to me and through my wings

No.56 Squadron's most famous combat took place on the evening of 23 September, when 'B' Flight's six SE5a scouts engaged a Fokker FI triplane (a prototype for the Dr I series) west of Poelcappelle. Its pilot was the German ace Leutnant Werner Voss, Staffelführer of Jasta 10. In a fighting career which lasted barely ten months, Voss had accounted for some 50 Allied aircraft – an achievement second only to that of Manfred von Richthofen at the time. McCudden's flight dived down onto the triplane, but failed to damage it during the initial attack. McCudden recalled that:

'The German pilot saw us and turned in a most disconcertingly quick manner, not a climbing nor Immelmann turn, but a sort of flat half spin. By now the German triplane was in the middle of our formation and its handling was wonderful to behold. The pilot seemed to be firing at all of us simultaneously and although I got behind him a

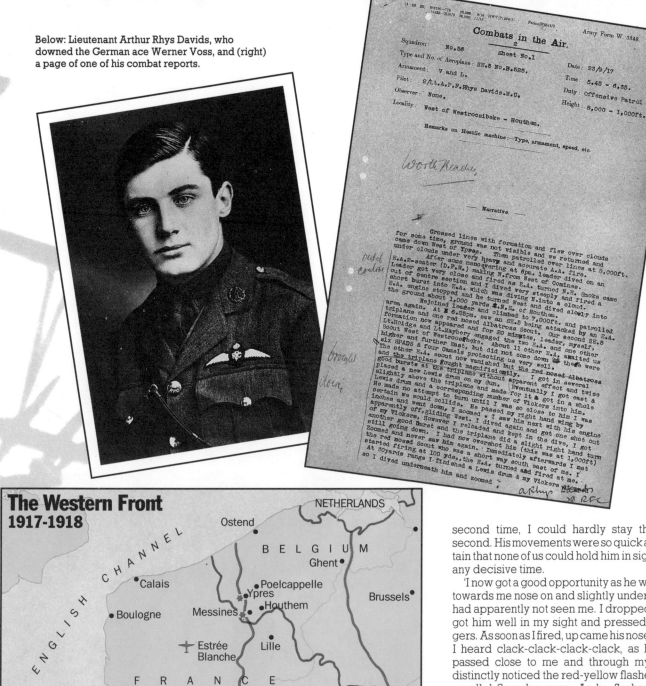

Below: Lieutenant Arthur Rhys Davids, who downed the German ace Werner Voss, and (right) a page of one of his combat reports.

The Western Front
1917-1918

NETHERLANDS

BELGIUM

Ostend

Ghent

Poelcappelle

Ypres

Houthem

Brussels

Messines

ENGLISH CHANNEL

Calais

Boulogne

Lille

FRANCE

Estrée Blanche

Arras

Doullens

Cambrai

Vert Galant

Dieppe

Amiens

St Quentin

Lavieville

Rheims

Paris

Key
* Major battles
— Front line, 9 April 1917
— Armistice line, 11 November 1918
✈ Airfields

Formed in 1916, No. 56 Squadron, Royal Flying Corps, was deployed to the Western Front early in April 1917. The squadron flew SE5 and SE5a biplanes in the 'scout' or fighter role. No. 56 Squadron was involved in the Battle of Messines during the summer of 1917, and later, in the Third Battle of Ypres and the attack on Cambrai.

During the German offensives of March 1918 the squadron was heavily engaged, and by the end of the war the aces of No. 56 Squadron had accounted for a total of 401 enemy aircraft.

second time, I could hardly stay there for a second. His movements were so quick and uncertain that none of us could hold him in sight at all for any decisive time.

'I now got a good opportunity as he was coming towards me nose on and slightly underneath and had apparently not seen me. I dropped my nose, got him well in my sight and pressed both triggers. As soon as I fired, up came his nose at me and I heard clack-clack-clack-clack, as his bullets passed close to me and through my wings. I distinctly noticed the red-yellow flashes from his parallel Spandau guns. As he flashed by me I caught a glimpse of a black head in the triplane with no hat on at all.

'By this time a red-nosed Albatros scout had arrived and was apparently doing its best to guard the triplane's tail, and it was well handled too... The triplane was still circling round in the midst of six SEs, who were all firing at it as opportunity offered, and at one time I noted the triplane in the apex of a cone of tracer bullets from at least five machines simultaneously and each machine had two guns. By now the fighting was very low and the red-nosed Albatros had gone down and out, but the triplane still remained. I had temporarily lost sight of the triplane whilst changing a drum of my Lewis gun and when I next saw him he was very low, still being engaged by an SE marked I, the pilot being Rhys Davids. I noticed that the triplane's movements were very erratic and then I saw him go into a fairly steep dive and so I continued to watch and then saw the triplane hit the ground and disappear into a thousand fragments.'

On 30 September Maxwell gained the squadron's 200th victory, but the following month was a period of heavy casualties. Eight pilots were lost, including the young and brilliant Arthur Rhys Davids who was killed in action on 27 October. The squadron also lost Maxwell, who was posted to Home Establishment, and at the end of the month Major Blomfield was relieved as CO by Major R. Balcombe-Brown. In November, No. 56 Squadron moved to Lavieville, near Amiens, in preparation for the Battle of Cambrai, during which it was heavily engaged despite periods of bad weather. Yet more experienced pilots were lost during the closing months of the year. Hoidge was posted to Home Establishment and Maybery (who had taken over from Maxwell as 'A' Flight's commander) was killed on 19 December.

December 1917 was chiefly remarkable for McCudden's outstanding fighting record, for of the 17 enemy aircraft brought down by the squadron during the month, 14 were his victories. His posting to Home Establishment in the following March marked the end of an era. During his period in command of 'B' Flight, No. 56 Squadron had gained 175 victories, of which his flight had contributed 77 and he himself no fewer than 52. When Captain Duncan Grinnell-Milne was posted to No. 56 Squadron in September 1918, he was told, 'You're in luck to be sent here. This is the most famous squadron in France.' With a final score of 401 victories, that fame had been hard earned.

THE AUTHOR Anthony Robinson was formerly on the staff of the RAF Museum, Hendon, and is now a freelance military aviation writer. He has edited the books *Aerial Warfare* and the *Dictionary of Aviation*.

Bottom: Riddled with holes, a German DFW CV lies crumpled in the mud. This type of plane, known as the 'C' class, was introduced by Germany in the spring of 1915 to fulfil general duties, and it was not until the advent of the first true single-seat fighter, the Fokker EI, that combat became a specialised role. The 'C' class aircraft were extremely vunerable to ground fire, though their chances of survival were later improved by the fitting of armour round the engine, the fuel tanks and the crew compartment.

Captain Albert Ball, No. 56 Squadron, RFC France 1917

Captain Ball is holding the propeller and red-painted propeller spinner of the Nieuport 17 scout which he flew in preference to his squadron's SE5s. He is wearing the field service dress of a Royal Flying Corps officer, which included breeches and high boots. The badge of the RFC is on his cap and lapel, and the badges of his rank are on his sleeve. Above the left pocket are the RFC wings and the ribbons of his DFC and MC. The uniform is completed by the Sam Browne belt.

Below: One of 85 Squadron's groundcrew tinkers with the engine housing of a Mosquito nightfighter. Left: A devastating team: John 'Cat's Eyes' Cunningham (above) and his navigator-radio, C. F. 'Jimmy' Rawnsley (below). Cunningham accounted for some 20 German aircraft during World War II.

NIGHT HAWKS

When streams of German bombers threatened to obliterate London, the nightfighter pilots of No. 85 Squadron rose to meet the challenge

ON THE NIGHT of 17/18 January 1943 the Luftwaffe despatched 118 bombers against London in reprisal for an RAF Bomber Command raid on Berlin. It was the biggest attack on the British capital since May 1941 and heralded an increase in Luftwaffe night-bombing activity which was to culminate in the 'Baby Blitz' between January and May 1944. Four of the raiders were claimed by the defenders, the only success by a Mosquito nightfighter going to No. 85 Squadron. Although this unit, which was based at RAF Hunsdon in Essex, had been operating Mosquito NF Mk IIs since the previous August, this was its first confirmed night victory with the new fighter. However, the squadron was soon to make up for this slow start and on 28 January Wing Commander John Cunningham. one of the top scoring nightfighter pilots, took command of the unit. Yet nightbombers proved to be elusive quarries and victories were hard won. Consequently, it was not until January 1944 that the squadron's score reached the 200 mark.

Cunningham and C.F. 'Jimmy' Rawnsley, his regular navigator-radio (as the nightfighters' radar operators were officially known), were in action on the night of 3/4 March when over 100 German bombers again raided London. Rawnsley recalled the beginning of the hunt:

> 'The sirens were howling and the guns in the estuary were already shaking the air as we raced for our aircraft. Mosquitoes were streaking off down the runway, hard on each other's heels. We elbowed our way into the stream and leapt into the air.'

Rawnsley soon made contact with an enemy bomber on his radar and Cunningham eased the Mosquito into position behind and below a Dornier Do 217. However, on attempting to shoot it down, Cunningham discovered that his guns refused to fire. It was found on return to base that the electrical lead to the firing solenoid had been accidentally disconnected during servicing. This failure was all the more frustrating since Cunningham and Rawnsley were the only No. 85 Squadron crew to make contact with a Luftwaffe bomber that night.

Late in March 1943 Oberst Dietrich Peltz was appointed Angriffsführer England (Attack Commander England) and he began to build up his bomber forces. In January 1943, about 120 Do 217s and Junkers Ju 88Ss were available for night attacks on Britain. A year later Peltz could draw on over 500 night bombers, including the Ju 188, Focke Wulf Fw 190 fighter-bombers, Messerschmitt Me 410s and twin-engined He 177s.

The RAF nightfighters were likewise improving in effectiveness. No. 85 Squadron began to convert onto the first of the improved Mosquito NF Mk XIIs in March and Cunningham was 'full of enthusiasm' for the new fighter. Its major innovation was its AI Mk VIII radar, a centimetric set with a scanner dish fitted beneath a bulbous radome in the aircraft's nose. This installation necessitated a reduction in armament from the Mosquito NF Mk II's nose-mounted battery of four .303in machine guns and four 20mm cannon, to four cannon only. Nevertheless, it was generally agreed that the performance of the new radar more than compensated for the loss. At about the same time, No. 85 Squadron received Mosquito NF Mk XV high-altitude fighters, which had been developed to counter the Luftwaffe's Ju 86P reconnaissance aircraft. Rather than integrating these specialised fighters into the normal squadron organisation, a third flight ('C' Flight) was formed within No. 85 Squadron for high-altitude operations. The performance of the Mosquito NF Mk XVs was impressive: for example, on 10 April Flight Lieutenant Nigel Bunting climbed one to an altitude of 44,500ft. However, no high-flying reconnaissance aircraft were encountered and 'C' Flight's role was consequently restricted to operational testing.

The first successful night interception by a Mosquito NF Mk XII was made on 14/15 April by the officer commanding 'A' Flight, Squadron Leader Peter Green. It was a busy night for No. 85 Squadron, with 12 operational sorties flown against raiders over the east coast. Shortly after Green's victory, a second German bomber fell to the guns of Flight Lieutenant Geoff Howitt. Both of these victims were Do 217s, a

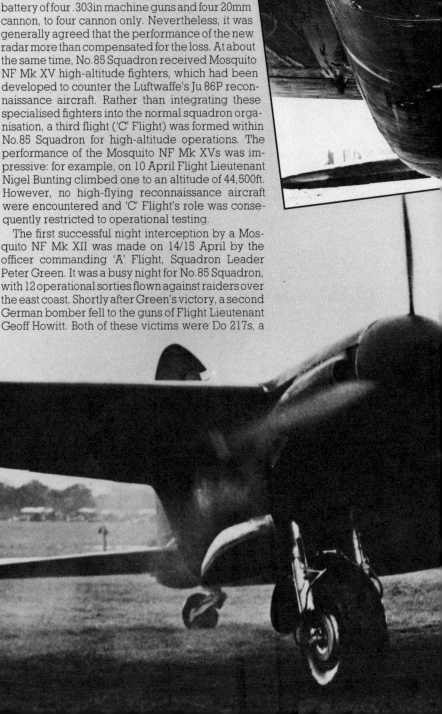

relatively easy target for the high-performance Mosquito. A far more formidable enemy made its appearance two nights later, when the Fw 190As of Schnellkampfgeschwader 10 began operations against Britain. Yet, when loaded with a heavy bomb (of 250kg or 500kg) and two underwing drop-tanks, the Fw 190's performance was sufficiently reduced to make its interception by a Mosquito nightfighter a realistic, if by no means easy, proposition.

The squadron took leave of its old airfield with an impromptu display of low-level flying

In order to improve No. 85 Squadron's opportunities of intercepting night raiders, and especially Fw 190s bound for London, the unit was moved from Hunsdon to West Malling in Kent on 13 May. The squadron took leave of its old airfield in the time-honoured manner, with an impromptu display of low-level flying. West Malling, surrounded by countryside 'alive and aglow with fruit blossom and spring flowers', was a grass airfield with a strip of Somerfield track (wire mesh) laid down to form the main runway.

On the night of 16/17 May, No. 85 Squadron succeeded in inflicting a serious defeat on the Fw 190 raiders. Squadron Leader Green and his navigator Flight Sergeant A. R. Grimstone were patrolling over the Channel at 10,000ft when they picked up a radar contact. At a distance of 1000ft they could identify it as a bomb-carrying Fw 190 and Green closed the range to 100yds before opening fire. The enemy aircraft blew up with a large red flash, the Mosquito having to dive sharply to port to avoid the burning debris'. A second Fw 190 was intercepted and shot down by Flight Lieutenant Howitt. Flying Officer Bernard Thwaites was even more successful, claiming one confirmed victory and another probable. A fifth Fw 190 fell to Flying Officer J.D. Shaw, whose Mosquito returned covered in soot as a result of the enemy aircraft exploding. Green's victory was celebrated as the first Fw 190 to be destroyed at night

Above: A Mosquito NF Mk XIII with its four 20mm cannon. Below: An early version of the nightfighter, the NF Mk II, equipped with the AI Mk VI radar, four machine guns and four cannon.

over Britain and the occasion was commemorated by the presentation of a silver model of a Mosquito to the squadron from Squadron Leader M.H. Bradshaw-Jones, the senior controller at Hunsdon.

Two more Fw 190s were shot down later in May, the successful pilots being Flying Officer J.P.M. Lintott and Squadron Leader Edward Crew, the officer commanding 'B' Flight. Lintott and his navigator, Pilot Officer G.G. Gilling-Lax, were again in action on the night of 29/30 May, intercepting a Ju 88S at 29,000ft, near Lewes. Attacking from below and behind, Lintott obtained hits on the enemy bomber's starboard engine and started a fire in the wing. The Ju 88S went into a steep dive and its crew baled out. It was the first example of this Ju 88 variant to be shot down over Britain. However, the very promising career of Lintott and Gilling-Lax came to a premature end on 9 July, when they intercepted a Do 217 near Maidstone. Both the German bomber and the Mosquito crashed shortly afterwards. It was thought that the RAF fighter had either been damaged by fragments from its victim, or had suffered a structural failure due to the vibration of its cannon fire.

'John very briefly touched the trigger and the guns gave one short bark'

Cunningham gained his first victory on the Mosquito during the night of 13/14 June. It brought his total of victories up to 17. Rawnsley remembered the kill:

'We had gone off on patrol just before midnight and we were beating up and down the Channel off Dungeness at 23,000ft when "Skyblue" warned us that a fast customer was on the way in. The controller timed our converging courses to a nicety and the blip came scuttling across my cathode ray rube only a mile-and-a-half ahead and well below us. I had no fears about overshooting, only of being outdistanced. John opened up the engines as I brought him around in a tight diving turn and we went howling down after the raider.

'The range closed only very slowly and the blip

HUNTING BY DAY AND NIGHT

Formed at Upavon on 1 August 1917, No.85 Squadron fought in the final stages of World War 1, carrying out ground attacks and offensive sweeps on the Western Front. The squadron remained on the continent until early 1919, when it was disbanded. Reformed at Debden on 1 June 1938, the squadron flew Hurricanes over France and the Low Countries until heavy losses forced its return to England, where the unit was made non-operational in May 1940. Over the following months, 85 Squadron was re-equipped and began flying night sorties over the south of England, claiming 44 kills in August. Throughout 1941 the squadron carried out night duties flying Hurricanes, Defiants and Havocs until August 1942 when the first Mosquitoes arrived.

Flying high-altitude intruder missions over Europe, the unit's tally of kills steadily mounted, reaching 200 by January 1944. As the RAF's bomber offensive against occupied Europe gathered momentum, 85 Squadron was placed under 100 Group Bomber Command to fly bomber-support missions and low-level intruder raids.

With the end of World War II, the squadron formed part of the RAF's nightfighter force until its disbandment in November 1958. However, No.89 Squadron was renamed No.85 at the same time and, after a series of organisational changes, was reformed as a target squadron to fly Meteors and Canberras in training exercises. No.85 Squadron was finally disbanded on 19 December 1975.
Above: No.85 Squadron's insignia with the motto: 'We hunt by day and night'.

was as steady as a rock. This must be a new boy, I thought; one of those they-will-never-catch-me-at-this-speed characters I had been hoping to meet. The only thing to worry about now was the searchlights. If only they would leave us alone!

'On the other aircraft went, hell bent for London and not the slightest sign of a light broke the soft velvet of the summer night. And all the time we were creeping in...

'At that moment John saw the other aircraft against a patch of cloud. I looked up from the AI set and there was no doubt about what we were after. It was an Fw 190 all right. The single exhaust flickered below the fuselage; the short, straight wings still had the drop tanks hanging from [them]; the big, smooth bomb was still clutched fiercely to its belly.

'John very briefly touched the trigger and the guns gave one short bark. The enemy aircraft reared straight up on its nose, flicking over and plunging vertically downward. It all happened with an incredible speed. Standing up and pressing my face to the window, I watched the blue exhaust flame dwindle as the aircraft hurtled earthwards.'

The twin-engined Messerschmitt Me 410 had begun to operate over Britain in June and No. 85 Squadron scored the RAF's first success against this fast, twin-engined fighter-bomber on the night of 13/14 July. The raider was detected coming in over Dover and flying northwards. Flight Lieutenant Bunting was directed into an interception over the east coast and spotted the glow from the Me 410's engine exhausts at a range of one-and-a-half miles. Climbing hard at full engine boost, he pursued the Me 410 for some 15 minutes before he was able to close to a range of 200yds. Bunting then gave the enemy aircraft a two-second burst of cannon fire and saw it turn onto its back and dive vertically. It crashed into the sea five miles off Felixstowe. Another three Me 410s were claimed by No. 85 Squadron during the following six weeks and for a short period these aircraft were used as intruders, attacking returning RAF bombers and their bases. The Fw 190s were also very active during the late summer months. Cunningham claimed one on the night of 23/24 August and a second on 8/9 September (when Thwaites also shot down two 190s). On the latter occasion, Cunningham's Mosquito was hit by debris and returned to base on one engine.

Above: One of No. 85 Squadron's Mosquitoes. This aircraft, an NF Mk XII, reached the unit during early 1943 and was credited with the destruction of a Ju 188S on the night of 29/30 May of that year. Below: Caught in the eerie glow of a Chance light, a Mosquito taxies along a runway prior to taking off to carry out an intruder mission over occupied Europe. Left: Interior detail of a Mosquito showing the navigator-radio's radar screen, used to track down the enemy's aircraft at night. Despite the undoubted sophistication of the fighter's equipment, most kills depended on the skill and judgement of the aircrafts' crews.

NIGHTFIGHTER ACE

John Cunningham was born at Addington in Surrey on 17 July 1917. He joined the de Havilland company in 1935 as a technical apprentice and trained as a pilot with the 'week-end flyers' of No.604 (County of Middlesex) Squadron of the Auxiliary Air Force. On the outbreak of war in September 1939, the squadron's Bristol Blenheim Mk If twin-engined fighters were assigned to convoy patrol duties and Cunningham carried out this monotonous work until June 1940.

No.604 Squadron then began training in the nightfighter role, receiving its first Bristol Beaufighters in September 1940. On 20 November Cunningham scored his squadron's first night victory with this aircraft and in January 1941, following his third victory, he was awarded the DFC. By April 1941 Cunningham had raised his score to 10 victories, three of them shot down on the night of 15 April, and he was awarded the DSO. In August Cunningham was promoted to the rank of wing commander and took command of No.604 Squadron. As the most successful and experienced British nightfighter pilot, he was involved in the development of new equipment and tactics, as well as operational flying. In June 1942, when he had gained 16 victories, he was given a staff appointment as a rest from operations.

During his period in command of No.85 Squadron he added a further four victories to his total, which was the second highest for an RAF nightfighter pilot.

After the war Cunningham returned to de Havillands, becoming the company's chief test pilot.

Right: Cunningham (left) examines his squadron's new crest during a parade in 1944. The badge includes the white hexagon carried by the unit during World War I.

October 1943 was a busy month for the squadron, which recorded 10 successful combats during this period. One of the most notable was fought by Squadron Leader Bill Maguire, 'a jovial, prosperous-looking man, an ex-instructor and a fine pilot,' who had recently taken over from Green as officer commanding 'A' Flight. On the night of 7/8 October he was directed to intercept an Me 410 and closed to within 2000ft of it. In the words of an official report:

'A violent dogfight now ensued with the enemy aircraft appearing to make repeated attempts to get on the tail of the Mosquito. After several minutes Maguire managed to get in two bursts and observed strikes on the port side of the fuselage and on the port wing.'

The Me 410 then dived away, but Maguire was able to fire on it again, before it disappeared into cloud. Another No.85 Squadron crew saw the blazing aircraft fall into the sea off Hastings. This combat suggested that the Germans had recently introduced tail-warning radars for their bombers, and POW interrogations revealed that they were also shortly to begin using Duppel (strips of radar-reflective foil, equivalent to the RAF's 'Window') in order to jam British radars. These developments were to make the job of RAF nightfighters in-creasingly difficult during the winter of 1943/44.

One answer to the Luftwaffe's use of Duppel was the introduction of the American SCR 720 radar (known to the RAF as AI Mk X), which was less susceptible to jamming than the AI Mk VIII. The new equipment was fitted on Mosquito NF Mk XVIIs, which began to reach No.85 Squadron in November. At first glance, the American radar sets were complex and daunting pieces of equipment. Rawnsley recalled that:

'My first impression of the new AI Mark X had been that we should have to breed a new race of radar navigators to handle it. They would have to be men with three or more hands to cope with the thing as it fairly bristled with controls.'

However, experience soon showed that many of these controls, once pre-set, could be left alone. A far more serious problem was that the Mosquito had only a small performance advantage over the Me 410. One solution to this handicap was to fit a number of Mosquitoes with a nitrous oxide injection system to boost performance for short periods.

It was while flying one of these specially modified Mosquitoes that Cunningham gained his twentieth victory, on the night of 2/3 January 1944. The Me 410 had dropped its bombs and was heading back for France when Cunningham was directed to intercept.

Above: No. 85 Squadron personalities and the unit's mascot pose for the camera. From left to right: Cunningham, Flight Lieutenant T. J. Molony, Squadron Leader W. P. Green and Squadron Leader E. A. Crew. Below: One of the squadron's Hawker Hurricane nightfighters in action.

Rawnsley picked up the enemy aircraft on his radar at one-and-a-half mile's range, but as the Mosquito closed in, the Me 410 began violent evasive action. Cunningham turned on the nitrous oxide injection system and Rawnsley could feel the Mosquito 'suddenly lengthen its stride'. This advantage allowed them to stay in contact with the Me 410, which they finally closed with and shot down over Le Touquet.

In February 1944 Cunningham was promoted to group captain and handed command of No.85 Squadron over to Wing Commander C.M. Miller. During the eventful 14 months under Cunningham's leadership, the squadron had gained a total of 46 victories – the highest score of a nightfighter squadron in RAF Fighter Command during this period by a considerable margin.

THE AUTHOR Anthony Robinson was formerly on the staff of the RAF Museum, Hendon and is now a freelance military aviation writer. He has edited the books *Aerial Warfare* and the *Dictionary of Aviation*.

Pilot, No. 85 Squadron, 1943

Wing Commander Cunningham wears pre-war black flying overalls, a silk scarf and black shoes. A leather flying helmet and oxygen mask are carried.

WILD WEASELS

In their F-105 Thunderchiefs the pilots of the 44th Tactical Fighter Squadron flew some of the most hazardous missions undertaken by the US Air Force in Vietnam

OPERATION 'Rolling Thunder', the United States Air Force (USAF) bombing offensive against North Vietnam from 1965 until 1968, was carried out in the face of an ever-growing threat from North Vietnamese air-defence systems. Initially, opposition was weak, but by the end of 1967 North Vietnam had deployed a total of more than 6500 anti-aircraft (AA) guns, ranging in calibre from 37mm up to 100mm, about 200 SA-2 Guideline surface-to-air missile (SAM) sites, and 40 interceptor aircraft. The AA guns and fighters could be dealt with using traditional methods: by assigning flak-suppression aircraft to accompany

the bombing force, and providing an escort of air-superiority fighters. The latter measure had proved to be particularly effective, as was shown by the reduction of the North Vietnamese interceptor force from a strength of nearly 100 aircraft in the spring of 1967, to under half that figure by the end of the year. However, SAMs were a comparatively new air-defence system that called for innovative counter-measures.

It was found that the SA-2s could be defeated by jamming their guidance radars and even, under certain conditions, outmanoeuvred in flight, but by far the surest method of dealing with them was to attack and destroy the missiles on their launchers before they could be fired against American aircraft. This defence-suppression mission, code-named 'Iron Hand', was the task of the 'Wild Weasel' crews flying F-105 Thunderchiefs, or 'Thuds' as they were invariably nicknamed in Southeast Asia. 'They had the most demanding job and the most hazardous,' thought Seventh Air Force commander General William Momyer, 'These flights were the first into the target area and the last out.' Moreover, in the autumn of 1967, just as the threat from enemy interceptors had been all but mastered, that from the SAMs intensified. It was at this crucial stage of the air war that the USAF's 44th Tactical Fighter Squadron (44th TFS), nicknamed the 'Vampires', became the 388th Tactical Fighter Wing's specialised Wild Weasel unit at Korat air force base in Thailand.

In December 1964 the 44th TFS became one of the first USAF Thunderchief squadrons to become involved in the war in Southeast Asia when six of its F-105s deployed from Okinawa to Da Nang in the Republic of Vietnam. On Christmas Day, the detachment flew its first combat mission, a dive-bombing attack on North Vietnamese Army barracks at Tchepone in Laos. A larger-scale air strike followed on 13 January 1965, the target being a bridge at Ban Ken, also in Laos. This had been identified as a potential chokepoint on the communications network linking North and South Vietnam through ostensibly neutral territory, which was to become known by the Americans as the Ho Chi Minh Trail. Sixteen F-105s drawn from the 44th TFS and the 67th TFS made up the bombing force. They were accompanied by eight F-100s armed with cluster bombs for flak suppression, one RF-101 Voodoo to act as pathfinder and another to obtain post-strike reconnaissance photos.

The first eight F-105s, armed with 750lb bombs, succeeded in cutting the bridge. Consequently, the following eight Thuds, carrying both bombs and two AGM-12B Bullpup air-to-surface missiles, switched their attack to the enemy's AA gun emplacements that the F-100s had not succeeded in completely silencing. This proved to be a tactical error. Each aircraft needed to make at least three passes to release its ordnance and, moreover, had to descend to within lethal range of the AA fire in order to guide its missiles onto the targets. As a result, one F-105 was shot down and four others were damaged for no

44TH TFS, USAF

The history of the 44th Tactical Fighter Squadron (44th TFS) began in January 1941 when the 44th Pursuit Squadron was activated as part of the 18th Pursuit Group. Operating Curtiss P-40s from Bellows Field, Hawaii, the unit suffered considerable losses during the Japanese attack on Pearl Harbor.

Renamed the 44th Fighter Squadron, it began operations from Guadalcanal in the Solomon Islands at the end of 1942. In 1944 the squadron re-equipped with P-38 Lightnings, and transferred to the Philippines in 1945.

The war over, the 44th Fighter Squadron remained in the Philippines as part of the 18th Fighter Group, operating the P-51 Mustang, the P-47 Thunderbolt, and its first jet, the F-80 Shooting Star. In 1954 the squadron converted to F-86 Sabres, moving with them to Kadena Air Base on Okinawa the following year. F-100 Super Sabres were received in 1957, and in 1963 the unit, by then designated the 44th TFS, part of the 18th Tactical Fighter Wing (TFW), was re-equipped with F-105 Thunderchiefs.

After the Vietnam War the Vampires rejoined the 18th TFW at Kadena on Okinawa to operate F4-D Phantoms. In 1980 they re-equipped with F-15 Eagle air-superiority fighters, which today proudly carry the unit's vampire insignia (above).

Far left above: F-105 crews of the 44th TFS pose for the camera in front of the squadron's distinctive vampire insignia at Korat air base in April 1967. Left: A line of F-105 Thunderchiefs of the 44th TFS at Korat. Left above: View from a Thunderchief of a knocked-out bridge in North Vietnam.

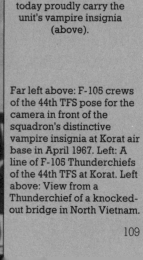

THUNDERCHIEF

The last aircraft built by Republic before the company became part of Fairchild Hiller, the F-105 Thunderchief was already on the drawing-board when its predecessor, the F-84F Thunderstreak, went into service in 1954. The F-105 was an ambitious and complex aircraft – more than 65,000 components went into the plane and more than five million engineering man-hours were spent in its creation. In compensation, it set standards of performance, ordnance and electronics capability, and mission adaptability which were only to be bettered in the late 1970s.

The prototype Thunderchief, powered by a Pratt & Whitney J57-25 engine, flew on 22 October 1955 and exceeded Mach 1. The Area Rule for shaping aircraft for minimum transonic or supersonic drag was then applied to the F-105 and a new version, incorporating a J75-P-3 engine, flew on 26 May 1956 and achieved a speed exceeding Mach 2. Introduced into service as the F-105B, this version was superseded by the F-105D in 1959, now powered by the new Pratt & Whitney J75-P-19W turbojet.

After 1966 nearly all the USAF's F-105Ds were flying combat missions over Vietnam. Fitted with 17 stores points, they were able to carry virtually every strategic air-to-ground weapon of the USAF. These planes were later joined by two-seater F-105Fs fitted out as Wild Weasel electronic warfare platforms and featuring the new Thunderstick computerised fire-control system.

The F-105s played a major part in air strikes on North Vietnam, and it was only the toll exacted by being constantly in the front line that caused them to be withdrawn in 1970.

worthwhile return, since the bridge had already been destroyed. Yet the mission's greatest mistake was made not by the Thud pilots, whose only fault had been a commendable excess of enthusiasm, but by the staff planners. This became apparent three days later, when the North Vietnamese converted the top of a dam just upstream of the Ban Ken bridge into an alternative route, thus completely negating the results of the bombing.

The 44th TFS remained in the combat theatre on temporary duty until May 1965, moving from Da Nang to Korat air force base in Thailand. One of its most memorable missions during this period was the attack on the Thanh Hoa bridge in Annam Province, North Vietnam, on 3 April 1965. This massive structure, spanning the Song Ma river, was known in Vietnamese as the Ham Rung (Dragon's Jaw). The 79-aircraft strong strike force was led by Lieutenant-Colonel Robinson Risner of the 67th TFS and included 46 F-105s armed with 750lb bombs and Bullpup missiles. The missile-armed aircraft were first into the target area, each Thud having to make two firing passes as the Bullpups needed to be guided individually.

The No.3 pilot in the third flight, Captain Bill Mayerholt of the 44th TFS, was surprised to see that the bridge was still undamaged as he guided his first missile onto the target. However, after watching the

Bullpup's 250lb explosive warhead detonate against the bridge's superstructure and do no more damage than scorch the steel and concrete, he wondered no more. It was like shooting shotgun pellets at a Sherman tank, he later reflected. In all, 32 missiles and 120 bombs had been aimed at the bridge and many of them had hit, yet it remained standing. It was only when laser-guided bombs were employed during the Linebacker I campaign in the spring of 1972 that American airmen succeeded in making any impression on this formidable structure.

In May 1965 the 44th TFS's period of temporary duty in Southeast Asia came to an end and it was not until April 1967 that the unit returned to the combat theatre. The squadron was then assigned to the 388th Tactical Fighter Wing at Korat, and for the following six months was employed in a tactical bombing role against targets in North Vietnam. Enemy interceptors were especially active during this period, and on 13 May one of the 44th TFS pilots was credited with the squadron's only MiG kill of the war. Major Maurice E. Seaver Jr. had just pulled out from his bomb run against the Vinh Yen army barracks when he saw a MiG-17, 1000ft ahead of him at the 10 o'clock position. Pulling in behind it, Seaver opened fire with his 20mm Vulcan cannon. The North Vietnamese pilot had not spotted him and took no evasive action. Seaver's fire took immediate effect. The North Viet-

Left: A flight of F-105 Thunderchiefs roars into action against a North Vietnamese railway bridge in 1965. Ordnance on the aircraft includes conventional bombs and AGM-12 air-to-surface Bullpup missiles. Below: The Princess Cheri, an F-105D of the 44th TFS. The F-105D was the definitive single-seat model of Thunderchief and over 600 of this variant were produced. The F-105D could carry a wide range of stores including bombs, missiles, mines, napalm and rockets. The F-105D was also armed with an M-61 20mm six-barrelled rotary cannon, mounted in the nose.

Thanh Hoa raid
44th TFS, 3 April 1965

Five months after its deployment in Vietnam, the 44th TFS participated in an air strike against the Thanh Hoa bridge. The mission was typical of long-range air-refuelled bombing missions flown from Thailand.

Map key:
CHINA · NORTH VIETNAM · Lang Son · Dien Bien Phu · Hanoi · Haiphong · Song Ma · LAOS · Thanh Hoa bridge · F-105s · Vinh · GULF OF TONKIN · Dong Hoi · F-100s · DMZ · F-105s and KC-135 tankers · Tchepone · Da Nang · THAILAND · Takhli · Korat · CAMBODIA · SOUTH VIETNAM

Key
→ Thanh Hoa raid, 3 April 1965

aircraft to detect the SA-2 sites' radar emissions and determine their position so that they could be attacked. It was the duty of the F-105's backseater (officially titled the electronic warfare officer, but more usually known as 'the Bear') to manage this equipment and direct his pilot into an attack. The SAM sites could be dealt with from stand-off ranges, by launching AGM-45A Shrike anti-radiation missiles against their radars. Alternatively, the Wild Weasels could make a direct attack on the entire complex, using free-fall bombs and cannon fire. Often though, the mere threat of a Shrike-armed Wild Weasel was sufficient to cause the North Vietnamese missile crews to shut down their radars. However, an optical tracking device for the SA-2 had recently been introduced as a partially effective counter-measure to the Wild Weasel's Shrike tactics.

Captain Don Carson has written a graphic account of one of the 44th TFS's Iron Hand missions over North Vietnam:

'"SAMs at two and five... guns at three", my Bear, Don Brian, coolly calls over the intercom, telling me where the threat is located.

'I light up the afterburner and our speed approaches 600 knots. I turn towards the SAM site, which is looking at my flight of four Weasels with its radar. We have the green light in the outboard weapons pylon buttons, indicating that

Below: US Thunderchief pilot Clarence H. Hoggard of the 44th TFS prepares to leave the cockpit of Princess Cheri after a mission over North Vietnam in July 1967. By 1967 Hoggard had flown over 100 missions with the Princess.

namese fighter broke sharply to the right and its wing exploded. From first to last, the combat had lasted just 90 seconds. It had been an outstandingly successful day for the USAF's fighter pilots, with a total of seven MiG-17s shot down – five of them by Thud pilots. Although the F-105 had not been designed for fighter-versus-fighter combat, it often proved to be a dangerous antagonist and 25 North Vietnamese fighters were shot down by Thuds during the conflict.

In October 1967 the 44th TFS took over the Wild Weasel missions for the entire 388th TFW, adopting the nickname Vampires which was also used as a radio callsign. They flew the F-105F two-seat version of the Thud, which had been specially modified for the defence-suppression role. Radar-homing and warning receivers were fitted, which enabled the

USAF 00429

when we're in range and position, we are armed and ready to fire our AGM-45 Shrike anti-radiation missiles.

'"SAMs at 12 o'clock... a three ringer." My Bear now has the SAM battery off our nose and is getting very strong signals on his indicating equipment. We press in, pull up our F-105 at the proper range and hose off a pair of Shrikes just as the SAM site fires at our flight. My skin crawls as the rattlesnake sound in my headset and the flash of the warning-gear light tells me that it is for real this time.

'"Valid launch.... 12 o'clock," yells my Bear. "Vampires... take it down," I call to my flight as I nose over and unload. "Taking it down" is the standard Wild Weasel manoeuvre of rapidly diving in full afterburner and picking up speed to avoid the SAMs being guided onto your aircraft.

'I see clouds of dust and the "telephone poles" [SA-2s] trailing fire as they climb. Our Shrikes are still guiding directly toward the radar van which controls them. Suddenly, however, the SAMs appear to go unguided and streak off well above our flight. This means the radar control van had shut down in hopes of foiling our Shrikes, but it doesn't work. Our Shrikes impact the van, and dust and smoke rises to mark the target area clearly.'

Ignoring the flak from gun emplacements ringing the SAM site, Carson's flight then completed its destruction by bombing, before heading out of the area to

Below: An F-105G, a twin-seat variant of the Thunderchief, on an 'Iron Hand' anti-SAM mission over Laos in December 1972. The aircraft is armed with two anti-radiation missile types: the outboard station mounts an AGM-45 Shrike and the inboard station carries the larger AGM-78 Standard ARM.

rendezvous with a tanker aircraft in order to top-up their tanks for the flight back to Korat.

As well as controlling the Wild Weasel flights, the 44th TFS was responsible for Ryan's Raiders, a select force of six F-105Fs converted under project 'Commando Nail' to specialised night-bombing aircraft for missions over North Vietnam. The aircraft radars were modified to give an expanded picture of the ground, which was of sharper definition than that obtained by the standard set. Using this information, the backseater was able to direct his pilot into a blind bombing-run against targets with a good radar return. The Commando Nail F-105Fs' weapons circuits had been modified to allow the backseater to release the bombload – the job of the pilot on standard aircraft. Ryan's Raider missions, nicknamed after General John D. Ryan, the C-in-C Pacific Air Forces, who originated the project, could be extremely hazardous. Don Carson thought:

'You've never lived until you've battled the Southeast Asia weather at night. A night thunderstorm, tanker join-up and aerial refuelling – with lightning and St Elmo's fire crackling around your canopy and pitot tube until they glowed with an eerie purple light – could be more frightening than the arcing red balls of 37mm or 57mm guns.'

Above: Personal insignia were popular with the 44th's pilots and aircraft were decorated with a variety of jokey motifs.

Nor were the enemy air defences less active by night than during daylight. However, Carson thought that because it was easier to see a SAM or AA gunfire at night, the pilot then had more time to react and this balanced out the handicaps of night operations. As the threat from radar-directed SA-2s was just as great during night missions, the Commando Nail F-105Fs were usually accompanied by a Wild Weasel escort. Carson remembered one such night mission in 1968:

'We trolled back and forth along the target area, listening and looking for any enemy SAM or AA activity. This was not unlike trolling for fish, except this time we were the bait. A couple of strobes from a radar-guided gun and a low-pulse repetition-frequency SAM radar light indicated that someone knew we were there. They probably also knew that since we were alone and carried no jamming pods, we were a Weasel bird.'

The Shrike lit off with a roar and left the F-105 with a burst of speed and a trail of brilliant fire

As the first Ryan's Raider approached the target area, enemy activity increased, with heavy fire from 37mm and 57mm AA guns. Then Don Brian picked up a strong SAM signal and his pilot launched a Shrike:

'It lit off with a roar and left the F-105 with a burst of speed and a trail of brilliant fire. I waited for Don to call the SAM launch, hoping the Shrike would get there first. The Shrike guided and, as we saw it impact, the SAM signal suddenly ceased.'

In April 1968 American bombing was limited to the southern provinces of North Vietnam, thus putting the heavily-defended Hanoi and Haiphong areas out of bounds. This measure was but a prelude to the complete halt of bombing raids against North Vietnam, which came into force at the end of October. During that month, the 44th TFS had been re-assigned to the 355th TFW at Takhli air force base in Thailand; a logical move since the other squadrons of the 388th TFW had converted onto the F-4E Phantom, whereas the Vampires' new wing continued to fly Thuds. The transition also marked the end of the 44th TFS's service as a Wild Weasel squadron. Because US strike forces no longer penetrated into the high-threat areas, the Weasels' services could be delegated to specialised flights within each squadron. Accordingly, the Vampires reverted to the tactical bombing role until the squadron was withdrawn from the combat theatre in March 1971.

THE AUTHOR Anthony Robinson was formerly on the staff of the RAF Museum, Hendon and is now a freelance military aviation writer. He has edited the books *Aerial Warfare* and the *Dictionary of Aviation*.

The pilots of Nachtjagdgeschwader 1 waited tensely during the night of 30 March 1944, expecting at any moment the order to take off against the British bomber streams heading for Nuremberg

NIGHT FIGHTING

Top and left: Lancasters of Bomber Command head for Nuremberg on 30 March 1944. In an ineffectual raid, the RAF lost over 100 aircraft to the Luftwaffe's pilots. Centre: German aces are congratulated by Hitler.

NJG 1

Nachtjagdgeschwader 1 (NJG 1) was the Luftwaffe's premier nightfighter unit of World War II; with over 2000 kills to their credit, its pilots accounted for nearly 40 per cent of all the RAF bombers destroyed at night over Western Europe. Within the ranks of NJG 1 were some of the top aces of the entire war, including Heinz Schnaufer, with 121 victories, and Helmut Lent with 120. At one time, 107 of the air force's top-scorers were members of NJG 1. The unit also pioneered the nightfighting tactics that enabled the Luftwaffe to inflict such heavy losses. An early commander of NJG 1, Wolfgang Falck, was a key figure in the development of radar-guided interception.

Falck was stationed at Aalborg in Denmark with the First Gruppe of Zeroströrergeschwader 1 (1/ZG 1) and, after several successes at night, both he and 1/ZG 1 were sent to Dusseldorf on 22 June. Here, with the blessing of the German Air Ministry, he began forming the Luftwaffe's first nightfighter unit, NJG 1.

Over the following years, NJG 1 formed the heart of the German nightfighter force and bore the brunt of the battle against the RAF's Bomber Command. By 1945, however, lack of fuel and stiff opposition forced NJG 1 onto the defensive. Although the unit continued to fight until the end of the war, its men were unable to compensate for the numerical superiority enjoyed by the RAF.

Above: Operational Flying Clasp, awarded to men of short-range nightfighter units.

ON THE night of 30/31 March 1944, the pilots and air-crews of the Luftwaffe's premier nightfighter unit, Nachtjagdgeschwader 1 (NJG 1), fought in one of the bloodiest and, for them, most successful air battles of World War II. In a running action over much of western Germany against the cream of the RAF's bomber squadrons heading for Nuremberg, the spiritual home of Hitler's Reich, they contributed to the destruction of over 100 British aircraft.

One of the first actions of the night was fought between a Bf 110 of the Third Gruppe, NJG 1 (III/NJG 1) and a Lancaster from No. 467 Squadron. Unteroffizier Erich Handke, the radar operator in the Bf 110, later remembered the ideal hunting conditions and the ease of one of the first German 'kills' of that fateful spring night:

'We were flying from Laon and had been told by the running commentary that the bombers were about five minutes away. I hadn't even switched on the SN-2 [airborne interception radar] set when the gunner poked me in the back and pointed, "There he is up there, the first one." As we came round we saw another straight away, about 200m directly above. I switched on my SN-2, but we had dropped 2000m behind in the turn and had lost them.

'When the set warmed up, I saw three targets on it at once. I headed for the nearest and Drewes [the pilot] picked it up at 600m. Weather was marvellous – clear sky, half-moon, little cloud and no mist – it was simply ideal, almost too bright.

'It was a Lancaster flying nicely on a steady course so that, when we were comfortably positioned underneath and from about 50m, Drewes opened fire with the upward firing cannon at one wing which immediately caught fire. We followed the Lancaster for five minutes until it crashed below with a tremendous explosion.'

At his command post at Deelen in Holland, the senior officer of the Luftwaffe's Third Fighter Division, Generalmajor Walter Grabmann, a 39-year-old veteran of the Spanish Civil War, had no hesitation in declaring that the force of bombers approaching his operational area, soon to cross the Belgian coast near Knokke, was the main raid and that the other force over the North Sea was a feint.

Immediately, Grabmann sent the message 'Fasan' (pheasant), indicating that enemy raids were expected, to his nightfighter units and ordered them to rendezvous at a radio beacon known as Ida, south of Cologne.

From airfields at Venlo and Saint-Trond, the pilots of I/NJG 1 and IV/NJG 1 took to the air in their Bf 110 and He 219 nightfighters. Other units, including the other two Gruppen of NJG/1 based at Saint-Dizier and Laon, were ordered to make for beacon Otto, lying a few kilometres to the northeast of Cologne. As the Pathfinder force and marker aircraft of Bomber Command reached the German border a little after midnight, over 200 of the Luftwaffe's nightfighters were circling the two beacons, poised to strike at the RAF's Lancasters and Halifaxes.

While the nightfighters awaited further orders, the German ground controllers assessed the information they had gathered. At their 'Battle Opera Houses', the co-ordinating centres for each of the Luftwaffe's five fighter divisions in northern Europe, the controllers plotted the course and strength of the raiders, and attempted to identify possible targets.

Working on the data provided by the Freya radar used for long-range detection and the Würzburg radar sets that gave a more accurate indication of the enemy force's direction, the controllers were able to

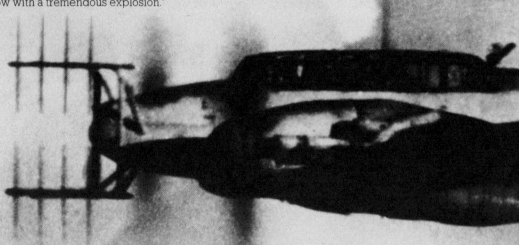

The deadly cat-and-mouse game between the Luftwaffe and the RAF had begun shortly before 2300 hours on the 30th, when the first link in the German defences had warned of an attack. In the early-warning radar station at Texel, operations had spotted the tell-tale plots on their radar screens, indicating a large force of bombers flying across the North Sea on a route threatening both Hamburg and Berlin. A few moments later, the same station detected signs of a second force massing in the area of East Anglia.

As further information became available, the Germans were able to forecast the routes that the two forces were likely to follow to the coast; if they stayed on the present headings, they were expected to cross the coast at two points some 480km apart.

build up a remarkably accurate picture of the Main Force of RAF aircraft. Consisting of over 770 bombers, the stream stretched for nearly 110km. Within this distance there were five waves of bombers in the Main Force preceded by 97 aircraft of the Pathfinder, marker and electronic-countermeasures wave. Each of the Main Force waves contained on average 133 bombers, including nine Pathfinders, five Lancasters carrying ABC jamming sets, 78 ordinary Lancasters and 46 Halifaxes.

At 2322 hours the leading elements of the Main Force crossed the Belgian coast, heading for the first turning point, a little northeast of Charleroi. To the surprise of the RAF crews, opposition was minimal: a little light flak that failed to reach their altitude of

Nachtjagdgeschwader 1 (NJG 1), the Luftwaffe's top-scoring nightfighter unit, played a key part in the attacks on RAF's bomber force, and many of its pilots were aces. Wolfgang Schnaufer (above) was credited with 121 victories by the end of the war, and Helmut Lent (above right) with 102 night kills by the time of his death in October 1944. Main picture: Although the Luftwaffe's night force was neglected by Hitler and had to fly older aircraft, the Bf 110 proved a lethal nightfighter in the hands of a skilled crew.

Below and right: Deployed by NJG 1 from the summer of 1943, the He 219 Uhu (Owl) was the Luftwaffe's most sophisticated nightfighter of the war. With a top speed of 630 km/h and a range of 2800km, armaments could include two 20mm MG 151 cannon in the wings, two 30mm cannon in a ventral tray and two upward-firing cannon in the rear fuselage.

5800m. Nuremberg, however, was still a good 670km away – 101 minutes' flying time through the heart of the Luftwaffe's night defences. Nevertheless, the force pressed on and crossed into Germany south of the city of Aachen. The RAF plan was to squeeze the bombers through a 32km gap lying between the heavily defended southern edge of the Ruhr and Koblenz, known as the Cologne Gap. The Luftwaffe, aware of this favoured route, had placed both the Otto and Ida beacons to cover this potential weakpoint in their night defences.

Ahead, the nightfighters of NJG 1 were listening to the running commentary provided by the ground controllers at Deelen. Almost unbelievably, they heard that the RAF's Main Force was heading directly towards them; usually they had to scour the night sky for the RAF, rather than have their targets served up on a plate.

Indeed, every possible advantage lay with the Luftwaffe: its nightfighters were available in massive strength, with two hours' flying time of fuel in their tanks and a beautifully clear night to aid the attack. To make their task of identifying the route of the bombers even easier, vapour trails, not usually seen below heights of 7600m, had begun to stream from each aircraft. Moments later, the deadly array of Bf 110 and He 219 nightfighters were unleashed against the 712 bombers that had crossed the Rhine.

The battle that followed was a perfect example of the 'Zahme Sau' (tame sow) tactic, a system used by the Luftwaffe's ground controllers to guide their nightfighters onto a formation of enemy aircraft. In each Battle Opera House, operators processed information and observations from radar, listening posts, reconnaissance aircraft and fighters already in action. Once correlated, the data was projected onto a huge panel made of frosted glass, using light spots and illuminated writing. The operators then provided a continuous running commentary to their nightfighters, whose pilots used the information to fly on an interception course from their holding beacons.

After reaching the stream, the nightfighters identified their own target, either by using their own short-range radar or by sight if conditions permitted. The nightfighters were armed either with forward-firing machine guns or cannon, or with a system known as 'Schräge Musik' (slanting, or jazz, music).

Both types required the nightfighter crews to manoeuvre their aircraft into a favourable position near the target before an attack could be launched.

The most usual form of attack was known by the Luftwaffe pilots as 'von unten hinten' (from under and behind). With this tactic, the nightfighter would make a long-range radar-guided approach to the stern of the bomber and, when a visual sighting had been made, would launch a rear attack at close range, below the line of fire of the bomber's rear-gunner. However, if the nightfighter was spotted, or the pilot inexperienced, the quick kill might be denied and an inconclusive positional battle would develop.

Schräge Musik was developed after pilots had discovered that it was completely safe to fly directly under both the Lancaster and Halifax without being

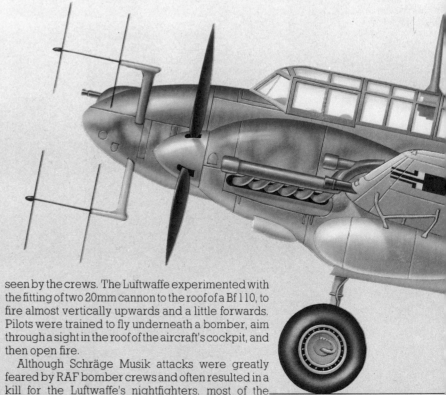

seen by the crews. The Luftwaffe experimented with the fitting of two 20mm cannon to the roof of a Bf 110, to fire almost vertically upwards and a little forwards. Pilots were trained to fly underneath a bomber, aim through a sight in the roof of the aircraft's cockpit, and then open fire.

Although Schräge Musik attacks were greatly feared by RAF bomber crews and often resulted in a kill for the Luftwaffe's nightfighters, most of the

The Ju 88 was, with the Bf 110, the backbone of the Reich's nightfighter force during the latter stages of World War II. Originally designed as a medium or dive-bomber, it was used in a variety of roles. Top and right: This model, the Ju 88G, was fitted with Lichtenstein radar and a mix of weapons including Schräge Musik cannon, four forward-firing cannon and a single flexible machine gun in the cockpit. Below right: The outdated Do 217 saw limited service as a nightfighter. Bottom: The Bf 110 nightfighter fitted with SN-2 radar and Schräge Musik.

aircraft that were lost during the Nuremberg raid fell to the more straightforward 'von unten hinten' tactic. The reasons for this were twofold; first, the Luftwaffe had only recently developed the Schräge Musik technique and, secondly, as nightfighter units were considered less important than other forces by Hitler, the funds to install the new weapons were not readily available – less than 40 per cent of the Luftwaffe nightfighters were fitted with upward-firing cannon at this stage of the war.

Stern attacks, however, were often successful. Oberleutnant Fritz Lau, a Bf 110 pilot from II/NJG 1, later remembered one such attack on a Halifax from No. 158 Squadron:

'I tried to put myself in position to attack but, whenever I thought I had got him in my sight, he had gone again and so it went, to and fro, for several minutes. My intention was to get within

MESSERSCHMITT Bf 110

Despite its limitations as a twin-engined dayfighter, the Bf 110 became one of the most successful nightfighters deployed by the Luftwaffe during World War II.

Initially, the Bf 110 was fitted with a variety of crude aids to visual identification, but these proved to be of only limited value.

Interception techniques were improved, however, with the introduction of the FuG 212 Lichtenstein airborne radar in July 1942; Lichtenstein was used to home onto enemy aircraft at short range.

By this stage the standard Bf 110 nightfighter, the F-4 version, was armed with four 7.92mm machine guns and a pair of Mauser MG 151/20 cannon. Specific modifications included two 300-litre tanks for extra fuel, flame-dampers on the engines' exhausts, and high explosive 'night-glimmer' rounds for the Bf 110's weapons.

During 1943 a number of Bf 110s were fitted with 20mm upwards-firing cannon. Known as 'Schräge Musik' (slanting, or jazz, music) these weapons proved extremely effective against the RAF's bombers.

The Messerschmitt Bf 110G equipped with FuG 212 and then Lichtenstein SN-2 (FuG 220) radar, was the mainstay of the Luftwaffe's nightfighter force until the end of hostilities.

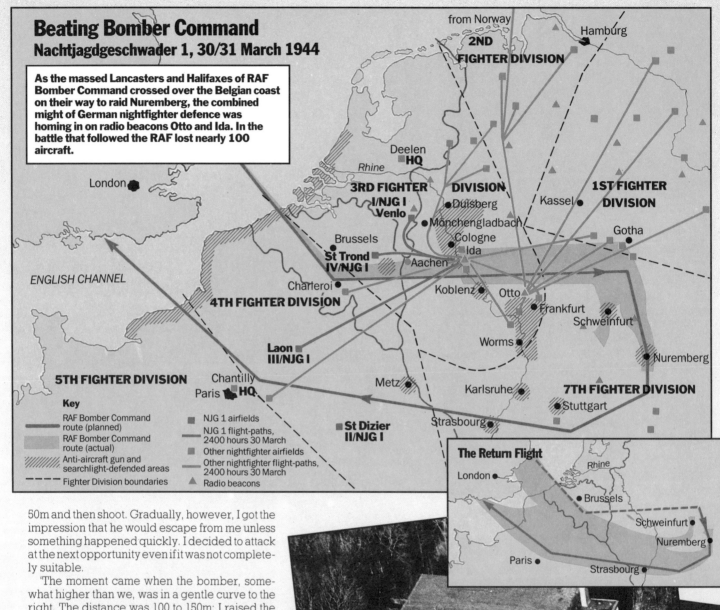

Beating Bomber Command
Nachtjagdgeschwader 1, 30/31 March 1944

As the massed Lancasters and Halifaxes of RAF Bomber Command crossed over the Belgian coast on their way to raid Nuremberg, the combined might of German nightfighter defence was homing in on radio beacons Otto and Ida. In the battle that followed the RAF lost nearly 100 aircraft.

Key

RAF Bomber Command route (planned)	■ NJG 1 airfields
RAF Bomber Command route (actual)	NJG 1 flight-paths, 2400 hours 30 March
▨ Anti-aircraft gun and searchlight-defended areas	■ Other nightfighter airfields
– – – Fighter Division boundaries	Other nightfighter flight-paths, 2400 hours 30 March
	▲ Radio beacons

The Return Flight

50m and then shoot. Gradually, however, I got the impression that he would escape from me unless something happened quickly. I decided to attack at the next opportunity even if it was not completely suitable.

'The moment came when the bomber, somewhat higher than we, was in a gentle curve to the right. The distance was 100 to 150m; I raised the nose, took aim and fired. Within seconds, the bomber burst into flames, banked to the left and lost height quickly. I flew above him and we were able to see one man jumping out by parachute. The bomber broke into two burning parts which soon afterwards hit the ground.'

The RAF's bombers faced the might of the Luftwaffe's nightfighters all the way from the German border to a point a few kilometres south of Gotha, where the Main Force turned towards Nuremberg at 0045 hours on the 31st. Despite the skill and ferocity of the German attacks, 643 bombers were poised to make the final approach. Nevertheless, the shattered remains of nearly 70 bombers littered the countryside between Aachen and Gotha.

Although some of the Luftwaffe's nightfighters continued the pursuit towards Nuremberg and beyond, many others were forced by this stage to land at the nearest airfield due to lack of fuel and ammunition. Most of the Lancasters and Halifaxes that reached the turning-point near Gotha were able to bomb targets in and around the Nuremberg area, but with little success. Many aircraft bombed Schweinfurt, some 80km north of the true target and others hit only the outskirts of Nuremberg, before returning to England via Strasbourg. By 0725 hours on the 31st the last aircraft had touched down; 105 others had failed to return

To the nightfighter crews gathered at airfields in the Frankfurt area, there was no mistaking the scale of their victory. Many were able to give graphic accounts of a kill, but others were more reflective. Oberleutnant Fritz Lau of II/NJG 1 viewed the celebrations at Hanau with mixed feelings:

'I was, of course, pleased to have shot down at least one but what I said about this was different from what my comrades were saying. Because of my age – I was 32 years old, about 10 years older than most of the others – I viewed everything more soberly. I had seen Nuremberg burning and, although I had seen many bombers shot down and already sensed that it would be an unusually large victory, this seemed to me to be not enough when measured against the destruction of our cities.'

Hauptmann Heinz Wolfgang Schnaufer of IV/NJG 1, destined to be one of the greatest nightfighter pilots of the war with 121 kills to his credit, also landed at Hanau. Although he had attempted an interception as the main bomber force had crossed the Belgian coast and had attacked other aircraft after rendez-vousing at the Ida beacon, he had failed to score.

For the RAF, the Nuremberg raid was a costly failure. Although 84 per cent of the bomber force was able to bomb a target, the resultant damage was limited. In Nuremberg itself, one factory was badly damaged and three others suffered minor damage. The bombs that fell on Schweinfurt did little to affect the production of ball-bearings, the city's main contribution to the war effort. In terms of the number of aircraft lost or damaged the picture was even bleaker: 95 aircraft were downed, 10 were lost in crashes over England, 70 suffered varying degrees of repairable battle damage and one other was written off.

In comparison, the Luftwaffe's losses were remarkably light. Bomber Command claimed to have shot down 10 German aircraft: four Ju 88s, three Bf 109s, two Fw 190s and a single Bf 110. The Germans acknowledged that three crew members were killed, eight were missing and one had been wounded.

Below left: Generalmajor Grabmann's Battle Opera House in Deelen, Holland. During the Nuremberg raid, its staff plotted the direction of the RAF raid and guided the nightfighters of the Third Fighter Division into the RAF's bomber stream. Below centre: The single-engined Fw 190 supplemented Germany's night defences from mid-1943. With only half the endurance of the Bf 110, it proved an inferior nightfighter. Below: Close-up of the radar aerials of a Bf 110. The outer elements were for SN-2 airborne interception radar; the inner for the more effective FuG 212 set.

The RAF admitted to 545 men killed.

Nightfighters accounted for the lion's share of the RAF's losses and Bf 110s claimed the greater part of the night's kills. The men of NJG 1, probably the largest and most experienced Geschwader in the Luftwaffe's nightfighter force, undoubtedly accounted for several of these scores, although precise figures for their total during the raid were never made clear.

In one of the largest bomber raids over Germany during World War II, the nightfighter Gruppen of NJG 1 met the RAF with the skill and determination that typified the spirit of the Luftwaffe's finest pilots. In a sprawling, often confused encounter in the night sky of Germany, they had come close to forcing a re-appraisal of Bomber Command's strategy for the destruction of Hitler's war industry.

THE AUTHOR Martin Streetly is an aviation and electronic warfare historian who has contributed to various military and aviation journals. His recent works include *World Electronic Warfare Aircraft*.

JAGDGESCHWADER 27

The early months of World War II found Jagdgeschwader 27 (JG 27), equipped with Messerschmitt Bf 109Es, assigned to the air defence of Germany. Consequently, it did not take part in the Polish or Norwegian campaigns of 1939 and 1940, but saw considerable action over the Saar during the eight-month 'Phoney War' period. During the Battles of France and Britain in 1940 it operated in support of the Ju 87 Stuka Gruppen of Wolfram Freiherr von Richthofen's VIII Fliegerkorps, under the command of General Hugo Sperrle's Luftflotte 3.

In June 1941, I and II Gruppen of JG 27 were assigned to the Russian campaign under Major Wolfgang Schnellmann, III/JG 27 already having been sent to North Africa under Hauptmann Eduard Neumann. The other two Gruppen were also assigned to North Africa under X Fliegerkorps after the initial German offensives in Russia. Following the German defeat in Africa, the battered JG 27 re-formed in Sicily and re-equipped with the Messerschmitt Bf 109G. Subsequently, all three Gruppen were transferred to Wiesbaden-Erbenheim for the air defence of Germany. Meanwhile, in April 1943, a fourth Gruppe – IV/JG 27 – had been formed in Greece under Oberleutnant Alfred Burk, and in August this unit scored numerous successes against American bombers during the first big attack on the Ploesti oilfields.

From June 1943, II/JG 27 under Hauptmann Werner Schroer operated in the 'Wilde Sau' (Wild Boar) nightfighter role alongside I/JG 302. All Gruppen with the exception of IV/JG 27, which stayed in the Balkans, continued to defend the Reich territory until the collapse of Germany.

Above: Hans-Joachim Marseille, the 'Star of Africa', demonstrates to his fellow pilots how another victim was added to his astonishing tally of kills. Left: A marshaller flags in a Bf 109 after a sortie over the desert.

THE STAR

In 1942, the North African skies were the hunting ground of JG 27's seemingly invincible fighter ace, Hans-Joachim Marseille

IT WAS 3 JUNE 1942, and for days the Afrika Korps, under the redoubtable Field Marshal Erwin Rommel, had been assaulting the British Eighth Army's Gazala Line defences in an attempt to achieve the massive breakthrough that was needed to take Axis forces to the ultimate prizes in North Africa – Cairo and the Suez Canal. But Rommel's outflanking tactics were being held up by the stubborn resistance of the Free French at Bir Hacheim, on the southern tip of the Gazala Line. On 3 June the French position was shrouded in smoke and dust, hurled up by incessant Stuka attacks; but the Stukas had suffered heavily at the hands of the Curtiss P-40B Tomahawks of No.5 Squadron, South African Air Force (SAAF), which was responsible for the Allied defence of that sector. Even the escort provided by the Messerschmitt Bf 109s of Jagdgeschwader 27 (JG 27), the Luftwaffe's desert fighter force, had not been able to prevent a massacre of the dive bombers.

Then the Stukas came again, and this time the fighter escort was led by the young and flamboyant commander of the Third Gruppe of JG 27 (III/JG 27), Hans-Joachim (Jochen) Marseille. Together with his wingman, Feldwebel Rainer Pöttgen, Marseille swept into the middle of the South Africans who, believing that they were being attacked by a far superior force, immediately formed a defensive

Background: Master of the desert skies – a Messerschmitt Bf 109E of I/JG 27 with the insignia of the group, a panther's head on the map of Africa, emblazoned on its nose.

circle. Marseille got inside it, turning steeply, and gave a P-40 a short burst. The fighter went down vertically and exploded in the desert.

Marseille's tactics were unorthodox. Turning continually inside the circle of enemy fighters, keeping his airspeed low, he fired in short, deadly accurate bursts. A second P-40 went down, followed quickly by a third. In less than 12 minutes the burning wrecks of six South African fighters were scattered over the desert. Circling over the mêlée, Pöttgen watched in fascination as one P-40 after another plunged to destruction. He later commented:

'I had my work cut out counting his victories, noting the times and position, and at the same time protecting his tail. His judgement of deflection was incredible. Each time he fired I saw his shells strike first the enemy's nose, then travel along to the cockpit. No ammunition was wasted.'

Marseille was a master of low-speed air combat. Supremely confident of his skill in handling a Messerschmitt – of remaining in full control in any attitude and speed range – his usual tactics involved the sacrifice of speed to gain manoeuvrability, enabling him to turn inside an opponent. Once in this position, his excellent deflection shooting did the rest. When Marseille landed after the battle with the South African P-40s, it was found that he had used only 10 20mm shells and 180 rounds of machine-gun ammunition in shooting down the six aircraft.

Together with III/JG 27, commanded by Captain Eduard Neumann, Hans-Joachim Marseille had arrived in North Africa in April 1941. The unit was equipped with 40 Messerschmitt Bf 109E-4 fighters, and had the task of providing air cover for the Afrika Korps. III/JG 27 was based at Ain-el-Gazala, and quickly scored a number of victories in the skies over the Tobruk sector – the first falling to Marseille, who destroyed a Hurricane.

Marseille was eager to prove himself the top

OF AFRICA

scoring Luftwaffe fighter pilot in North Africa, and it was almost his undoing. Time after time, regardless of personal danger, he dived straight into the middle of a British formation and often returned to base with his aircraft full of bullet holes. On one occasion, as he leaned forward in the cockpit during a dogfight, a burst of machine-gun bullets ripped the back of his helmet. Had it not been for his sudden movement, the bullets would have shattered his head. During another dogfight over Tobruk, Marseille's Messerschmitt was badly damaged and he had to make a forced landing in no-man's land; but he managed to reach the German lines safely. A few days later, after his Bf 109 was hit in the engine, he crash-landed at Gazala but managed to walk away unscathed.

After Neumann threatened to ground him on account of his maverick approach to flying, Marseille concentrated on improving his tactics. He practised

North Africa 1942

MEDITERRANEAN

Gazala
Tobruk
El Adem
Bir Hacheim
Bardia
Sidi Barrani
Mersa Matruh
Fuka
To Alexandria
El Alamein

L I B Y A

E G Y P T

Key
→ Axis forces
ↄ Allied defensive lines

shooting from every angle, making dummy attacks on the other aircraft of his squadron; and as the weeks passed his skill increased. During Rommel's summer offensive of 1941, Marseille's score grew to 18 aircraft destroyed and his name was frequently mentioned in despatches. The high point of this period came on 24 September, when Marseille destroyed a Martin Maryland bomber in the morning, and, later in the afternoon, shot down four Hurricanes in a fierce half-hour battle between Halfaya Pass and Sidi Barrani. The British fighters had tried to form a defensive circle, but the Messerschmitts broke it up and Marseille destroyed his last victim after a hectic chase that led him over Sidi Barrani itself.

Right: Trailing plumes of sand, a swarm of Bf 109s gets airborne from a forward landing strip. Top left: Major Edouard Neumann, the commander of I/JG 27, in a typical mixture of German and Italian tropical kit.

In October the rains came, flooding Allied and German airstrips alike and severely curtailing air activity on both sides. The British Eighth Army used this opportunity to launch an autumn offensive, pushing Rommel back to the point from which he had started several months earlier. During this defensive period Marseille's score rose to 48 kills, bringing the award of the Knight's Cross. He was also accorded certain privileges within the Gruppe; he flew his own 'personal' Messerschmitt, with a large and distinctive yellow '14' painted on the fuselage.

By April 1942 the Luftwaffe's small fighter force in North Africa had re-equipped with the greatly improved Messerschmitt Bf 109F. Marseille was promoted to the rank of Oberleutnant and given command

Background: Hauptmann Karl-Wolfgang Redlich (left foreground) briefs pilots of I/JG 27 before their departure for Gambut, Libya, in April 1941. The air intake on the Bf 109E has been fitted with a tropical filter in readiness for desert operations. Bottom left: A camera is prepared for installation in a Bf 109. Tactical reconnaissance formed part of JG 27's role.

of III/JG 27. When one of the Jagdgeschwader's sister units, I/JG 27, arrived in North Africa after operating in the early stages of the campaign in Russia, Rommel's fighter strength was effectively doubled. In the late spring of 1942, II/JG 27 was also transferred to the North African theatre. Rommel now had some 120 Messerschmitt Bf 109Fs at his disposal – at least in theory. In practice, the number of serviceable 109s seldom exceeded 60 or 70.

Jochen Marseille's score continued to mount, and he and his 'Yellow 14' rapidly assumed a legendary reputation on both sides of the front. His exploits during the Bir Hacheim battle in June 1942 underlined his extraordinary skill. On 10 June the Luftwaffe made a final all-out assault on the fortress; in the course of the day 250 German bombers – including Junkers Ju 88s drawn from X Fliegerkorps in Greece and Crete – carried out three massive raids on Bir Hacheim, dropping 140 tons of bombs. As the dust and smoke settled, the German infantry launched their attack. High overhead, fierce air battles raged as JG 27's Messerschmitts joined combat with the Hurricanes, Spitfires and P-40s of the Royal Air Force (RAF), Royal Australian Air Force (RAAF) and SAAF. Both sides sustained considerable losses, but Marseille destroyed four more enemy fighters, bringing his score to 81.

'Yellow 14' roared across the airfield, rocking his wings three times to signify three kills

Bir Hacheim surrendered on 11 June. Rommel's rear was now secure and his panzers pushed forward, forcing the Eighth Army to retreat towards the Egyptian frontier. The pilots of JG 27 flew almost without rest during the next three days, and Marseille shot down a further six aircraft. On 15 June, another day of heavy fighting, Marseille destroyed four aircraft over the El Adem sector. His score was now 91 and, as he approached the magic figure of 100, the tension among the personnel of JG 27 became almost unbearable – particularly as Marseille had vowed to shoot down his 100th aircraft within the next 48 hours.

On the morning of 16 June, III/JG 27 carried out two sorties without sighting a single enemy aircraft. A third sortie was flown in the early afternoon, and when the Messerschmitts landed their pilots were jubilant; Marseille had got four more. But there was only a day to go before his self-imposed deadline expired, and even his more ardent admirers wondered if he would achieve his target in time. They were not kept in suspense for long. The next morning, the whole of JG 27 took off on a fighter sweep. Large numbers of British fighter bombers were

attacking the German forces and their supply lines, and there was certain to be action. Shortly after mid-day, excited lookouts sighted Marseille's flight returning to base. A minute later, 'Yellow 14' roared across the airfield, rocking his wings three times to signify three kills. Then Marseille made a second run at low level and rocked his wings three more times. Six enemy aircraft down in a single sortie – that brought the ace's score to 101!

An elated crowd converged on Marseille's fighter as it taxied in. Fellow pilots jumped on the wing, ready to lift him from the cockpit and chair him shoulder-high in triumph. But Marseille waved them away; his face was ashen and he was trembling. He climbed down and lit a cigarette with hands that shook heavily. He was drenched in sweat and seemed hardly able to stand. His commanding officer, Eduard Neumann, recognised the classic symptoms of advanced combat fatigue. The next day, Marseille was on board a Junkers Ju 52 transport, heading out over the Mediterranean for Italy on the first leg of his journey home. He was away for two months, and when he returned he found that considerable changes had taken place.

In an incredible 10-minute period Marseille claimed no fewer than eight Kittyhawks

A fierce argument had broken out between Rommel and Field Marshal Kesselring, the commander of the Mediterranean theatre. In June, when Tobruk fell to the Germans, Rommel had declared his intention to push straight on to the Nile delta and Cairo, giving the British no time to regroup their forces. Kesselring's argument was that such a move would create an enormous logistics problem for the Luftwaffe, whose crews were exhausted and aircraft badly in need of overhaul. Moreover, the strength of the British Desert Air Force was continuing to grow and the Luftwaffe was in no position to mount attacks on its airfields; this meant that if Rommel persisted in an all-out push towards Cairo, there was no guarantee that the Luftwaffe would be able to provide the necessary air support. Rommel, however, emerged victorious from the contest of wills and the advance continued. The Luftwaffe threw its dwindling resources into the battle, attacking enemy supply depots and troop concentrations. At the end of June, JG 27 took its Bf 109F-4 fighters up to Sidi Barrani, and

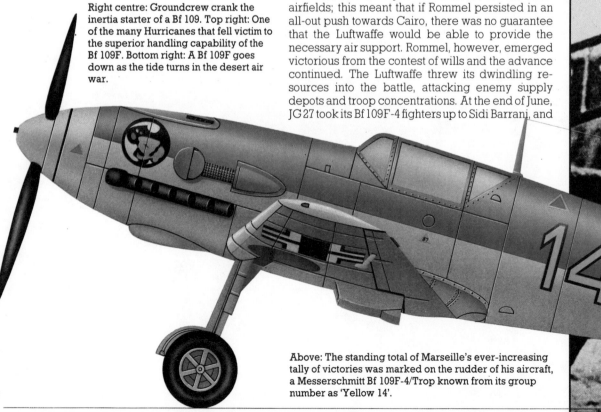

Right centre: Groundcrew crank the inertia starter of a Bf 109. Top right: One of the many Hurricanes that fell victim to the superior handling capability of the Bf 109F. Bottom right: A Bf 109F goes down as the tide turns in the desert air war.

Above: The standing total of Marseille's ever-increasing tally of victories was marked on the rudder of his aircraft, a Messerschmitt Bf 109F-4/Trop known from its group number as 'Yellow 14'.

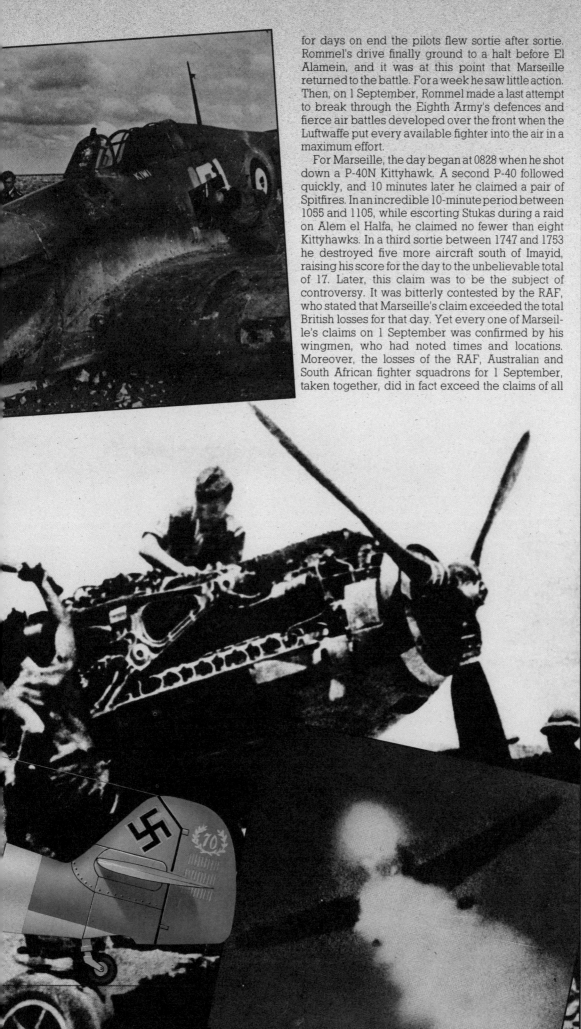

for days on end the pilots flew sortie after sortie. Rommel's drive finally ground to a halt before El Alamein, and it was at this point that Marseille returned to the battle. For a week he saw little action. Then, on 1 September, Rommel made a last attempt to break through the Eighth Army's defences and fierce air battles developed over the front when the Luftwaffe put every available fighter into the air in a maximum effort.

For Marseille, the day began at 0828 when he shot down a P-40N Kittyhawk. A second P-40 followed quickly, and 10 minutes later he claimed a pair of Spitfires. In an incredible 10-minute period between 1055 and 1105, while escorting Stukas during a raid on Alem el Halfa, he claimed no fewer than eight Kittyhawks. In a third sortie between 1747 and 1753 he destroyed five more aircraft south of Imayid, raising his score for the day to the unbelievable total of 17. Later, this claim was to be the subject of controversy. It was bitterly contested by the RAF, who stated that Marseille's claim exceeded the total British losses for that day. Yet every one of Marseille's claims on 1 September was confirmed by his wingmen, who had noted times and locations. Moreover, the losses of the RAF, Australian and South African fighter squadrons for 1 September, taken together, did in fact exceed the claims of all

HANS-JOACHIM MARSEILLE

Officer cadet Hans-Joachim (Jochen) Marseille joined the Third Gruppe of Jagdgeschwader 27 (III/JG 27) in late 1940, having seen action over the English Channel. His score at this time amounted to eight aircraft destroyed. Although Marseille should rightly have been accorded the rank of Oberleutnant, his superiors had consistently frowned on his lack of flying discipline and instead gave him the inferior rank of officer cadet.
Shortly after his arrival in Africa, Marseille's aircraft suffered an engine failure and, 500 miles from base, he had to make a forced landing in the desert. Hitching a ride on an Italian truck, Marseille reached a supply depot where he managed to convince a German general that he was a flight commander. The general placed his staff car at the young airman's disposal and sent him on his way with the following valedictory message: 'You can repay me with 50 victories.' Marseille promised to do his utmost to achieve this, without dreaming that his promise would be fulfilled three times over.
During a two-month leave in Germany, Marseille became the idol of the whole nation. He was the archetype Teutonic knight – dashing, chivalrous and bubbling over with a zest for life and adventure. His leave was one long round of parties; women vied for his attention, and his fan mail was enormous when he arrived back in North Africa. Dozens of letters arrived at the airstrip addressed simply to 'The Star of Africa'.
When he died in September 1942, Germany mourned him. He was just 23 years old.

German fighter pilots by approximately 10 per cent. Two days later, Marseille was awarded the Diamonds to the Knight's Cross. He was now the Luftwaffe's most highly-decorated pilot, possessing the Knight's Cross with Oak Leaves and Swords, and the Italian Gold Medal for Bravery, the latter being one of only three awarded in World War II.

During September, Marseille's score rose to 158 enemy aircraft destroyed. His 158th victim, a Spitfire, almost succeeded in shooting him down, but Marseille gained the advantage and despatched his opponent after a savage dogfight that lasted over 15 minutes. It was his last victory. On 30 September, together with eight other Messerschmitts of III/JG 27, he took off to provide top cover for a formation of Stukas. The dive bombers attacked their targets without incident; no enemy aircraft were sighted and the Bf 109s turned for home, their job completed.

The smoke grew worse, pouring back from the cockpit and engulfing the rear fuselage and tail

At 1135, as the fighter formation cruised at 4500ft, Marseille's voice suddenly came over the radio, telling the others that there was smoke in his cockpit and that he could no longer see clearly. The other pilots saw him open the small ventilation hatch in the side of the canopy, and a stream of dense smoke poured out. Marseille kept repeating that he was unable to see, and the others passed directions to him over the radio. Ground control, which had heard his radio call, advised him to bale out, but the Messerschmitts were still three minutes' flying time away from the German lines and Marseille refused. He had a horror of being taken prisoner.

The smoke grew worse, pouring back from the cockpit, and engulfing the rear fuselage and tail. The seconds dragged by endlessly. At last, the formation entered friendly territory. Marseille called: 'I've got to get out.' The others saw his jettisoned canopy whirl away in the slipstream. A second later the dark bundle of Marseille's body fell from the cockpit as he turned the Messerschmitt over on its back. It seemed to strike the tailplane a glancing blow, then dropped away towards the desert. Horrified, Marseille's fellow pilots saw his body dwindle to a tiny speck, merging with the tawny background of sand and scrub. There was no parachute. They buried him where he fell, and his weeping batman – a South African negro called Matthias – placed a few person-

Below: Groundcrew hold down the tail of Oberleutnant Ludwig Franzisket's Bf 109E as the engine is warmed up prior to the flight of I/JG 27 from Catania in Sicily to its new theatre of operations in North Africa. In April 1942, the three groups of JG 27 were re-equipped with the much-improved Bf 109F. With a maximum speed of 388mph and a rate of climb that allowed it to reach 3000m in two minutes and 36 seconds, this aircraft proved more than a match for the Hawker Hurricane and Curtiss P-40N Kittyhawk of the Allied Desert Air Forces.

al trinkets in the grave before the sand closed over the remains of the 'Eagle of the Desert'. Later, in the wake of the Battle of El Alamein, General Montgomery's Eighth Army rolled past the very same spot. For Jochen Marseille, the Desert Star had set; for the Afrika Korps, it was already on the wane.

THE AUTHOR Robert Jackson is a professional aviation historian who has contributed a number of articles to military publications. He is the author of over 50 books, including *Fighter Aces of World War II*.

Oberleutnant Hans-Joachim Marseille, III/JG 27, North Africa 1942

Marseille wears a mixture of civilian and military clothes. Over his Luftwaffe light khaki drill trousers and non-issue pullover he carries an inflatable life jacket.

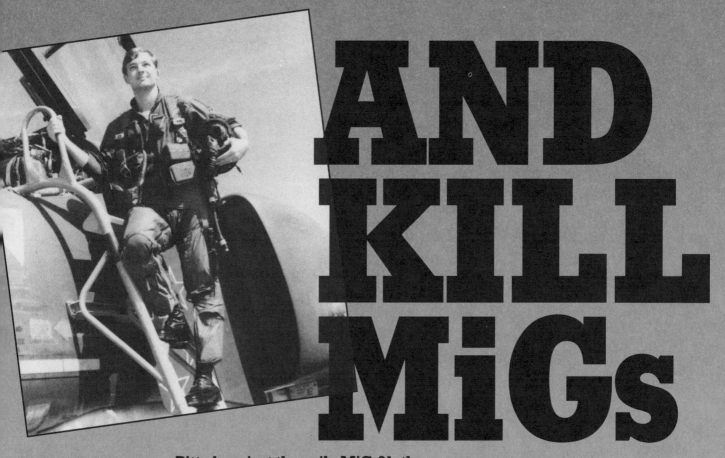

AND KILL MiGs

Pitted against the agile MiG-21, the pilots of the 'Triple Nickel' Squadron emerged from the Vietnam War with an unparalleled record

Above: Weapons systems officer Captain Charles B. DeBellevue, credited with six victories, was the United States Air Force's leading MiG killer of the Vietnam War. The F-4 Phantom II (below) was originally developed as a fleet air interceptor, its missiles intended for use against enemy bombers. However, by equipping the F-4D with an impressive array of avionics, the Phantom could be employed in land-based missions against ground targets.

ON THE NIGHT of 21 February 1972, a McDonnell Douglas F-4D Phantom of the 555th Tactical Fighter Squadron (TFS), based at Udorn in Thailand, was flying a MiG combat air patrol (CAP) mission over north-eastern Laos. Its role was to prevent North Vietnamese interceptors from penetrating Laotian airspace and attacking American strike aircraft. Shortly after 2100 hours, Red Crown (the call sign of a US Navy control ship operating in the Gulf of Tonkin) warned the F-4's crew of enemy aircraft in their vicinity, and directed them to intercept. As the pilot, Major Robert A. Lodge, followed the controller's instructions, his weapons systems officer (WSO),

Lieutenant Roger C. Locher, picked up the target on the Phantom's radar. It was heading straight for them, on the same level, and at a speed of over 900 knots. Closing to a range of 11 nautical miles, Lodge fired an AIM-7E Sparrow radar-guided missile at the enemy aircraft, and shortly afterwards launched his remaining two Sparrows. He saw the warhead of the first missile detonate and then the second. This was followed by a massive explosion and fireball – Lodge's only sight of his adversary throughout the brief engagement. When radar detected two more MiGs closing in, Lodge immediately dropped down to low altitude and accelerated away. With his Sparrow missiles expended, he had no other means of engaging the North Vietnamese fighters. Major Lodge's victory was significant in two respects: it was the United States Air Force's (USAF) first successful night engagement of the Southeast Asia conflict and, by shooting down the first North Vietnamese aircraft

for four years, it signalled the opening of a new phase in the air war.

President Lyndon Johnson's decision, in 1968, to halt the bombing of North Vietnam had given the Vietnam People's Army Air Force opportunity to build up its resources. Thus, by the spring of 1972, it had grown to a strength of some 200 interceptors, doubling its numbers since the late 1960s. In contrast, the USAF's strength in Southeast Asia had declined during this period – in line with the policy of 'Vietnamization'. As a result, when bombing operations over North Vietnam were resumed in May 1972 – in response to the Spring Invasion of South Vietnam – the USAF had to fight hard to regain air superiority. The 555th TFS, known as the 'Triple Nickel' Squadron, was destined to play a major role in this new campaign.

Originally a component of the 8th Tactical Fighter Wing – the famous 'Wolfpack' – the 555th TFS had been re-assigned to the 432nd Tactical Reconnaissance Wing (TRW) in June 1968. Its mission had been to protect the wing's RF-4C reconnaissance aircraft, but, as air operations against the North resumed, it began to specialise in providing escorts and combat air patrols in support of the strike aircraft. Usually operating in flights of four Phantoms, the escorts would stick closely to their charges and only attack enemy aircraft that constituted a direct threat to the strike force. The F-4s on MiG CAP, however, had a more free-ranging mission and could search out the North Vietnamese MiGs before they reached an attacking position. Their patrols were often flown in close proximity to the enemy airfields so as to increase the chances of enticing the MiGs into combat.

On 8 May 1972 Lodge and Locher were again in action, flying a MiG CAP in support of an air strike in the Hanoi region. Lodge, leading a flight of four F-4Ds, intercepted two MiG-21s and fired a pair of AIM-7 Sparrows at the wingman. Both missiles hit their target and the enemy aircraft disintegrated. The leading MiG broke away and escaped. Two days later, Lodge and Locher gained their third kill. Operating on MiG CAP ahead of the strike force, they picked up several enemy fighters on radar and Lodge led the four Phantoms of Oyster Flight into a head-on engagement. He and his wingman, Lieutenant John Markle, both fired AIM-7 Sparrows that knocked down two of the MiG-21s. The two remaining enemy fighters salvoed their Atoll heat-seeking missiles into the American formation before flashing past the F-4s – it was an empty gesture, since the Atolls could not guide from head-on. Lodge pulled his Phantom around into the six o'clock position of one of the MiG-21s. He was too close, however, to fire a missile and the F-4D had no gun. While attempting to gain sufficient separation from the enemy fighter, Lodge was attacked from behind by four MiG-19s. Markle spotted them and called out a warning, but Lodge was intent on nailing the MiG-21 and ignored his colleague. The Phantom was hit by enemy cannon shells and exploded, Locher recalled: 'we immediately went out of control, flopping from side to side. Then fire started coming in the back of the cockpit.' The weapons systems officer ejected, but Lodge crashed to his death. Locher came down in jungle and survived for 23 days on nuts and berries before a combat rescue team was able to reach him.

At a range of some 6000ft he locked-on his radar and fired two AIM-7 Sparrows in quick succession

Meanwhile, Oyster 3 had gained the Triple Nickel Squadron's third kill of the combat. Its crew, Captain Richard S. Ritchie and his 'backseater', Captain Charles B. DeBellevue, were to finish the war as the USAF's top-scoring pilot and weapons systems officer. Yet their first experience of actual combat was as bewildering as that of any other inexperienced crew. Ritchie later recalled that: 'things really got confusing once the engagement started. There were missiles in the air all over the place, fireballs, smoke trails, debris and airplanes everywhere.' When Lodge had turned to engage one of the surviving MiG-21s, Ritchie positioned his F-4D for an attack on the other. At a range of some 6000ft he locked-on his radar and fired two AIM-7 Sparrows in quick succession. The first passed just beneath the target and failed to detonate, but the second found its mark. The MiG-21 exploded in a yellow ball of fire and, as the Phantom flashed past, DeBellevue noticed the North Vietnamese pilot's parachute deploying. The next day, the honours went to Captain Stephen E. Nichols, who shot down a MiG-21 with an AIM-7 Sparrow – but not before enemy fighters had themselves accounted for a Republic F-105 Thunderchief and an F-4 Phantom. The 555th TFS's fifth victory in three days went to the squadron's commanding officer on 12 May. Flying in the vicinity of Yen Bai airfield, Lieutenant-Colonel Wayne T. Frye was able to attack four MiG-19s just after they had taken off. He launched three AIM-7s at the rearmost enemy fighter and it disintegrated into a cloud of debris. Frye later jokingly claimed the world record for the combined age of a MiG-killing crew: he was 41 years old and his WSO, Lieutenant-Colonel James P. Cooney, was 44.

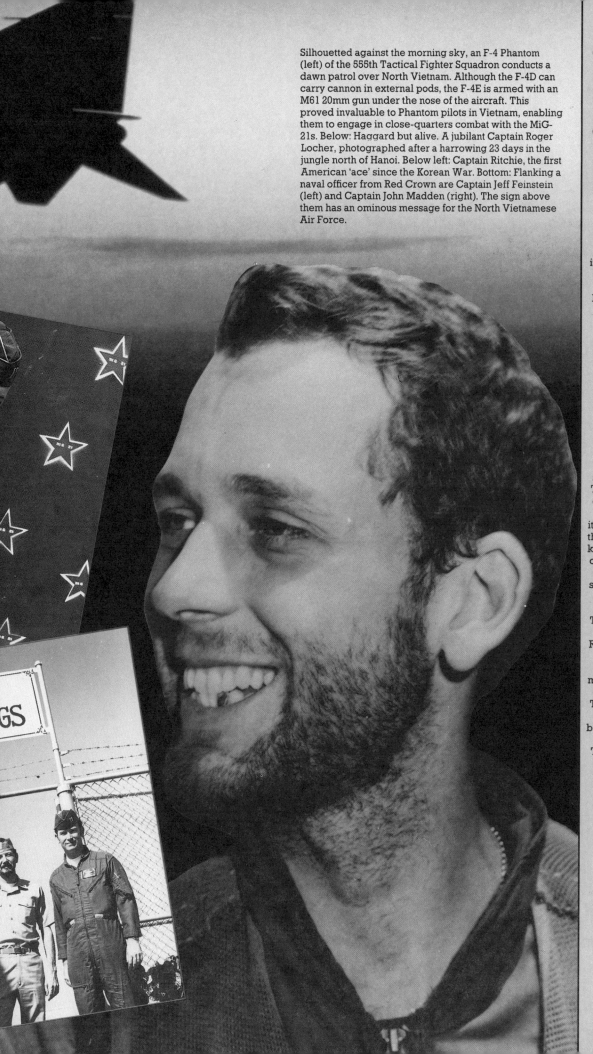

Silhouetted against the morning sky, an F-4 Phantom (left) of the 555th Tactical Fighter Squadron conducts a dawn patrol over North Vietnam. Although the F-4D can carry cannon in external pods, the F-4E is armed with an M61 20mm gun under the nose of the aircraft. This proved invaluable to Phantom pilots in Vietnam, enabling them to engage in close-quarters combat with the MiG-21s. Below: Haggard but alive. A jubilant Captain Roger Locher, photographed after a harrowing 23 days in the jungle north of Hanoi. Below left: Captain Ritchie, the first American 'ace' since the Korean War. Bottom: Flanking a naval officer from Red Crown are Captain Jeff Feinstein (left) and Captain John Madden (right). The sign above them has an ominous message for the North Vietnamese Air Force.

THE 'TRIPLE NICKEL' SQUADRON

Unlike many of the famous fighter squadrons of the United States Air Force (USAF) that won their spurs during the air battles of World War II, the 555th Tactical Fighter Squadron (TFS) did not enter the order of battle until the mid-1960s.

Activated at MacDill Air Force Base, Florida, in January 1964 as part of the 12th Tactical Fighter Wing, it was equipped with the F-4 Phantom. At the end of the year it was deployed to Naha Air Base on Okinawa, Japan, and remained there for three months, on attachment to the 51st Fighter Interceptor Wing. In February 1966 the unit was attached to the 8th Tactical Fighter Wing at Udorn in Thailand, flying combat operations over Southeast Asia. The following month, the temporary detachment became a permanent assignment, and the squadron was stationed in Thailand for the remainder of the conflict. On 23 April 1966 the squadron gained its first two victories, and by the end of the year it had six kills to its credit. By the time of the March 1967 bombing halt, the squadron's score stood at 18 MiGs destroyed in combat.

On 1 June 1968, the 555th TFS was re-assigned to the 432nd Tactical Reconnaissance Wing, and in May 1972 it became committed to escort missions with the launching of Operation Linebacker. The 555th TFS remained in Thailand until July 1974, before being re-assigned to the 58th Tactical Fighter Training Wing at Luke Air Force Base, Arizona, responsible for training pilots on the F-15 Eagle.

Ritchie's second victory came at the end of the month, when he was flying a MiG CAP northeast of Thai Nguyen, with Captain Lawrence H. Pettit in the back seat. Red Crown directed him into an interception of two MiG-21s and he fired all four of his AIM-7s at the wingman. It was none too many, for the first missile failed to guide properly, the next two detonated early and only the fourth found its target. The 555th TFS claimed no further kills in June 1972, but

saw were those missiles coming at him.' It was Ritchie's last successful combat; but DeBellevue, then with four enemy aircraft to his credit, was to gain a further two kills flying with another pilot. No other USAF or US Navy fighter crew member was to equal

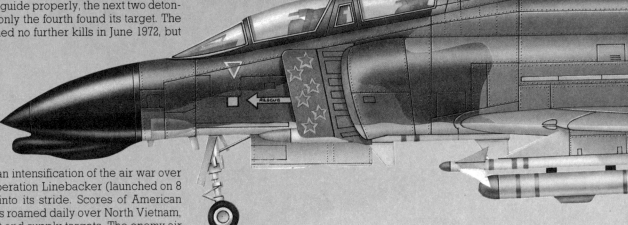

the month saw an intensification of the air war over the north, as Operation Linebacker (launched on 8 May) got fully into its stride. Scores of American fighter-bombers roamed daily over North Vietnam, hitting transport and supply targets. The enemy air defences fought back fiercely, however, and the MiG interceptors proved to be especially effective, claiming many more kills than surface-to-air missiles and anti-aircraft fire combined.

On 8 July Ritchie, again teamed with DeBellevue, was leading four Phantoms of Paula Flight on a MiG CAP south of Yen Bai. Red Crown and Disco (a USAF C-121 airborne command aircraft flying over northern Laos) advised them of bandits to the southeast, and Ritchie led his flight into a head-on interception with two MiG-21s. He then pulled round onto the enemy wingman's five o'clock position and fired two AIM-7s. The first missile hit, and the MiG-21 exploded in a large yellow fireball. Ritchie then turned hard right in pursuit of the leading MiG which was threatening Paula 4. He fired a single Sparrow, that again found its mark and the enemy fighter disintegrated in mid-air.

Competition was now fierce for the honour of becoming the first USAF ace of the war – hitherto, the magic five victories had eluded even the legendary Colonel Robin Olds. Ritchie, with four kills, was the leading contender, but on 29 July Captain Jeffrey Feinstein, a WSO with the 13th TFS (another of the 432nd TRW's F-4 squadrons), gained his fourth victory. The contest was decided on 28 August when Ritchie and DeBellevue shot down a MiG-21 – again with the fourth and last AIM-7. 'I don't think the MiG pilot ever really saw us,' commented Ritchie, 'all he

his score.

DeBellevue's pilot on 9 September was Captain John A. Madden, and appropriately enough they were leading Olds Flight. One of the most experienced of the Triple Nickel Squadron's pilots, Madden was to complete over 250 combat missions in Southeast Asia. The flight was flying to the west of Hanoi, when they were warned that MiGs were airborne. Anticipating that the enemy fighters would land back at the Phuc Yen airfield, Madden positioned his flight in ambush. When DeBellevue picked up the MiGs on radar, Madden led Olds Flight in for the kill:

'We got a visual on a MiG about 5 miles out on final approach with his [landing] gear and flaps down. Getting a [radar] lock on him, I fired my missiles but they missed. We were coming in from the side-rear and slipped up next to that MiG no more than 500ft apart. He got a visual on us, snatched up his flaps and hit afterburners, accelerating out. It became obvious that I wasn't going to get another shot at the MiG. That's when Captain Tibbett closed in...'

Captain Calvin B. Tibbett and Lieutenant William S. Hargrove, flying in Olds 3, had seen Madden's two AIM-7 missiles fail to guide onto the MiG-21. Tibbett therefore positioned his F-4 behind the enemy aircraft and, when Madden had cleared him to fire,

Above: This particular F-4D Phantom II, in which Captain Richard S. Ritchie scored his first and fifth victories, was the most prolific MiG-killing aircraft of the war – being used in an additional four successful combats. The Phantom II was, by a wide margin, the most potent fighter of the late 1950s and it smashed every existing record for fighter aircraft. It is still the most numerically important aircraft in the USAF, its air-combat manoeuvrability enhanced by the fitting of large outer-wing slats to the F-4E to allow greater acceleration. The F-4D is powered by two General Electric J79-15 turbojets, providing a combat-loaded speed of 910mph. The F-4Ds of the Triple Nickel Squadron were also equipped with a receptacle for the 'flying boom', allowing inflight refuelling (below).

launched two AIM-9 Sidewinder heat-seeking missiles. These were no more successful than the radar-guided Sparrows – but Tibbett's F-4D was also carrying a 20mm cannon pod. Closing the range, Tibbett opened fire with this impressive weapon. He saw his shells impacting on the MiG-21's fuselage and port wing, its pilot ejected, and the enemy fighter nose-dived into the ground on the perimeter of Phuc Yen airfield.

Olds Flight then turned away to return to their original CAP station, but were warned by control that two more enemy fighters were closing in astern of them. Madden pulled around to engage and shortly afterwards DeBellevue picked them up on his radar. Olds 2, Captain Mike Francisco, sighted two MiG-19s

Triple Nickel's Area of Operations February-December 1972

Yen Bai • Red • Thai Nguyen
• Phuc Yen • Kep
Hanoi •
• Haiphong

• Luang Prabang

NORTH VIETNAM

GULF OF TONKIN

L

Vientiane •

A

✈ Udon Thani

O

S

Mekong

DMZ

Hue •

THAILAND

Da Nang •

NORTH VIETNAMESE AIR FORCE

Although the Vietnam People's Army Air Force (VPAAF) was a relatively small air arm, it proved a difficult opponent for the USAF during the 'Linebacker' campaigns of 1972.

Formed in May 1955 after the French withdrawal from Indochina, it developed slowly and did not form its first fighter regiment until February 1964. This unit, organised along Soviet lines, entered action the following spring. Individual pilots were trained in the Soviet Union and the fighter regiments were formed in the People's Republic of China, where they carried out their training before transferring to their operational airfields in North Vietnam.

Their fighters were all Soviet designs, although some Chinese-built MiGs were supplied to the VPAAF in the late 1960s. By the spring of 1972, the North Vietnamese fighter force comprised some 200 aircraft: 93 MiG-21s, 33 MiG-19s and a mixture of MiG-17s and MiG-15s (the latter being advanced trainers rather than operational fighters).

They operated from 13 main airfields, many of which were concentrated in the Hanoi/Haiphong area. The most important of these were Phuc Yen, Kep, Gia Lam, Cat Bi and Kien An. The MiG-21 – using hit-and-run tactics against the USAF strike aircraft and operating under ground control – often proved an elusive target for the USAF's escorts and MiG combat air patrols (CAPs). At the sub-sonic speeds at which most combats were fought, the MiG-21 could both out-manoeuvre and out-accelerate the F-4 Phantom.

at one and a half miles range in the 11 o'clock position – Madden ordered the flight to turn in towards the enemy:

'We pulled hard, about 6 Gs, and went through about 90 degrees of turn before they spotted us. When they saw us they began a hard turn towards us and punched their wing tanks off. I increased my turn to about 8 Gs. It was all I could do to get the [gunsight's] pipper on the trailing MiG. After about 180 degrees of turn, I fired a Sidewinder. It was a reasonably high-angle off shot, but the missile guided perfectly, exploding close to the MiG's tail.'

The MiG-19 crashed and burned out on the runway at Phuc Yen. Madden then switched his attention to the second enemy fighter, destroying it with an AIM-9 Sidewinder. The victorious F-4Ds headed back for Udorn air base at high speed and low level. However, Olds 4 was hit by AA fire and its crew, Captain Bill Daleky and WSO Captain Terry Murphy, had to eject over northern Laos, but were later picked up by a rescue helicopter.

Madden then cleared Tibbett to open fire – he responded by launching four Sidewinders

Tibbett and Hargrove fought their second successful combat on 16 September, while flying an escort mission. The flight leader, Madden, had given chase to a MiG-21 spotted flying at low level down the Red River. He fired two AIM-7 Sparrow and four AIM-9 Sidewinder missiles at the enemy, but all failed to guide properly. Madden then cleared Tibbett to open fire – he responded by launching four Sidewinders. The last of these hit the MiG in the rear fuselage, and the pilot ejected seconds before his aircraft hit the ground. As this and previous engagements had shown, the air-to-air missiles of the Vietnam era were far from reliable weapons – even though they eventually accounted for the majority of the USAF's kills during the air war over Southeast Asia. Nevertheless, skilful flying was sometimes all

that was needed to achieve a victory, as Madden was to demonstrate on 12 October. Engaging a MiG-21 head-on at 20,000ft, Madden turned hard to get behind his adversary. The MiG evaded by rolling onto its back and diving down into a cloud layer 2000ft below. When Madden dived down after him and closed in to re-engage, the enemy fighter again dived for a lower level of cloud. But the North Vietnamese pilot had miscalculated his recovery and flew straight into the ground. It was Madden's third victory and the second for his WSO Captain Lawrence Pettit.

One of the problems with using radar-guided missiles over North Vietnam was that of positive identification of the target. The AIM-7 Sparrow could be fired from beyond visual range, but if there were any friendly aircraft in the vicinity the launch aircraft was required to sight the target and positively identify it as being hostile. This situation arose on 22 December, when Lieutenant-Colonel James E. Brunson was leading Buick Flight on a MiG CAP mission. He was advised by Red Crown of MiGs at 46 miles' range, but also warned that there were friendly aircraft between him and the enemy. Accordingly, Brunson followed Red Crown's directions for a head-on interception and at a range of 16 miles he got a radar lock-on. The flight then jettisoned their centre-line tanks and accelerated to engage. Since the enemy aircraft was about 10,000ft above his Phantom, Brunson pulled his fighter's nose up as the range closed. By centring the radar steering dot in his gunsight, he was able to pick up the enemy almost immediately and identify it as a MiG-21. Only then, was he allowed to open fire. Keeping his Phantom in a steep climb towards the MiG, Brunson loosed off four AIM-7 Sparrows in rapid succession. One of these hit, knocking the tail section off the enemy fighter and sending it plummeting towards the ground in an uncontrollable spin.

All appeared to guide perfectly, and suddenly a large fireball appeared some four miles off

The 555th TFS's last victory of the war was another radar-guided missile engagement, but, unlike Brunson's combat, there was no need to identify the enemy aircraft visually prior to the attack. On 28 December, Major Harry L. McKee and WSO Captain John E. Dubler were on MiG CAP west of Hanoi when they were directed onto an enemy fighter. Dubler obtained radar contact at a range of 90 miles. Closing in from astern, McKee and his wingman, Captain Kimzey W. Rhine, obtained a radar lock-on 10 miles out and then launched three AIM-7 Sparrows. McKee fired the first and third, his wingman the second. All appeared to guide perfectly, and suddenly a large fireball appeared some 4 miles off the Phantoms' noses.

Two days later, Operation Linebacker II came to an end. Only one more enemy fighter was destroyed in combat by the USAF, the victory going to another unit of 432nd TRW, the 4th TFS. Yet the Triple Nickel Squadron had no cause for complaint – with 39 aerial victories to its credit, it was, by a comfortable margin, the highest-scoring USAF tactical fighter squadron of the Vietnam War.

THE AUTHOR Anthony Robinson was formerly on the staff of the RAF Museum, Hendon, and is now a freelance military aviation writer. His books include *American Air Power* and *Aerial Warfare*.

The F-4 Phantom claimed 107 victories during the Vietnam War, and the air-to-air missile accounted for 60 per cent of these. Four AIM-7 Sparrows (below) could be carried in recesses on the underside of the Phantom's fuselage, together with four infra-red homing AIM-9B Sidewinders (below left) on the external pylons. Above: Fitting avionics to the nose of an F-4. Left: Enemy MiGs, spotted from high altitude by a Phantom's oblique camera.

In October 1938 No. 1 Squadron was equipped with its first Hawker Hurricanes. Immediately on the outbreak of war, No. 1 moved from its peacetime station at RAF Tangmere in Sussex to northern France, beginning operations from Octeville near Le Havre. It was one of four RAF fighter squadrons comprising the Air Component of the British Expeditionary Force, assigned to provide air support for the landing on the shores of northern France. At the end of September 1939 No. 1 Squadron moved to Norrent-Fontes near St Omer. Transferred to Vavincourt near Bar-le-Duc in the following month, the squadron's primary role was then to protect the Fairey Battle light bombers of the Advanced Air Striking Force (AASF), which had been badly mauled by Luftwaffe fighters. No. 1 and No. 73 Squadrons were transferred to the operational control of No. 67 Wing for this purpose. Weather conditions and a prolonged German build-up along the French border resulted in a lull for the squadron during the first eight months of the war. However, the experience gained by No. 1 Squadron during their patrols along the Franco-German frontier was later to prove invaluable. On 31 October 1939 Pilot Officer Peter Mould opened the squadron's scorebook, shooting down a Dornier Do 17 reconnaissance aircraft. Further victories followed on 23 November, but after this, operations virtually ceased until March 1940. During this month, No. 1 Squadron scored a number of triumphs. On the 29th, a Messerschmitt Bf 109 was brought down by Flight Lieutenant Paul Richey, and the first Bf 110 fell to the guns of Flight Lieutenant 'Johnny' Walker the same day. On 1 April, faced with the superior cannon armament of the Bf 110, three pilots of 'B' Flight engaged nine German fighters near the Luxembourg border, and each succeeded in bringing down an opponent.

As the German armies moved on France and the Low Countries on 10 May 1940, the Hurricanes of No. 1 Squadron, RAF, were scrambled to meet the invaders

THE FIGHTING WITHDRAWAL carried out by No. 1 Squadron during the Battle of France merits recognition as one of the finest examples of a successful battle, against overwhelming odds, in the history of the Royal Air Force. During 10 days in May 1940, the squadron's Hawker Hurricanes were in continuous action, often flying several missions in a day, against Luftwaffe formations of considerable strength. In the same period it was forced to move its base on three occasions, amid the chaos and confusion of the French army's retreat. Yet, throughout this testing ordeal, the squadron remained a cohesive and effective fighting unit, and for the loss of only five pilots, was able to claim a total of at least 87 victories.

Squadron Leader P. J. H. Halahan, who had led the unit since May 1939, said of No. 1: 'No commanding officer could wish for a better squadron.' Halahan, nicknamed the 'Bull', had trained his pilots to fight together as a team, discouraging lone-wolf tactics. 'The squadron's watchword was caution', remembered Flying Officer Paul Richey, 'no fooling, no dare-devil stuff, no individual seeking the limelight.' It was a sound doctrine that was to be fully vindicated by the squadron's heroic performance during the intense air battles to come.

By the spring of 1940, the experience of the previous two months had shown No. 1 Squadron that the RAF's Fighter Area Attack tactics, in which they had been carefully drilled in peacetime, were totally unsuited to wartime conditions. Their main drawback was that they took no account of the possibility of meeting escorted bomber formations. In order to deal with enemy fighters effectively, it was essential to maintain a good lookout; accordingly, the squadron began to employ the two rearmost aircraft in a five-fighter formation as weavers, or in pilots' jargon, 'arse-end Charlies', to guard against surprise attacks from the rear. Halahan was determined to engage enemy formations at full strength, with one flight detailed to fend off the fighter escort, while the other attacked the bombers. The squadron's historian Michael Shaw has captured the mood of the time:

'At Vavincourt the promise of a fine summer wafted the scents of the countryside over the crouched shapes of the waiting Hurricanes in the lengthening evenings. The air was full of wild rumour. A feeling of uneasiness began to spread throughout the squadron that this must be the lull before a mighty storm.'

The long-awaited blow fell on the morning of 10 May. The sound of heavy artillery fire had given the squadron a clear indication of what was to come. 'B' Flight was scrambled into the air at 0500 hours and 'A' Flight followed shortly afterwards. Both engaged enemy aircraft, and each claimed a bomber shot down. No. 1 Squadron was then ordered to move to Berry-au-Bac, from where it was to fly bomber escort missions, in addition to providing the bases of the Advanced Air Striking Force (AASF) with air cover. En route to the new airfield, 'B' Flight ran into a formation of German bombers, shooting down three of them. Pilot Officer L. Lorrimer's Hurricane was hit by return fire and he was forced to bale out. That afternoon Berry-au-Bac came under attack from German bombers, catching the squadron unawares,

but luckily they escaped without casualties.

Although the Hurricanes became fully operational on the morning of 11 May, they were not scrambled to meet a Luftwaffe raid on Reims; the squadron's responsibilities were at that time restricted to defence of the bomber airfields. However, as the AASF Headquarters were located in the town, Squadron Leader Halahan was amused, but not entirely surprised, when his orders were modified to include responsibility for its protection. At 0800 hours an enemy formation was reported heading for Berry-au-Bac. The squadron scrambled to intercept and forced the intruders to turn away from their target. Richey claimed a hit on a Dornier Do 17, but his own fighter was damaged after the combat when he landed on the bomb-cratered French airfield at Mézières. That same afternoon 'B' Flight escorted a formation of Battle bombers to Rethel, and after sighting a group of Bf 109s, they engaged the enemy and shot down three of the German aircraft.

The most intense action of the day, however, was to come soon after 'B' Flight had returned. A heavy raid was reported approaching Reims and five Hurricanes from 'A' Flight were scrambled to meet it. They intercepted a group of 30 Do 17s, escorted by

15 Bf 110s. Honours were equally divided, with 'A' Flight's commander, Flight Lieutenant P.R. 'Johnny' Walker, Richey, Flying Officers M.H. 'Hilly' Brown and J.I. Kilmartin and Sergeant F.J. Soper all claiming two kills. Richey's Hurricane was set aflame during a head-on attack on a Bf 109, but he managed to escape unscathed and parachuted to the ground. Richey's account of the opening moves of this combat gives a good indication of the speed of action, and the

The men of No.1 Squadron were moulded into a highly efficient fighting unit by their CO, the formidable P.J.H. Halahan, seen below centre in his leather flying jacket. Standing behind, and to his right is Pilot Officer Peter Mould, who scored the squadron's first kill over France. Above: Hurricanes break their tight formation following a sighting of the enemy. Above left: A Heinkel He 111 erupts in a ball of smoke and flame.

HURRICANE FORCE

confusion, that is so typical of a dogfight:

'We went in fast in a tight bunch, each picking a 110 and manoeuvring to get on his tail. I selected the rear one of two in line-astern who were turning tightly to the left. He broke away from his No. 1 when he had done a half-circle and steepened his turn, but I easily turned inside him, holding my fire until I was within 50 yards and then firing a shortish burst at three-quarters deflection. To my surprise a mass of bits flew off him – pieces of engine-cowling and lumps of his glass-house [hood] – and as I passed over the top of him, still in a left-hand turn, I watched him in a kind of fascinated horror as he went into a spin, smoke pouring out of him. I remember saying "My God, how ghastly!" as his tail suddenly swivelled sideways and tore off, while flames streamed over the fuselage. Then I saw a little white parachute open... Good!

'Scarcely half a minute had passed, yet as I looked quietly around me I saw four more 110s go down – one with its tail off, a second in a spin, a third vertically in flames, and a fourth going up at forty-five degrees in a left-hand stall turn, with a little Hurricane on its tail firing into its side, from which burst a series of flashes and long, shooting red flames. I shall never forget.'

On 12 May No. 1 Squadron took part in the Advanced Air Striking Force's most famous bombing mission: the attack on the Meuse bridges. This operation was to earn No. 12 Squadron's Flying Officer D. E. Garland and his observer Sergeant Thomas Gray the post-humous award of the Victoria Cross. Halahan himself led the eight escorting Hurricanes, which were to sweep the target area ahead of No. 12 Squadron's Battle bombers, and – it was hoped – fully occupy the attention of the German fighters.

Bf 109s were attacking from all directions and the Hurricane pilots were fighting for their lives

Many small formations of Bf 109s were encountered by the Hurricanes en route to the bridges, but it was not until the Battles actually began their bombing run that a dogfight developed above them. Yet, although No. 1 Squadron had succeeded in keeping the Luft-waffe fighters away from their vulnerable charges, the flak gunners surrounding the bridges cut the bombers to pieces. By that time Bf 109s were attacking from all directions and the Hurricane pilots were fighting for their lives. The commanding officer accounted for one of the attackers, before his fighter was hit by a cannon shell and, with his engine running roughly, he left the fight and headed for friendly territory. Before he crash-landed, however, he ran into a group of slow-flying German liaison aircraft, and promptly shot two of them down. Flying Officer Leslie Clisby, a tough and aggressive Australian, met more of these sluggish aircraft on his way back to base and knocked down a further three. Only he, Kilmartin and Brown returned to Berry-au-Bac. Pilot Officer Lewis had baled out of his crippled Hurricane, while the other pilots had successfully force-landed away from base. Despite the day's heavy

Main picture: A well earned, if brief, rest for the pilots of No. 1 Squadron. Top left: Sergeant Arthur Clowes had a unique method of recording his kills; each time an enemy aircraft was shot down, an extra stripe was painted on the wasp. Top centre: A lean, hungry look on the face of Flight Lieutenant Richey, one of No. 1's leading aces.

Right: P3395 'JK B', the Hawker Hurricane Mark I flown by Sergeant Clowes. No. 1 Squadron received its first delivery of Hurricanes immediately prior to the outbreak of World War II.

On 10 May 1940, the German army launched its offensive against France and the Low Countries. As the British and French armies struggled to contain the advance, No.1 Squadron, RAF, engaged the Luftwaffe, contesting with the enemy for control of the skies. No.1 Squadron's Hurricanes saw action continuously until 18 June when the squadron was withdrawn.

THE HAWKER HURRICANE

A successor to Hawker's successful Fury biplane, the Hurricane was numerically the most important British fighter in service until the end of 1940. It was the first combat aircraft to be adopted by the RAF that was capable of speeds in excess of 300mph, and was to shoulder the lion's share of Britain's defence during the Battle of Britain. The speed with which the Hurricane was brought into operational service was remarkable; deliveries were made to No.111 Squadron only two months after the aircraft made its first production flight. This rapid deployment demonstrated the faith of the service chiefs in the extremely versatile Hurricane. Powered by a Rolls Royce Merlin II engine, the Hurricane had a maximum speed of 316mph at 17,500ft, and a normal range of 525 miles. The Mark I was armed with eight .303in machine guns, four mounted in each wing to fire outside the propeller arc. Later variants carried different armaments: for example, the Hurricane IIB had 12 Browning machine guns, with the wings strengthened to support two 250lb or one 500lb bomb. Although the speed of the Hurricane was slower than the Luftwaffe's Bf 109, it proved itself more than capable of holding its own against the Messerschmitts by virtue of its superior manoeuvrability. The last Hurricane was delivered to the RAF in September 1944.

The invasion of France and Belgium
May 1940

Key
✈ Airfields used by No. 1 Sqn, RAF
→ German forces

action, none of the squadron's pilots was seriously injured, and between them they accounted for a total of 12 enemy fighters destroyed.

Pilot Officer Billy Drake became No. 1 Squadron's first casualty, on 13 May, when he was shot down and wounded by an attack by Bf 110s. However, the Hurricanes continued to give a good account of themselves, claiming 16 victories the following day for the loss of only one fighter force-landed. The day's action was particularly successful for Clisby. He had attacked a Heinkel He 111 bomber, forcing it to crash-land in a large field. Seeing the crew about to make good their escape, he promptly landed beside his victim and, drawing his revolver, rounded up the German airmen.

On the afternoon of 15 May the squadron suffered its most serious losses of the French campaign. 'B' Flight's six Hurricanes, led by Flight Lieutenant Prosser Hanks, engaged a formation of 30 Bf 110s over Laôn. The German pilots, outnumbering their opponents by five to one, fought well – with the confidence inspired by overwhelming odds. Faced with this situation, No. 1 Squadron fought with unparalleled tenacity. Prosser Hanks, after knocking down one of his opponents, was forced to take to his parachute. Pilot Officer Peter Mould was more fortunate and shot down two enemy fighters before he ran out of ammunition and broke away from the engagement. Two further pilots claimed victories, but on return to base it was discovered that Clisby and Lorrimer were missing. They never returned and had to be presumed killed in action.

The advancing German armies forced No. 1 Squadron to abandon their airfield on 16 May and

The Hawker Hurricane, a remarkably sturdy aircraft, possessed impeccable handling characteristics. Moreover, its basic metal tube construction, covered with fabric, made the task of the groundcrews (bottom) considerably easier. The cockpit design afforded the pilot good all-round visibility, while a wide-track carriage provided the stability essential for landing on the makeshift, often bomb-cratered runways of northern France. Below: A formation of Hurricanes, silhouetted against the early morning sky, conducts a dawn patrol. Below left: A cause for celebration in the officers mess. After notching up six more victories, three pilots from No. 1 examine souvenirs from the aircraft they have shot down.

move back to Conde-sur-Marne, where they shared a base with the Bristol Blenheims of No. 114 Squadron. By now, all of the pilots were suffering from fatigue – exhausted by the unremitting strain of combat flying. Halahan recalled that everyone fell asleep over their meal that evening. Two days later they were on the move again, settling into a makeshift airfield at Anglure near Pleurs.

Yet No. 1 Squadron remained a force to be reckoned with, despite the stress that its pilots had endured. On 19 May, 10 Hurricanes waded into a formation of He IIIs, bringing down eight of them. A leading part was taken by Richey, who destroyed three bombers before he was forced to crash-land, having been seriously wounded. He was rushed to a Paris hospital and later evacuated to England.

The hard-pressed veterans of No. 1 were at last relieved on 23 May, when replacement pilots were posted in and a new commanding officer, Squadron Leader D.A. Pemberton, was transferred from the Headquarters of No. 67 Wing. Two of the original pilots, Sergeant Arthur Clowes and Hilly Brown stayed on; the latter being promoted to Flight Lieutenant, officer commanding 'A' Flight. The remaining pilots followed Halahan back to the United Kingdom. This transfer proved to be invaluable; as Operational Training Unit instructors, these veterans were able to pass on their tactical experience to newly qualified fighter pilots, destined to defend their own shores during the Battle of Britain.

No. 1 Squadron remained in France until 18 June,

steadily retreating in the face of the German advance, before flying back to Tangmere in order to prepare for the imminent onslaught on Britain. Many of the pilots of the French campaign went on to distinguished careers in the RAF.

THE AUTHOR Anthony Robinson was formerly on the staff of the RAF Museum, Hendon, and is now a freelance military aviation writer. His books include *American Air Power* and *Aerial Warfare*.

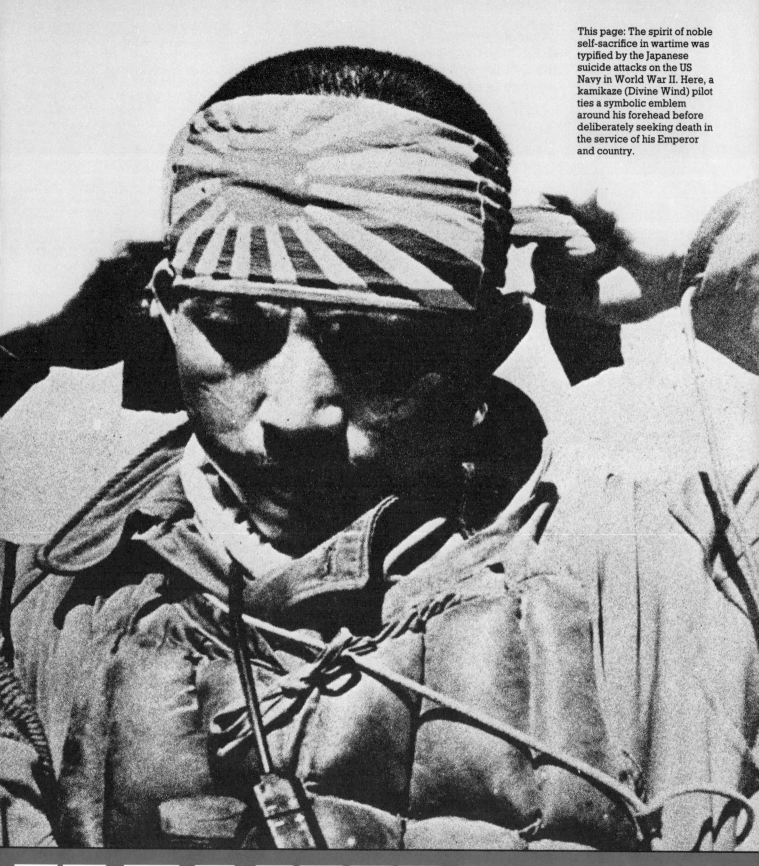

This page: The spirit of noble self-sacrifice in wartime was typified by the Japanese suicide attacks on the US Navy in World War II. Here, a kamikaze (Divine Wind) pilot ties a symbolic emblem around his forehead before deliberately seeking death in the service of his Emperor and country.

KAMIKAZE!

The first Japanese air unit devoted specifically to suicide attacks on warships, was formed on 19/20 October 1944, by the 26 pilots of 201st Air Group, First Air Fleet, Imperial Japanese Naval Air Force, at Mabalacat airbase on the Philippines. The unit, called 'Kamikaze' (Divine Wind) was set up at the instigation of Vice Admiral Takijiro Ohnishi, commander First Air Fleet. Within days, the number of these special attack units, as they were known, had multiplied. On 26 October, Second Air Fleet joined with First Air Fleet, in a combined special attack corps to which almost all their aircraft were devoted. The Army Air Force also began to form suicide units, known as *tokubetsu*

The First and Second Air Fleets, supplied with fresh pilots from a kamikaze training centre established on Formosa, sustained operations on the Philippines until 9 January 1945. The remnants then regrouped on Formosa as First Air Fleet. During February and March, a reorganisation of the Naval Air Force created Fifth and Tenth Air Fleets, based in Kyushu and Honshu, in southern Japan.

In mid-March, these two air fleets were combined with part of Third Air Fleet and with *tokubetsu* units of the Army Air Force in a mass special attack formation known as the *kikusui*, or floating chrysanthemum, under the command of Vice Admiral Matome Ugaki. The *kikusui* units carried out a concentrated suicide campaign against the Allied fleet off Okinawa from April to late June 1945, after which air activity declined as losses exceeded replacement of pilots and aircraft.

Like modern-day Samurai, inspired with divine purpose, the Japanese suicide pilots made the ultimate sacrifice in defence of their homeland

IN THE AUTUMN of 1944, Rear Admiral Masafumi Arima, commander of the 26th Air Flotilla of the Imperial Japanese Naval Air Force, was serving with the occupation forces on the Philippines. Stationed at Nichols Field outside Manila, he shunned the comfort of the officers' quarters, preferring an austerely furnished hut near the airbase. There he meditated on Japan's desperate plight in the Pacific war and the decimation of the once powerful Naval Air Force. After deep reflection, he took a momentous decision.

On 15 October 1944, US warships were spotted off Luzon, the main island of the Philippines. Immediately, every available aircraft on Nichols Field was mobilised for action. As the second wave – about 100 Suisei dive-bombers and Zero fighters – prepared to take off, Arima declared his intention of leading the attack in person. Since admirals were forbidden to take part in aerial combat, Arima calmly stripped off his insignia of rank before climbing into the cockpit of a Suisei. He was the first to take off.

At 1553 hours, Arima sighted the American vessels. Exploiting cloud cover, he evaded the US fighter screen and emerged into clear sky above the carrier USS *Franklin*. Holding his aircraft in an unwavering dive straight at the warship, he made no attempt to release his bomb load. The Suisei plunged on to the carrier's flight-deck and exploded in a ball of orange-red flame.

Arima's self-immolation was a purely personal action, not part of a general tactical plan. But, unknowingly, he had acted out the prelude to a full-scale campaign of suicide attacks which was to become Japan's last hope in the desperate months ahead.

Two days after Arima's death, the Japanese Imperial General Headquarters learnt that an American invasion of the Philippines was imminent. But the Naval Air Force was in a poor position to contribute to the supreme effort that was now demanded. Japanese losses had been appalling: for example, in the Battle of the Philippine Sea (19-20 June 1944) alone, some 400 aircraft had been lost. The Philippines-based First Air Fleet was now reduced to an effective operational strength of less than 100 aircraft.

At 0830 hours on 19 October, Vice Admiral Takijiro Ohnishi, who had arrived in Manila only two days previously to assume command of the First Air Fleet, was informed that a massive American invasion force had been sighted in Leyte Gulf. Later that afternoon, Admiral Ohnishi appeared unannounced at Mabalacat airfield 50 miles from Manila, and invited the commanders of 201st Air Group to a conference at headquarters in Mabalacat town. Ohnishi seemed tired and strained as he began to address the assembled officers. First he explained their vital mission – to provide air cover for the Japanese Navy which was setting out to engage the Americans in Leyte Gulf. The only way to protect the Japanese vessels from air attack would be to neutralise the US carriers. He communicated his strategy:

'In my opinion, there is only one way of assuring that our meagre strength will be effective to a maximum degree. That is to organise suicide attack units composed of Zero fighters armed with 550lb bombs, with each plane to crash-dive into an enemy carrier… What do you think?'

The duty of answering fell to Commander Asaichi Tamai, executive officer of 201st Air Group. After brief consultation, Tamai agreed to implement the suicide plan. It was instinctively felt that such missions would have to be voluntary, however, so Tamai presented the proposition to his 23 non-commissioned pilots. Their response was unanimous and enthusiastic. Before the night was over, the new special attack unit had been dubbed 'kamikaze' (also written as *shinfu*), meaning the Divine Wind, in reference to a typhoon which had saved Japan from invasion in the 13th century. Lieutenant Yukio Seki was the pilot chosen to head the first kamikaze unit.

On 20 October, Admiral Ohnishi addressed the newly formed unit at Mabalacat airfield. 'You are already gods, without earthly desires,' he declared.

The first Zero dived straight into the USS *Santee*, blowing a large hole in the flight deck

To emphasise the pilots' divine purpose, he devised a ritual to precede suicide missions: lined up on the airfield, the pilots would solemnly drink a glass of *sake* or water, sing a traditional war song, and don the *hachimaki*, the folded white headband once worn into battle by the samurai. Nothing was to be spared in the effort to sustain morale in those effectively condemned to death.

The 26 aircraft of the first kamikaze unit were divided into four groups – Yamazakura, Yamato, Asahi and Shikishima. The Yamato group left Mabalacat as soon as Ohnishi had finished his address, moving to the base at Cebu in the south. There, they quickly persuaded other pilots to form special attack units, and over the following days the example spread. But at first the would-be suicide pilots, both at Cebu and at Mabalacat, experienced only frustration. Plagued by bad weather and hampered by US air attacks on their bases, for four days they failed to locate the enemy vessels and not a single crash-dive could be attempted. On 24 October the massive naval battle of Leyte Gulf began without the Japanese having achieved any success in their plan to disable the all-powerful US carriers.

Then, on 25 October, at the height of the naval conflict, the kamikazes struck. At 0740 hours, six Zeros from Cebu surprised a force of four escort carriers and seven destroyers north of the island of Mindanao. The Americans watched paralysed as the first Zero dived with all guns blazing straight into the carrier USS *Santee*, blowing a large hole in the flight-deck as it exploded in a ball of flame. Quickly a barrage of anti-aircraft fire was mounted, but one more aircraft got through to crash onto the deck of the carrier USS *Suwanee*. Damage was considerable.

Further north, Seki's Shikishima group from Mabalacat was in the air still searching for a target, but in official mythology it was Seki who was to be credited with the first successful kami-

Far right: A kamikaze pilot stands in mute contemplation as a comrade places a *hachimaki*, the Samurai symbol of courage and pre-battle composure, around his head. **Right:** A Zeke fighter makes its final plunge onto the deck of the USS *Missouri*. **Above right:** Hit by a suicide plane, the flight-deck of the USS *Saratoga*, covered with wreckage and aviation fuel, burns fiercely.

THE A6M (ZERO) FIGHTER

The first shipboard fighter capable of beating land-based opponents, the A6M first entered frontline service in mid-1940. Its origins, however, stretch back to the 1930s when the Imperial Japanese Navy issued specifications for a new aircraft; it had to have a speed of 300mph, with an endurance of eight hours, and be heavily armed. Jiro Horikoshi, a designer with Mitsubishi, produced the winning aircraft, the A6M – A for carrier-based and 6M for the sixth such type made by Mitsubishi. The A6M's more popular name was the Reisen (Zero fighter).

Over the next few years, the A6Ms were built in their thousands, and numerous modifications were made to keep up with Allied air design. Despite its fearsome reputation, the A6M airframe was light, and vital parts were technically inferior to those produced by Britain and the US. The A6M7 Model 63 (shown below) was an attempt to off-set the shortcomings of the original design. Armament was improved with the addition of two wing machine guns; a new engine, the Sakae 31 was fitted, and extra underwing fuel tanks gave the A6M7 greater range. A single 551lb bomb could be carried on the belly.

kaze mission. At 1050 hours the Shikishima group attacked a force of four carriers and six destroyers already heavily engaged against Japanese sea-borne forces. First to be hit was the escort carrier USS *Kitkun Bay* – ironically, struck by the kamikaze's bomb which fell off as the plane itself narrowly missed the ship and plunged into the sea. Then it was the turn of another escort carrier, USS *St Lô*. Diving too fast for the AA gunners, a Zero crashed through the flight-deck, dowsing the hangars below in burning gasoline. Within seconds, the heat ignited ammunition stores and the *St Lô* was ripped apart by a violent explosion. Less than an hour later, she sank.

Attacks continued, and by the end of the day kamikaze raiders had accounted for a total of one carrier sunk and six damaged. The kamikaze operation stood out as an isolated success in a day otherwise utterly disastrous for the Japanese, since their fleet had been effectively eliminated as a fighting force in the naval battle. Those officers who had previously opposed the principle of suicide missions found themselves unable to resist what now appeared to be Japan's best remaining card to play. The Second Air Fleet under Vice Admiral Shigeru Fukadome, which had been moved to the Philippines to face the US invasion, had been used in conventional mass air attacks – 250 planes at a time – during 24-25 October. They had suffered heavy losses and achieved minimal success. Admiral Ohnishi now convinced Fukadome to join with the First Air Fleet in a unified special attack corps, which Fukadome would head. By the end of October, kamikaze operations had become the central element of the naval air force strategy, and the Army Air Force had also begun to form suicide attack units.

From the start, kamikaze attacks were mounted by small groups of aircraft operating independently. It was soon agreed that the optimum formation was three to five suicide bombers – usually Tenzans, Gingas, Suiseis or Zeros – escorted by at least two fighters. Technically, the most difficult task lay with the escort pilots, who had to hold off attacks by Grumman Hellcats until the suicide pilots could start their dive. As a consequence, the most experienced crew flew escort and the newest recruits – with perhaps two weeks' basic flight training in Japan and a ten-day special attack course in Formosa behind them – carried out the crash-dives. This tactic also had the advantage of keeping a nucleus of good quality pilots alive.

Once enemy shipping had been spotted, the suicide pilot would accelerate to maximum speed, and fuse his bomb – that was the moment of no return. Now the unit would come under air attack, but the kamikazes were instructed to ignore the fighting around them, heading implacably for their target. At a signal from the formation leader – a raised arm – each pilot would select his target and begin the attack run through the curtain of flying steel thrown up by the American naval gunners, ending with a steep dive for maximum momentum. Many, despite their training, instinctively covered their faces with their hands at the last moment.

Suicide attacks were a more or less daily occurrence throughout the Philippines campaign, generally piecemeal, but with the occasional concerted effort. On 25 November, for example, a total of 35 aircraft was involved in attacks on US warships, damaging three fleet carriers – USS *Essex, Intrepid* and *Hancock* – and the light carrier USS *Cabot*. During the following week, two battleships, two cruisers and two destroyers were hit. But despite the triple blow of a kamikaze attack – the impact of the plane hitting the ship, the bomb exploding and the aircraft's fuel catching fire – the damage was rarely sufficient to force a vessel to withdraw from action.

US carriers were damaged mainly because they had unarmoured wooden decks, easily penetrated by the crashing aircraft.

By January 1945, the position of the Japanese forces in the Philippines was hopeless. With rapidly diminishing resources, the naval air force special attack units continued to mount operations until 9 January – sometimes little more than solo efforts by the sole survivor of a decimated unit – but they could do nothing to turn the tide of battle. Still, in less than three months, kamikaze attacks had sunk 16 US vessels and damaged a further 87, while 480 naval air force aircraft had been lost on suicide missions. Even allowing that many army air force planes had also been destroyed in suicide attacks, this was an impressive record.

With the loss of Luzon in January and the fall of Iwo Jima to the Americans the following March, Japan was reduced to its last line of defence before the homeland itself. On 1 April the invasion of Okinawa began. Japan's remaining airpower had been totally reorganised to face this long anticipated challenge, and the pilots were imbued with the kamikaze spirit which now permeated all Japanese military thinking. The remnants of the original special attack corps had regrouped in Formosa, but on the southern Japanese island of Kyushu, a new and formidable kamikaze

Main picture: Shrouded in flames, with one wing shot away, a Kate torpedo-bomber dives to destruction. Below left: Pre-raid briefing for suicide pilots. Bottom: Two men study the flag one of them will carry in his cockpit. It reads, 'All for the Emperor, we are happy to die for him.'

THE OHKA PILOTED BOMB

The first prototype of the Ohka ('Cherry Blossom') piloted bomb (left) was produced in September 1944. Made chiefly of wood, it was 19ft long and had a wingspan of 16ft. Its metal nose section was packed with 2640lb of explosive.

Five rockets, based on a German design, were built into the tail to boost the diving speed. The first production model, the Fuji MXY-8, appeared in October.

A modification of the Mitsubishi G4M Type-1 twin-engined bomber, the G4M 2E, was developed to carry the Ohka partially set into its bomb-bay. The Ohka pilot rode in the mother plane until it drew near to the target, when he climbed into the tiny Ohka cockpit. The Ohka was released at a distance of about 20 miles from the target and at a height of 20,000-26,000ft. The bomb would glide at 300mph until the pilot sighted his target. Then he would put the Ohka into a 50 degree dive and ignite the rockets. In the final dive, the Ohka could reach speeds of 575 to 650mph – astonishing at that period.

Some 800 Ohkas were manufactured, but only 74 were sent into combat and, of these, only four are known for certain to have hit their target. In most cases, the G4Ms were shot down before they could release the Ohkas – 16 were lost in this way on the first mission on 21 March 1945.

143

MASTERMIND OF THE KAMIKAZES

Vice Admiral Takijiro Ohnishi (1891-1945) was a career naval officer obsessed with aviation. An experienced pilot, he had personally led sorties during Japan's war in China in the 1930s, when he commanded Second Combined Air Group. In 1941, as a recognised leading authority on naval aviation, he was responsible for preparing detailed plans for the attack on Pearl Harbor which began the Pacific War. During 1943-44, while in control of aircraft production at the Ministry of Munitions in Tokyo, he became convinced that training sufficient pilots to successfully fly the aircraft being produced was impossible, and he became a leading advocate of suicide tactics as the best use of existing resources. He also argued that the navy should virtually abandon its warships, including carriers, and concentrate on land-based airpower.

His appointment to command First Air Fleet in the Philippines in October 1944, was an invitation to put these ideas into effect.

Having set up the kamikaze corps on the Philippines, Ohnishi remained with the formation when it withdrew to Formosa in January 1945.

Then, in May, he was recalled to Tokyo as Vice-Chief Naval General Staff. Ohnishi argued constantly against surrender under any circumstances. When Japan did surrender on 15 August, he committed ritual suicide.

force the *kikusui* (floating chrysanthemum) had been assembled under the command of Vice Admiral Matome Ugaki. From mid-March, Ugaki had control of both naval and army air force units on Kyushu, a total of some 2000 aircraft dedicated to suicide attacks on the Allied fleet. His aim was simple – to inflict such losses on the Americans and their allies that they would be forced to withdraw from further combat. Okinawa was to be the killing ground.

The main naval air force components of Ugaki's formation, Fifth Air Fleet and Tenth Air Fleet, were already blooded in kamikaze combat. They had carried out a number of attacks in February and March, which had also seen the first use of the Ohka manned bomb. But now Ugaki was planning a suicide attack on a scale never previously envisaged. Reversing entirely the earlier tactic of the small special attack group, Ugaki intended to swamp American defences with waves of a hundred aircraft at a time. The first of the *kikusui* suicide wave attacks was set for 6 April.

In the early afternoon, the first of the 355 assorted aircraft, assembled at airfields across Kyushu, took off for the south. Preceded by fighter decoys, the kamikazes flew in units of 20 or 30, choosing different

THE KAMIKAZE SPIRIT

The motivation behind the adoption of suicide tactics, not only by the Japanese air forces, but also by sea and ground units, was largely practical. Inferior in training and technology and outnumbered, many Japanese officers and men felt that suicide attacks offered the only hope of success.

But it is also true that the religious devotion to the emperor and the homeland that had been cultivated in Japan for centuries – and especially emphasised by Japan's military rulers since the 1930s – predisposed men to the ultimate sacrifice. The influential *Bushido* code of the Samurai warrior class, called for loyalty to the emperor, endurance of pain, and a readiness for death at all times. It was the positive attraction that so many Japanese found in the concept of a 'good death' that seemed most alien to their enemies.

This attitude was expressed in the last writings of kamikaze pilots. 'I have been given a splendid opportunity to die,' writes one. 'This is my last day ... I shall fall like a blossom from a radiant cherry tree ... How I appreciate this chance to die like a man!' Another writes: 'We are 16 warriors manning the bombers. May our death be as sudden and clean as the shattering of crystal.' Yet another: 'It will be glorious to die in action. I am grateful to die in battle ...'

flight paths and angles of attack. The first targets to be struck were two US destroyers on picquet duty at the perimeter of the fleet, USS *Bush* and USS *Colhoun*. Hit by three kamikazes, the *Bush* broke her back and sank. The *Colhoun* was struck by four aircraft and had to be scuttled. Soon the air above the

Above left: A chubby-faced youngster, imbued with the Samurai creed, accepts a bunch of flowers from his commander before leaving on a suicide mission. Most pilots, usually volunteers, received only rudimentary flight training from their instructors. Above: Six men pose for the camera wearing the emblems of their corps and carrying Samurai swords. Treated like young gods in their own country, they were seen as the living embodiment of the Japanese martial tradition.

widely scattered fleet was swarming with kamikazes, boring towards their targets through the searing white lines of tracer fire and the dark smokebursts of 5in shellfire. The minesweeper USS *Emmons* took no less than five direct hits and was sunk; the destroyer USS *Newcomb*, struck by three aircraft, disappeared in billows of smoke and flame, but miraculously stayed afloat. By the time the onslaught ceased at 2000 hours, four vessels had been sunk and some 20 damaged. But the Japanese had paid a fearful price: as commanders and groundcrew counted the aircraft returning, they found that 248 had crash-dived or had been shot down.

For the US and Allied sailors, a nightmarish war of attrition had begun. The mass raids, interspersed with smaller-scale attacks, inflicted a steadily mounting toll of damage; casualties rose and nerves were stretched to breaking point. Yet, in fact, Ugaki's gamble had already failed. He could never again

hope to mount a raid on quite the scale of 6 April, and even that one had not inflicted losses anything like sufficient to stop the Allied offensive. Through April and May, a total of seven raids involving over 100 aircraft at a time were carried out; by June, no more than 50 planes could be assembled for a mass attack.

At Kanoya, the main naval air force base on Kyushu, the pilots lived under constant threat from B-29 bomber raids. Many were housed in half-ruined buildings, bedding down on the bare floor in rooms with window panes shattered by bomb blasts. Instead of the dedicated fighting men who had made up Ohnishi's first special attack unit, the pilots were almost all recently drafted students, numbly resigned to a fate which dictated they should die young. The volunteer principle, never fully operative in the Army Air Force, was now no more than a form of words in the Naval Air Force also. Imperial propaganda did succeed in filling some young pilots with an arrogant self-importance, but no-one could confuse this with the heroic enthusiasm of the early days in the Philippines. Ohnishi's original plan had been a ruthless but rational attempt to pit idealism against hopeless odds; now Ugaki was merely herding young men to the slaughter.

The last *kikusui* raid on 21-22 June mustered 45 aircraft; five vessels were damaged for the loss of 30 raiders. After that only sporadic kamikaze missions could be mounted, although the US destroyer USS *Callaghan* was sunk by a suicide attack as late as 28 July. In all, at Okinawa the kamikazes had sunk 44 vessels and damaged 198, a staggering performance. But in the process the Naval Air Force had lost another 930 aircraft and the Army Air Force about the same. As a result, the Japanese no longer had the resources to carry out a coherent air offensive.

Had the Americans gone on to invade Japan, a final desperate kamikaze campaign would no doubt have been mounted. But on 6 August and 9 August atomic bombs were dropped on Hiroshima and Nagasaki. On 15 August, the emperor broadcast Japan's surrender. Admiral Ugaki had already decided what course of action to adopt. Having listened to the emperor's announcement on the radio at Otei airbase, he stripped off his insignia of rank and led 10 of his pilots out to their aircraft for the last kamikaze mission. Once in the air and heading for Okinawa, he broadcast a final message:

'I alone am responsible for our failure to defend the homeland and destroy the arrogant enemy... I am going to make an attack at Okinawa where my men have fallen like cherry blossoms. There I will crash into and destroy the hated enemy in the true spirit of Bushido... *Banzai!*'

He was never seen again.

As for Ohnishi, who was now occupying a staff post in Tokyo, on the night of the surrender he retired to his room and, following the prescribed ritual of Japanese suicide, first cut open his belly with a sword and then cut his throat to apply the *coup de grâce*. But the second cut failed in its object, and Ohnishi did not die until the following evening, having refused all medical assistance.

The effectiveness of the kamikaze tactic has been much discussed. The balance sheet for all suicide air attacks was 1228 naval air force aircraft lost, and probably a somewhat smaller number of their army equivalent, for 34 vessels sunk and 288 damaged.

THE AUTHOR R. G. Grant graduated in Modern History from Trinity College, Oxford. He has written extensively on recent military campaigns.

EAGLES ALOFT

The 4th Fighter-Interceptor Wing of Korean War fame originated in the three American Eagle Squadrons that fought in RAF Fighter Command during World War II. Before the United States entered the conflict, American volunteers joined the RAF, underwent training, and formed three units: No. 71 Eagle Squadron organised in September 1940, No. 121 Eagle Squadron in May 1941, and No. 133 in July of the latter year. Together, the three Eagle Squadrons downed 73½ German planes. In September 1942, some 10 months after the United States went to war, the Eagle Squadrons transferred to the US Army Air Force, becoming the 4th Fighter Group in the American Eighth Air Force, which was taking shape in the United Kingdom. The former No. 71 Squadron became the 334th Fighter Squadron, No. 121 Squadron was renamed the 335th, and No. 133 Squadron became the 336th. Conducting fighter sweeps over western Europe, escorting daylight bombing missions, and strafing German airfields, the so-called Debden Eagles destroyed more than 1000 German planes. Because of its accomplishments during the fighting in Europe, the 4th Fighter Group, soon redesignated a fighter-interceptor wing but consisting of the same three squadrons, became an element of the postwar US Air Force, which emerged as an independent service in 1947. The former American Eagle Squadrons and Debden Eagles adopted an emblem (shown above) that included an arrow adorned with three eagle feathers and chose the motto: 'Fourth but First'.

MIG ALLEY

In the battle for air supremacy in Korea, Sabres clashed with MiGs in a stretch of airspace known as 'MiG Alley'

DURING THE Korean War the United States suffered a series of shocks. The conflict began in June 1950 with a sudden, unprovoked, and unexpected attack by North Korea, whose troops advanced southwards across the 38th Parallel that served as the border with South Korea. After the United States intervened on behalf of the United Nations (UN) to defend South Korea against the communist assault, the invaders overwhelmed the first American ground troops to oppose them, thus administering a second shock. The third surprise of that year was the Chinese intervention in November. Despite clear

indications that China would take action to protect its border from the advancing UN forces, the move caught a complacent headquarters completely unprepared.

More than three weeks before launching the ground offensive that sent the UN divisions reeling back, the Chinese committed fighter units to the Korean War. Relying on equipment rather than training or experience, these so-called volunteers flew the Soviet-built MiG-15, a stubby, swept-wing jet fighter designed by Artem Mikoyan and Michael I. Gurevich. Although designed and built in the Soviet Union, the interceptor was powered by an engine based on the Rolls Royce Nene, which the British government had made available for export. This powerplant gave the fighter a speed in excess of 600mph and provided rapid acceleration even in the thin air at 30,000ft or higher.

The MiG-15 made its combat debut on 1 December 1950, and within six weeks had demonstrated its superiority over the American fighters being used in the Far East. Although one of the US Navy's Grumman Pantherjets downed a MiG during mid-November, the enemy plane was faster and

Above: Colonel Ben Preston (centre), the 4th Wing's senior officer, holds a sign commemorating nine kills scored on 16 October 1951. Below: 'El Diablo', flown by 335th pilot Captain Chuck Owens, displays the squadron's tally of victories and missions. Bottom left: Lieutenant 'Dusty' Showen's Sabre, 'Screamin' Eagle'. Bottom right: 'The Chopper', the mount of Major Asla.

147

ACES OF THE KOREAN WAR

As the negotiations that ended the Korean War drew to a close, three pilots competed to become the leading American ace of the conflict. Two were members of the 4th Fighter-Interceptor Wing: Major James Jabara of Wichita, Kansas, and Captain Manuel J. Fernandez of Key West, Florida. The third, also an F-86 pilot but assigned to the 51st Fighter-Interceptor Wing, was Captain Joseph C. McConnell Jr.

A veteran combat pilot, Jabara had shot down one German plane during World War II and shared in the destruction of another. Over North Korea, he became America's first jet ace by downing five Soviet-built MiG-15s. After his sixth victory, however, his tour of duty ended and he returned to the United States. He volunteered to return to Korea, and between January 1953 and the end of the war in July of that year he claimed nine more kills.

A latecomer to the Korean fighting, Fernandez had taught aerial gunnery at Nellis Air Force Base, Nevada, before going to Korea, and in combat he proved himself the deadliest marksman in the wing. His skilful shooting enabled him to score 14½ aerial victories during a single combat tour.

Neither of the pilots from the 4th Fighter-Interceptor Wing could equal McConnell's 16 victories. Jabara ranked second among the aces and Fernandez third. Two of the three had their careers cut short by fatal accidents. McConnell died in 1954 when the plane he was testing crashed and Jabara, a colonel at the time, was killed in an auto accident at Delray Beach in Florida during November 1966.

Top: James Jabara of the 334th Squadron strolls by a row of tents at K-2 airbase in early 1951. Jabara, a veteran of World War II, downed 16 MiGs in two tours of Korea. Above: Another ace, Pete Fernandez, poses for the camera after his 10th kill. During his only stint in the war, he was credited with 14½ confirmed victories.

148

more manoeuvrable than the Pantherjet, the Lockheed F-80 jet flown by the Air Force, or the piston-powered F-51s and Marine Corps Corsairs.

To deal with the MiG, the Air Force turned to an elite unit, the 4th Fighter-Interceptor Wing, equipped with an exceptional aircraft, the North American F-86A Sabre. On 8 November, when the wing received orders to go to the Far East, its headquarters was located at New Castle County airport, Delaware. The pilots of the unit's three squadrons and their F-86 Sabres were carrying out the mission of protecting the cities of the eastern seaboard against possible attack by Soviet bombers.

The Sabre had been chosen for this assignment because it was the best and most modern of America's daytime interceptors. It was as fast as the Soviet-built jet and better armed, inasmuch as its six 50-calibre machine guns had a uniform trajectory and a more uniform pattern of dispersion than the MiG's mixed armament of two 23mm and one 37mm cannon, even though the slow-firing cannon had greater destructive power. The swept-wing Sabre jet had slightly more sluggish acceleration at high altitude, and the two fighters shared a common failing: engines that gulped fuel at a discouraging rate. A Sabre carrying two jettisonable 120-gallon fuel tanks had a combat radius of just 490 miles, excluding the distance flown while patrolling on station prior to engaging in a few minutes of combat.

Handicapped by its short range, the Sabre could not provide close cover for the B-29s and the fighter-bombers that were being threatened by the MiGs. Such tactics would have cut too deeply into the time available for combat. Instead of accompanying the strike force, the F-86s, initially based at Kimpo airfield,

took off in four-plane flights at intervals of perhaps five minutes and formed an aerial barrier near the Yalu river, which marked the boundary between North Korea and Chinese Manchuria, while air operations were underway to the south. Since American policy forbade the Sabres from penetrating Chinese airspace, the skies over Manchuria remained a sanctuary for the MiGs. The American pilots tried to spot the enemy as they approached the Yalu, ideally while they were still climbing from one of the Manchurian airfields, and pounce as soon as they entered North Korea.

The F-86s of the 4th Fighter-Interceptor Wing approached this aerial battlefield in northwestern Korea, nicknamed 'MiG Alley,' at an altitude of about 30,000ft and, if combat seemed likely, at a speed of about Mach 0.86. At first, the F-86s had approached MiG Alley at a slower speed, accelerating only when the enemy was in sight, but experience soon showed that the fighter gained speed too slowly, unless in a dive. Higher speed proved necessary if the Americans were to gain the initiative and bounce the enemy, even though the faster approach cut into the supply of fuel, reducing the time available for combat to about 10 minutes.

Even though the F-86A and the MiG-15 were evenly matched in performance, the American pilots who entered combat in December 1950 enjoyed a decisive edge in experience and skill over their Chinese opponents. Officers of the 4th Fighter-Interceptor Wing included Lieutenant-Colonel John C. Meyer, who had shot down 24 German planes in World War II and Lieutenant-Colonel Glenn Eagleston with 18½ aerial victories. Another member of the wing, Captain James Jabara, who had downed only one German during the recent conflict and shared in a second kill, became the first American jet ace over Korea. On 20 May 1951, he downed a fifth MiG to earn that title and for good measure gained a sixth as well.

Above: Illuminaries of the 4th. From left to right: Colonel Eagleston, Colonel Schmidt, Captain Kaminski and Colonel Mayer. Below: 'Mende's Menace', flown by Jabara on his second kill.

Sabre vs MiG

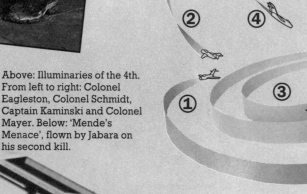

Left: The defensive split. A flight of two Sabres attacks a pair of MiGs. The MiG wingman breaks ① while his leader goes into a steep climb ②. The Sabres, with their slower rate of climb, are forced ③ to follow the MiG wingman. The MiG leader ④ loops into position to attack the Sabres.

Above: The low-speed yoyo. A Sabre chases a MiG. In level flight the Sabre is unable to gain on his target and reach an attacking position. The Sabre ① goes into a shallow dive, gaining speed. When the Sabre pulls out of the dive ② the extra acceleration has enabled it to gain on the MiG and attack.

Korea
Nov 1950–July 1953

CHINA

MANCHURIA

Fencheng · Siuho ·
Antung · Chosan
Takushan · Unsan
Tatunkou · Kuna-ri
Sinanju

NORTH KOREA

Chongjin

Chosin reservoir

Iwon

SEA OF JAPAN

YELLOW SEA

Pyongyang · Wonsan

38°N

Seoul
Inchon
Kimpo
Suwon

Taejon

SOUTH KOREA

Pusan

Naktong

Imjin

Key
→ Chinese forces
→ UN forces

▨ MiG Alley
✈ Chinese airbases
✈ UN airbases

Front lines during Chinese offensive
······ 24 Nov 1950
----- 26 Dec 1950
——— 25 Jan 1951

Front lines during UN counter-offensive
----- 28 Feb 1951
——— 21 Apr 1951

Armistice line
27 July 1953

In November 1950 the steady UN advance northwards through Korea turned into a retreat in the face of the intervention of the Chinese. Shortly afterwards the MiG-15 made its combat debut over the skies of North Korea. Throughout the rest of the war, US F-86 Sabres were embroiled in a bitter air-war over MiG Alley to hold the Chinese at bay.

In contrast, China seemed from the outset to be using the Korean War to train its airmen. A group of obviously inexperienced pilots would appear, perform cautiously at first, and grow bolder and deadlier as they learned how to handle the MiG-15 in combat. Then, as they began fighting on nearly equal terms with the Americans, a new group would arrive, enter combat, and so dilute the level of experience in the Chinese fighter force that the learning process would have to begin anew.

The Chinese, who usually operated in several elements of two aircraft each, used a variety of tactics, the choice reflecting the skill of the pilots involved. New men were content to take advantage of the greater ceiling of their aircraft, dive on the Americans, climb away after firing a single burst, and bolt for the sanctuary provided by the Manchu-

and Colonel Harrison Thyng with five. In MiG Alley Mahurin scored three-and-a-half kills and Thyng another five. Jabara returned for a second tour of combat to claim nine more victims; his total of 15 placed him second to Captain Joseph C. McConnell of the 51st Fighter-Interceptor Wing, who downed 16 MiGs. Ranking third behind McConnell and Jabara was Captain Manuel Fernandez, an instructor in fighter gunnery before joining the 4th Fighter-Interceptor Wing in Korea. He shot down 14 of the enemy and shared the credit for another. The 4th also boasted the oldest ace of the Korean War, Colonel Vermont

Far left: A Chinese MiG-15 captured by the nose-camera of a Sabre over the Yalu, moments before its destruction. Nearly 800 enemy fighters were destroyed by US pilots during the conflict. Left: Lieutenant-Colonel Robert Dixon surveys flak damage to his aircraft's tail. Below: The F-86 Sabre.

Left: Lieutenant Harry Jones of the 4th Wing's 335th Squadron leads a flight of Sabres back to K-14 field after an unusually uneventful combat patrol over the Yalu river in the summer of 1953, the year of the armistice that ended the war.

rian border. The veteran fliers, however, tried a number of variations, often using a decoy to attract the attention of the Americans, while other MiGs attacked from above, from both flanks simultaneously, or even from below.

The 4th Fighter-Interceptor Wing scored its first victory on 17 December 1950, when Lieutenant-Colonel Bruce N. Hinton and his flight of four F-86As saw an equal number of MiGs about 7000ft below them. He led his formation in a diving turn towards the Chinese, who responded by climbing towards the attackers. When the Americans continued closing the range, the inexperienced enemy airmen scattered to head for the Yalu and the safety of Manchuria, but Hinton caught one of the MiGs with three bursts from his 50-calibre guns. The Soviet-built jet began trailing smoke after the first armour-piercing incendiary bullet struck home, the smoke gave way to flames, and the plane flipped onto its back and began spinning to earth.

The 4th Fighter-Interceptor Wing remained an elite organisation throughout the war, as new pilots demonstrated the same skill as those they replaced. Joining the unit in 1952 were Colonel Walker S. 'Bud' Mahurin with 20 aerial victories over Europe in World War II

Garrison, a 37 year-old veteran of World War II; in Korea he added 10 victories to his earlier total of seven-and-one-third.

Fernandez demonstrated his shooter's eye by downing two MiGs in a matter of seconds during a battle that began when his four-plane flight encountered 10 times that number of Chinese. Alerted by radar operators on the ground that the enemy was approaching, Fernandez spotted more than 40 of the Soviet-built interceptors at a slightly greater altitude. Covered by the other section of two F-86s, the captain and his wingman cut off two MiGs, which tried to dive away. Fernandez set the leader on fire, followed up with a burst that blew up the Chinese wingman's MiG, and then finished off the other.

Ralph Gibson, who scored five victories to become another of the 4th Fighter-Interceptor Wing's 24 aces, had a close call while patrolling just south of the Yalu to prevent MiGs from jumping a formation of fighter-bombers attacking supply lines in North Korea. Upon seeing some three dozen contrails approaching from Manchuria, Gibson and the others dropped their external fuel tanks and turned to attack. He was flying high cover when the F-86s made their turn, his attention riveted on the approaching MiGs. These enemy aircraft proved to be the bait in a trap, for another formation of MiGs flashed past from above, one of them passing within 10ft of Gibson's canopy. When he recovered from the shock, he dived after the Chinese, downing two of the fighters in a brief but furious battle. One of the enemy aircraft burst into flames before plummeting to earth; the second shed a wing when

Bottom: Lines of F-86 Sabres flank the apron of K-13 airbase at Kimpo in April 1951. Below: The 4th Wing's victory board listing kills.

Gibson's bullets struck home.

The replacements who joined the wing in Korea thus maintained the high standards of the pilots who had entered combat in December 1950. Just as the roster of pilots had changed, so too did the wing's equipment. A new Sabre, the F-86E, made its debut in the summer of 1951 and more than matched the improved performance of its latest adversary, the MiG-15bis. In its final form, the E model had a more powerful engine than the F-86A and a larger wing, swept back somewhat more sharply and without the leading-edge slats of the older Sabre. The slats had been designed to open automatically at low speed, increasing lift and enabling the plane to land on a comparatively short runway. Unfortunately, they sometimes deployed during tight turns, while the Sabre pilot was trying to get a MiG in his sights, and thus caused a loss of speed at a critical moment.

The latest version of the Sabre also had hydraulically operated control surfaces and an 'all-flying tail'. The entire horizontal stabiliser moved in conjunction with the elevator, increasing responsiveness along with the danger of overstressing the tail section. Indeed, a British pilot once tore the elevators from an F-86E as the result of a violent manoeuvre, but the moveable horizontal stabiliser provided sufficient control for a recovery and safe landing.

The combination of aircraft, pilots, and mechanics that made up the 4th Fighter-Interceptor Wing destroyed 502 enemy planes at the cost of 57 Sabres during 45,854 sorties. Jabara, Fernandez, and the others accounted for 54 per cent of the total losses suffered by Chinese and North Korean aviation units. Included in the wing's kills were 481½ MiGs, 60 per cent of the aircraft of that type destroyed by American airmen. Clearly the 4th Fighter-Interceptor Wing had earned its place on the exclusive list of top-notch combat organisations.

THE AUTHOR Bernard C. Nalty has written extensively on aviation history and has a particular interest in the Korean and Vietnam Wars and is author of *Air Power and the Fight for Khe Sanh*.

Operating from makeshift airfields, the Kittyhawks of No.112 Squadron became the scourge of the Luftwaffe over the Western Desert

IT WAS DURING the fierce air battles over the Western Desert in 1942 that the Royal Air Force (RAF) first employed fighter-bomber aircraft for ground-attack missions during World War II. Although this employment was no great tactical innovation, as fighters had first been used in this way in World War I and the Luftwaffe had been deploying fighter-bombers since 1940, for the Allied fighter squadrons in the Desert it marked an important turning point. Poorly-

Below: A shark-mouthed Kittyhawk Mk III of No.112 Squadron is directed into the aircraft dispersal area of Zuara airfield. Bottom: Kittyhawk pilots of the squadron pose before their savage-looking aircraft. The squadron's shark-mouth motif was also adopted by the American Volunteer group, The 'Flying Tigers', operating in China.

into an eager fighting aeroplane that made you itch to get your hands on her.' One of nine fighter squadrons controlled by Air Headquarters, Western Desert, in September 1941, No.112 Squadron was attached to No.258 Wing, together with No.3 Squadron, RAAF, No.2 Squadron SAAF and No.250 Squadron, RAF.

As the British Eighth Army geared up in Egypt for Operation Crusader, an offensive, due to begin on 18 November, which was intended to drive Rommel out of eastern Libya, No.258 Wing was ordered to carry

SHARK SQUADRON

equipped and inexperienced compared to their German opponents, the fighter pilots of the RAF, the Royal Australian Air Force (RAAF) and the South African Air Force (SAAF) had struggled long and hard to gain some measure of air superiority over the Luftwaffe. Only when this was achieved were they able to intervene effectively in the ground battle.

The pioneer fighter-bomber formation in the Western Desert was No.112 Squadron, RAF. In May 1941, after seeing service in East Africa, the Western Desert, Greece and Crete, the squadron had been withdrawn to Fayid in Egypt. In the following month it began to replace its ageing Gloster Gladiator biplanes with US-supplied Curtiss Tomahawk monoplane fighters, and in September 1941 the unit was declared operational on its new aircraft. Under the command of Squadron Leader D. W. Balden, it moved to Sidi Heneish in the Western Desert. It was at this time that the squadron adopted the strikingly effective shark-mouth aircraft marking which it was to retain throughout its subsequent service. In the words of one pilot, 'that glaring mouth transformed the appearance of the stubby machine

out fighter sweeps and bomber-escort missions over the German-held territory of Cyrenaica. In anticipation of a fast-moving campaign, the squadron groundcrews were made fully mobile and divided into two servicing parties, plus a rear party comprising headquarters, workshops and stores. This form of organisation allowed one party to move forward to a new base while the other was servicing the aircraft.

Desert conditions were trying for air and groundcrew alike. The flying sand made maintenance very difficult and engines and guns were particularly prone to failure after storms. Pilot Officer Neville Duke, who joined No.112 Squadron in November 1941, found that:

'Life in the Desert was hard but healthy, and we

were all very fit. With nowhere to go, we were thrown together a good deal and the squadron tended to be much more of a unit than those in other areas as a result. The sandstorms were bad, but generally it was a matter of adapting to the conditions and getting the "feel" of the Desert.'

One hazard of Desert fighting was brought home to No.112 Squadron on the night of 24/25 November, when German armour threatened to overrun its base at LG122 (Landing Ground 122). 'We had 175 aircraft on the "drome"', recorded the squadron's diarist, 'and as the Hun column passed only 10 miles north of us they missed a glorious opportunity of wrecking most of our fighters.'

The main threat during November and December, however, came from the Luftwaffe's fighter force. During a fighter sweep in the afternoon of 22 November, the Tomahawks of No.112 Squadron flying with those of No.3 Squadron, RAAF, encountered the Messerschmitt Bf 109s of Jagdgeschwader 27 southeast of El Adem. As the German fighters had the advantages of superior speed, rate of climb, and ceiling, the Tomahawks went into defensive circles in order to exploit their superior manoeuvrability. These tactics were only partially successful, as seven Tomahawks fell to the enemy's guns, but both Pilot Officer Duke and Pilot Officer J. P. Bartle of No.112 Squadron claimed enemy fighters shot down. After the failure of his reflector gunsight, Duke used the Tomahawk's antiquated fixed ring-and-bead sight to aim and was rather surprised to see his victim blow up. After 30 minutes of combat, evening was closing in and the Bf 109s broke off the engagement, thus allowing the surviving Tomahawks to make good their escape. The majority of the casualties were borne by No.3 Squadron, RAAF, and only Sergeant H. G. Burney of No.112 Squadron failed to return. He was forced to crash-land in the desert. He was spotted there by Wing Commander F. E. Rosier, who gallantly landed his Hurricane nearby to pick him up. Unfortunately, the Hurricane burst a tyre in the process and so both pilots were forced to walk 30 miles to the nearest friendly troops.

'Occasionally we came across Italians in the Macchi M.C.200 and Fiat G.50, slippery customers and very manoeuvrable'

The squadron was not always so fortunate in escaping casualties. Duke, who was himself shot down twice within the space of five days, recalled that, 'in only four sorties we lost 14 Tomahawks, most of them shot down by 109s. Occasionally we came across Italians in the Macchi M.C.200 and Fiat G.50, slippery customers and very manoeuvrable.' In general, though, the Italians, while often fine aerobatic pilots, lacked tactical sense and 'seemed to enter combat more in the spirit of medieval joust than of a life-and-death struggle.'

On 5 December Duke was engaged in a combat which illustrated how the hostile desert environment, poor aircraft maintenance, and an enemy flying a superior machine could combine to defeat even the most able of fighter pilots:

'I was leading a section of four and not feeling particularly happy. On take-off clouds of sand raised by the leading section resulted in my perspex canopy becoming thickly coated with dust, restricting my vision. Then my radio packed up and I felt very lonely, not being able to hear what was going on; but as our numbers were few

No.112 SQUADRON

The increase in German bombing raids on England in 1917 brought about an expansion of Home Defence squadrons. No.112 Squadron was formed on 30 July with the nucleus of 'B' Flight of No.50 Squadron, and was soon flying daylight patrols in Sopwith Pups, switching to night flying in Sopwith Camels in 1918. Although it was re-equipped with Sopwith Snipes after the Armistice, disbandment followed on 13 June 1919.

On 16 May 1939 the squadron was re-formed, equipped with Gloster Gladiator biplanes and shipped to Egypt as part of the Suez Canal defence force. Following the outbreak of war, the squadron conducted patrols over the Western Desert, then participated in the defence of Athens and the support of British forces retreating from Greece. Moved again to Egypt in 1941 and re-equipped with Curtiss Tomahawk and Kittyhawk fighters, No.112 Squadron began a long and distinguished career of fighter-bombing. After the North African campaign it operated from Malta, then Sicily and Italy, where it supported the Allied force at Salerno. Following missions in Yugoslavia, the squadron was re-equipped with North American Mustangs. These were flown against rail and canal targets, and then in support of the Allied invasion of southern France in 1944. Though disbanded for a second time on 31 December 1946, the squadron was reformed at Fassberg in Germany on 12 May 1951 as part of the 2nd Tactical Air Force. It served until 1957; when defence cuts caused its disbandment on 31 May. No.112 Squadron's badge is shown above.

155

and there was a hope of meeting the enemy circus, I decided against leaving the formation and going home.

'The sun was brilliant, almost blinding when I glanced towards it occasionally, knowing it was from that direction we could expect trouble from 109s; and the combination of the sanded canopy and the glare of the sun had me blinking and peering. I felt a little blind and, without the radio, quite deaf. I hung onto the formation and soon I saw our leader breaking down into a gaggle of Ju 87s and a close escort of Macchis and Fiat G.50s.

'Down we went but there was to be no joy for me. There was a top cover of 109s all right, but with my sanded-up canopy and the sun I had missed them. One of them did not miss me. There was an abrupt bang in the cockpit on the starboard side. My foot was knocked off the rudder pedal. I felt a violent blow on my right leg and the cockpit filled with smoke. The banging continued, making the Tomahawk shudder, and I took some pretty quick evasive action, knowing that the aircraft had been badly hit.

'At 10,000ft the Tomahawk went into a spin; its right elevator was completely shot away, the right wing torn at the trailing edge by a cannon shell and the right aileron control shot through. Though I did my best to straighten out, the aircraft spun – and spun. Time to get out, I thought. I undid my safety straps, opened the hood and got ready to leave; and then, at about 2000ft, the machine began to behave itself again. It straightened out.'

Duke managed to bring his Tomahawk into besieged Tobruk for a crash-landing, but it was a complete write-off. After his wounded leg had been treated, he was flown out that evening to rejoin No.112 Squadron at LG122.

Caldwell concluded his dive-bombing trials with an attack on enemy positions at Martuba

By late December the wear and tear of relentless combat had reduced No.112 Squadron to a strength of only five serviceable aircraft, and at the end of the year it was re-equipped with the Curtiss Kittyhawk. The new fighter was an improved Tomahawk with a more powerful engine and increased armament. However, it was still no match for the Luftwaffe's ubiquitous Bf 109F. Because of its similarity to the Tomahawk, conversion onto the Kittyhawk posed few problems and by 9 January 1942 the squadron was back in action. Shortly afterwards, Squadron Leader C. R. Caldwell, an Australian, took over command, having previously served as a flight commander with No.250 Squadron. Destined to finish the war as the top-scoring fighter pilot of the Royal Australian Air Force, Caldwell already had 18 victories to his credit. He was to add a further two kills plus one shared victory to this total over the following two months, but perhaps his most important work during

Top right: A Kittyhawk armed with a 250lb bomb takes off in a cloud of dust from a rudimentary airstrip in the Western Desert. Centre right: A shattered German PzKpfw Mk III tank, its turret blown clear off its mounting, amply testifies to the efficacy of the Desert Air Force. Right: Sergeant Pilot Alec Rowe, one of No.112 Squadron's most distinguished airmen, and (far right) Squadron Leader C.R. 'Killer' Caldwell, who led the squadron in the early months of 1942.

this period was the development of dive-bombing techniques for the Kittyhawk. His first test flight on 10 March was intended to discover whether a bomb could be dropped without carrying away the aircraft's propeller. Fortunately, this was accomplished safely and Caldwell concluded his dive-bombing trials on the following day with an attack on enemy positions at Martuba.

Meanwhile, the Crusader offensive had achieved many of its objectives, having relieved Tobruk and driven the enemy from Cyrenaica. However, these gains proved difficult to consolidate, and on 21 January Rommel counter-attacked, driving back the Eighth Army. During the 400-mile retreat to Gazala, Neville Duke flew with No 112 Squadron on a number of strafing missions against enemy motor convoys:

SQUADRON LEADER NEVILLE DUKE

Neville Duke was born at Tonbridge in Kent on 11 January 1922 and in 1940 he volunteered for pilot training with the RAF. He was awarded his pilot's wings in February 1941 and in April was posted to No.92 Squadron at Biggin Hill, which was then the top-scoring squadron in RAF Fighter Command. Duke took part in numerous fighter sweeps and bomber-escort missions over France, and on 25 June 1941 he gained his first combat victory.

In October, with two victories to his credit, Duke was posted to Egypt and joined No.112 Squadron at Sidi Heneish. Duke remained in Egypt after the end of his first combat tour with No.112 Squadron in April 1942, serving as a fighter instructor until November 1942. He then rejoined No.92 Squadron, which had followed him to Africa and was operating Spitfire Mk VCs from Gambut in Libya.

In January 1943 he was promoted to flight lieutenant and became a flight commander. By March he was credited with 18 enemy aircraft destroyed and was awarded the DSO.

After another period of instructing, Duke began his third operational tour as commanding officer of No.145 Squadron, which flew Spitfire Mk VIIIs from Caserta in Italy. In September 1944, when his combat career came to an end, he was credited with 28 victories, making him the top-scoring pilot of the Desert Air Force.
Below: Squadron Leader Neville Duke in 1944.

THE CURTISS HAWKS

The Curtiss P-40 Warhawk was the last of a long series of single-seat fighters that began in 1926 with the introduction of the P-1, the first of the new Pursuit-class of fighters and the first Curtiss plane to bear the name Hawk. The P-40's performance was not outstanding when compared to some of the great Allied and Axis fighters of World War II, but more than 14,000 were produced over six years and they acquitted themselves well in every theatre of operation.

The first P-40 variant to enter service with the RAF was the Hawk 81-A1, ordered by France and diverted to Britain after the German Occupation. Designated the Tomahawk Mk I by the RAF, the 185 examples were mostly used for training. The RAF then received 930 examples of the Hawk 81-A3, a superior plane with self-sealing tanks, armour, and six wing-mounted .303in machine guns. This model was designated the Tomahawk Mk IIB by the British.

Dissatisfied with their aircraft's performance, the Curtiss company redesigned the P-40 in 1941. The powerplant was uprated to a 1150hp Allison V-1710-39 engine, armour was added, and the armament was replaced by four 0.5in machine guns. After adding a further two guns, 1500 examples of this type (the P-40E or Hawk 87-A3) were produced for Britain, where it was designated the Kittyhawk Mk IA. Further Kittyhawk variants were introduced into RAF service as the war progressed, and No.112 Squadron received Kittyhawk Mk IIIs in October 1942 and Kittyhawk Mk IVs in April 1944. After June 1944 the squadron flew North American Mustangs. Production of the Warhawk series ceased in December 1944.

'It was . . . risky if you returned for a second run; for by then all the ack-ack was prepared . . . Once you began firing you could see the bullets spurting up the sand; then you lifted the nose of the aircraft slightly until they were going right into the lorries; another slight lift and you were up and over the convoy, skimming low again seeking the cover of any slight dip.'

A notable victory was gained by the Kittyhawks of No.112 Squadron and No.3 Squadron, RAAF, on 14 February. They intercepted a formation of Ju 87 Stukas, escorted by Macchi M.C.200s and Bf 109s, in all numbering some 32 aircraft, in the vicinity of

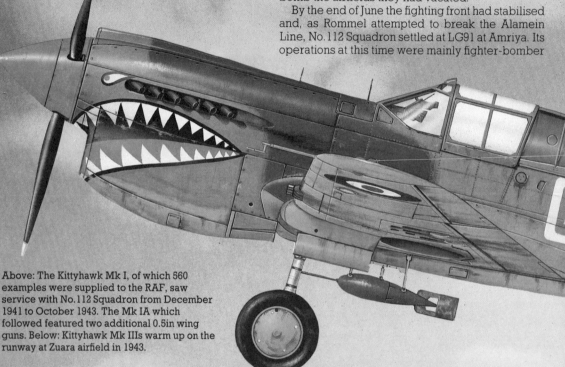

Above: The Kittyhawk Mk I, of which 560 examples were supplied to the RAF, saw service with No.112 Squadron from December 1941 to October 1943. The Mk IA which followed featured two additional 0.5in wing guns. Below: Kittyhawk Mk IIIs warm up on the runway at Zuara airfield in 1943.

Acroma. Of these, 20 were claimed as destroyed, two probably destroyed and 10 damaged. Neither Allied squadron suffered any casualties, and all 10 of the No.112 Squadron pilots who participated in the engagement submitted victory claims.

A lull in the fighting preceded the opening of the Battle of Gazala on 26 May 1942, but the Allies could do little to make good their losses. The first Spitfire unit was not to reach the desert until June and so the Kittyhawk units continued to bear the brunt of the fighting. Squadron Leader Billy Drake took command of No.112 Squadron in May, and on the 16th the squadron began dive-bombing operations in ear-

nest. However, the increased emphasis on ground-attack operations did not mean the end of air fighting. On 4 June Drake led a particularly effective dive-bombing attack in support of the defenders of Bir Hacheim, who signalled, 'Bravo! Merci pour la RAF.' The reply was, 'Bravo à vous! Merci pour le sport!' Two days later, when on a fighter-bomber mission in the same area, the squadron encountered a formation of Bf 109s and shot down two of them, with Drake claiming a third as a probable victory. The British defeat at Gazala led to a further retreat back to the Alamein line during June. During one hectic period in late June, No.112 Squadron was forced to move no fewer than four times in 10 days – often returning to bomb the airfields they had vacated.

By the end of June the fighting front had stabilised and, as Rommel attempted to break the Alamein Line, No.112 Squadron settled at LG91 at Amriya. Its operations at this time were mainly fighter-bomber

and bomber-escort missions, although as the day for Montgomery's counter-stroke approached, the emphasis shifted to air superiority missions. By a stroke of good fortune, heavy rains in early October waterlogged the German airfields in the El Daba and Fuka regions, while the RAF landing grounds around Amriya remained usable. Thus the Allied fighter-bombers and medium bombers were able to attack the grounded German aircraft and enemy troop

The war in the desert
Nov 1941–Nov 1942

On 18 November 1941, the British Eighth Army launched Operation Crusader, driving Rommel back through Cyrenaica and lifting the siege of Tobruk on 10 December. Rommel held the Agheila line and launched his counter-offensive, reaching Mechili in February and laying siege to Tobruk on 18 June. By the end of the month the Allies had been thrown back to El Alamein. Throughout the campaign, No.112 Squadron, RAF, was in action, distinguishing itself in the bomber-escort and ground-attack roles.

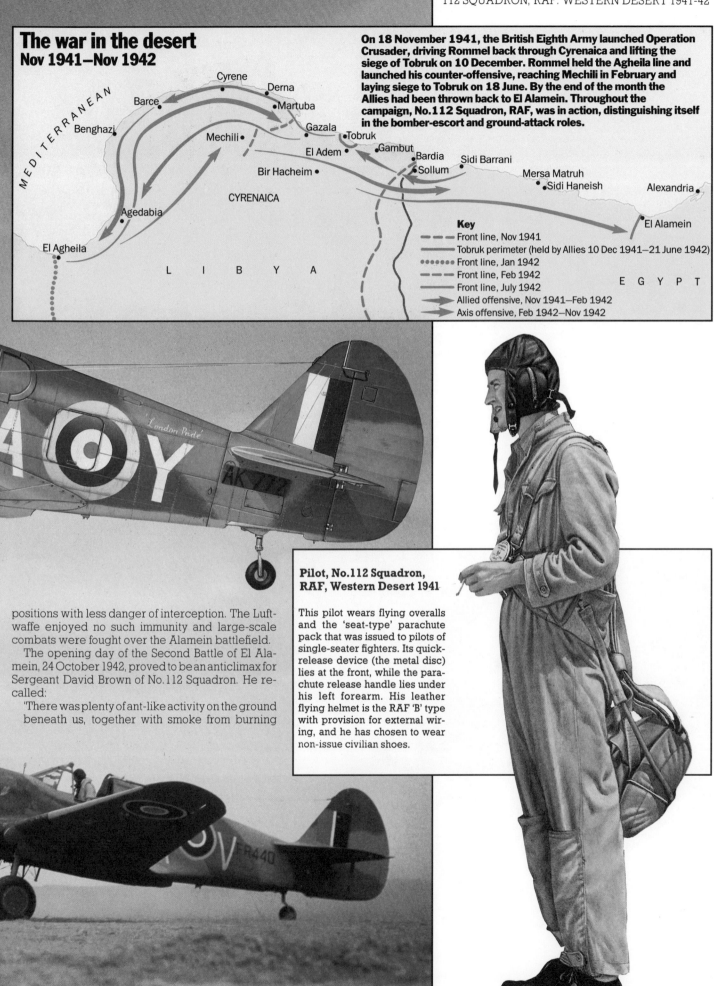

Key
— – — Front line, Nov 1941
——— Tobruk perimeter (held by Allies 10 Dec 1941–21 June 1942)
••••••• Front line, Jan 1942
– – – Front line, Feb 1942
——— Front line, July 1942
➤ Allied offensive, Nov 1941–Feb 1942
➤ Axis offensive, Feb 1942–Nov 1942

positions with less danger of interception. The Luftwaffe enjoyed no such immunity and large-scale combats were fought over the Alamein battlefield.

The opening day of the Second Battle of El Alamein, 24 October 1942, proved to be an anticlimax for Sergeant David Brown of No.112 Squadron. He recalled:

'There was plenty of ant-like activity on the ground beneath us, together with smoke from burning

Pilot, No.112 Squadron, RAF, Western Desert 1941

This pilot wears flying overalls and the 'seat-type' parachute pack that was issued to pilots of single-seater fighters. Its quick-release device (the metal disc) lies at the front, while the parachute release handle lies under his left forearm. His leather flying helmet is the RAF 'B' type with provision for external wiring, and he has chosen to wear non-issue civilian shoes.

159

vehicles and stores, but on our armed recce we had little trouble. We saw a couple of Bf 109s high above but, having manoeuvred into our six o'clock position, they changed their minds: perhaps they sensed our mood.'

Two days later, however, the enemy fighters were less reluctant to engage. A dozen of the squadron's Kittyhawks, carrying out a bomber-escort mission, were bounced by Bf 109s. Squadron Leader Drake and Pilot Officer Wright each claimed one of them, but two Kittyhawks were lost. On the morning of 27 October the squadron fought with Macchi M.C.202s, claiming three of them for the loss of one Kittyhawk.

By early November the enemy was in retreat, with No.112 Squadron attacking their motor convoys wherever they could be found. There followed a frantic leapfrogging from airfield to airfield in an attempt to keep up with the rapid advance. By January 1943 the Axis forces had retreated past Tripoli and the long campaign in the Western Desert was at an end. In March 1943, No.112 Squadron claimed its 200th air victory, but henceforth it increasingly specialised in ground-attack work. It went on to take part in the breaking of the Mareth Line and then the campaigns in Sicily and Italy. Yet, it was in the Western Desert that the squadron gained its greatest triumphs, flying the shark-mouthed Tomahawks and Kittyhawks that were an inspiration to the hard-pressed Commonwealth troops on the ground.

THE AUTHOR Anthony Robinson was formerly on the staff of the RAF Museum, Hendon, and is now a freelance military aviation writer. He has edited the books *Aerial Warfare* and the *Dictionary of Aviation*.

Above: A Curtiss Tomahawk Mk IIB (distinguishable from the Kittyhawk by its less pronounced nose air intake) on a strafing run over the desert. Left: Damaged German Ju 88 bombers on a Tunisian airfield after a raid. Note the burnt-out aircraft to the left. Top: Pilots of No.112 Squadron pose for the camera at a temporary base in Tunisia. Centre: The Desert Air Force was deployed in support of the invasion of Italy, and No.112 Squadron personnel are here seen entering Rome.

Fighter ace Adolf Galland honed his Jagdgeschwader 26 into the most feared German fighter unit of the Battle of Britain, 1940

ON 24 JULY 1940 Major (Squadron Leader) Adolf Galland led the Third Gruppe of Schlageter Jagdgeschwader 26 (III/JG 26), a Luftwaffe fighter unit, on its first mission of the Battle of Britain; providing escort for Dornier Do 17 bombers attacking shipping in the Thames Estuary. Galland's flight of Messerschmitt Bf 109s was intercepted by RAF Spitfires of No. 54 Squadron and a fierce dogfight ensued. Galland managed to surprise a section of the attackers from above:

'I glued myself to the tail of the plane flying outside on the left flank, during a right-hand turn. I managed to get in a long burst and the Spitfire went down almost vertically. I followed it until the cockpit cover came flying towards me and the pilot bailed out, then I followed him down until he crashed into the water. His parachute had failed to open.'

The pilots of III/JG 26 claimed three victories in this combat (in fact, only two of No. 54 Squadron's Spitfires were lost), but three Bf 109Es failed to return. 'We were no longer in any doubt that the RAF would prove a most formidable opponent,' said Galland.

In the summer of 1940, the 28-year-old Galland, 'moody, self-analytical, given to alternate flashes of gloom and gaiety', was fast developing into one of the Luftwaffe's most effective fighter commanders. Oberleutnant (Flying Officer) Gerhard Schöpfel, an office in III/JG 26, remembered Galland's qualities:

'He had a good nose for the enemy, probably because hunting was one of his favourite sports. But he was not easy to fly with. He flew over Dover and southern England at 1000m and the flak was terrible . . . but he was the leader and we followed him. He was an outstanding fighter leader in my experience.'

Many of his pilots found him equally difficult to keep up with on the ground and his love of high living was legendary. Galland smoked up to 20 cigars a day and even had a special cigar holder fitted in the cockpit of his Bf 109E.

Like Galland, the Luftwaffe's pilots were at the peak of their performance and were looking forward with confidence to the imminent battle with the RAF for the control of the skies over southern England. Their high morale appeared to be well-justified, as

Main picture: Adolf Galland flying his personal Bf 109, with its distinctive 'Mickey Mouse' emblem directly beneath the cockpit, on a cross-Channel Frei Jagd (Free Chase) in the opening stages of the Battle of Britain. Within weeks, he would become a living legend and one of the deadliest enemies the RAF had to face. Galland was a 'natural' pilot and had learnt to fly during the 1920s. His first combat missions, however, were flown with the Condor Legion in the Spanish Civil War. Below right: A lull in the battle for air superiority against the Republican Air Force in Spain. Galland is seated on the right. Right: Göring and Galland in conference. Their relationship was marred by frequent and often violent disagreements over strategy.

SPEARHEAD
OF THE LUFTWAFFE

during the early battles of World War II German fighter pilots had swept all before them. In the campaigns in Poland, Norway, the Low Countries and France the Luftwaffe had consistently outfought its opponents. Germany's Messerschmitt Bf 109E single-engined fighter aircraft was considered to be the finest warplane of its kind in the world, and the tactics evolved by the Luftwaffe's master tactician, Werner Mölders, had been proved time and again in the acid test of combat. Yet RAF Fighter Command, equipped with modern fighter aircraft and manned by resolute and courageous airmen, was to prove by far the toughest opponent yet faced by the Luftwaffe. The outcome of the Battle of Britain, the first major battle in history to be fought in the air, was far from being a foregone conclusion.

The preliminary combats of the Battle of Britain were fought over the English Channel in July, between Luftwaffe forces attacking British coastal convoys and the RAF fighter patrols covering these important shipping movements. On the German side

JAGDGESCHWADER 26

Jagdgeschwader 26 (JG 26) was formed in 1937 under the designation JG 234. Its unofficial title 'Schlageter' commemorated a National Socialist hero who had been executed by French forces occupying the Rhineland during the 1920s. By the outbreak of World War II, JG 26 was flying the potent Bf 109 fighter and was ready for action.

The unit, however, missed the Polish campaign and did not see combat until 18 December 1939 when a single Staffel, 10 (Nacht)/JG 26, helped to shoot down 12 RAF Wellington bombers over the Heligoland Bight. Following the German campaign in the Low Countries and France in the summer of 1940, JG 26 was withdrawn to rest and re-equip prior to the air assault on Britain.

JG 26 was organised in three Gruppen, each having a strength of some 30 aircraft. In addition, there was a Geschwader Stabs Schwarm (Staff Flight) of four fighters, manned by the Geschwader Kommodore and his staff officers. This gave JG 26 a nominal strength of 94 aircraft but the number of available fighters varied. On 17 August 1940, for example, JG 26 had a total of 112 Bf 109Es, 24 of which were unserviceable, while on 7 September the unit's strength was down to 92 fighters, 15 of them undergoing repairs.

MESSERSCHMITT Bf 109

Nicknamed 'Emil', the Bf 109 was the brain child of Willy Messerschmitt's design team and first shot to prominence in October 1935 when it won a fighter competition held at Travemünde.

During the pre-war years the Luftwaffe requested more powerful models. Of these, the Bf 109B and C versions were blooded with Jagdgruppe 88 of the Condor Legion during the Spanish Civil War. Their undoubted success against Republican fighters was noted by the Luftwaffe, who then placed large orders with their manufacturers. After playing a major part in the invasion of Poland in September 1939, the Bf 109-equipped units were ordered to convert onto the latest E version. By August 1940, 23 Gruppen were deployed along the Channel coast.

The Bf 109E-3 mounted two MG17 machine guns in its nose cowling, two in the wings and a 20mm cannon, capable of unleashing 60rpm, housed in the spinner. The other variant to see service in the Battle of Britain, the Bf 109E-4 was armed with two MG17s on

the engine crankcase and two 20mm cannon mounted in the wings.

The Bf 109 was capable of 570km/h at 4000m, able to dive faster than its opponent and was a match for most British fighters.

Above: Bf 109s of III/JG 26 undergoing engine checks prior to a sortie. Right: Schöpfel (seated, far left) and Galland (seated, with map) planning a sortie. Below: Galland's Bf 109 and cockpit interior (far right). Main picture: A flight of Do 17s on a raid over southern England.

PROTECTING THE BOMBERS

As the Battle of Britain progressed, German bomber losses became so great that JG 26, along with other fighter units, had to fly escort missions. Henceforth, Bf 109s flew high cover sorties over the bombers, while other fighters provided close support.

The Luftwaffe's escort fighters favoured a position a little above and behind the bombers and, despite the disquiet of some pilots at being tied to the Heinkels and Dorniers, they still represented a major threat to RAF pilots trying to get to grips with the bombers.

Although the RAF attempted to solve the problem by detaching a flight of aircraft to tackle the German fighters, while the remainder pressed their attack against the bombers, the British force was usually outnumbered and unable to compete on even terms. The Luftwaffe's tactics forced the senior officers of RAF Fighter Command to reconsider their fighter tactics. It was not until larger formations of Spitfires and Hurricanes were brought together to launch an attack that the Luftwaffe's bombers and their dogged fighter escorts could be separated. Once this had been achieved, however, the slow-moving and poorly-armed bombers were easy meat.

the brunt of the early fighter combats was borne by Jagdgeschwader 51 and it was not until the end of the month that it was joined by JG 26 and the other fighter units of Luftflotte (Air Fleet) 2 in the Pas de Calais area. These forces, under the command of Jagdfliegerführer 2, the World War I veteran Oberst (Group Captain) Theo Osterkamp, were to form the spearhead of the Luftwaffe's assault on Britain.

JG 26 occupied three airfields in the Pas de Calais area. The Geschwader Stabs Schwarm (Staff Flight), under the Kommodore, Major Gotthard Handrick, and I Gruppe, commanded by Hauptmann (Flight Lieutenant) Kurt Fischer, were based at Audembert; Hauptmann Karl Ebbighausen's II Gruppe was at Marquise; and Galland's III Gruppe was at Caffiers. The latter airfield, near Guines, was an unsurfaced landing strip on requisitioned farm land with none of the facilities of a permanent airbase. Accommodation was in tents and makeshift huts improvised by the airmen, and the aircraft were dispersed around the field in sand-bagged blast pens, which had been carefully camouflaged against air reconnaissance. Such primitive conditions were typical of the Luftwaffe's fighter airfields on the Channel coast in the early stages of the war.

The Bf 109E's combination of cannon and machine guns served the good marksman well

In terms of performance, the Messerschmitt Bf 109E and the Spitfire Mk1 were evenly matched, but the Hurricane Mk1 (in 1940 the most numerous RAF fighter) was decidedly inferior to the Bf 109E. Schöpfel recalled that the Bf 109E 'was superior to the Hurricane and, above about 6000m, faster than the Spitfire also. I believe that our armament was the better. It was located more centrally, which made for more accurate shooting.' Galland disagreed with this view, believing that, whereas the Bf 109E's combination of cannon and machine guns served the good marksman well, the shot-gun effect of the British eight-gun armament (.303in calibre Browning machine guns) was more effective for the average squadron pilot. Schöpfel acknowledged that 'the British fighters could turn tighter than we could. Also, I felt that the Messerschmitt was not so strong as the British fighters and could not take so much punishment.' The Bf 109E's greatest disadvantage when operating over Britain, however, was its limited tactical radius (some 200km), putting it in similar predicament to a dog on a chain, as Galland commented.

In the field of tactics the Luftwaffe had a clear advantage over the RAF. Its basic combat unit was the Rotte of leader and wingman, flying in a widely-spaced formation about 200m apart. Two Rotten combined to form a Schwarm and larger formations were built up of these sections of four stepped up at different altitudes. This arrangement allowed the German pilots to concentrate on keeping a good lookout for the enemy, rather than on flying a close formation. In Galland's words:

'The first rule of combat is to see the opponent first. Like the hunter who stalks his prey and then manoeuvres himself unnoticed into the most favourable position for the kill, the fighter in the opening of a dogfight must detect the opponent as early as possible to obtain a superior position for the attack.'

An additional advantage of the German system was that when formations broke up in combat, the wing-

Lieutenant Müncheberg, JG 26, France 1940

Wearing Luftwaffe officers' uniform, this ace carries the awards of Knight's Cross and Iron Cross 1st and 2nd class, plus pilot and wound badges.

Top: Oberleutnant Joachim Müncheburg (right), the senior officer of 7/II JG 26, scored his twentieth victory of the Battle of Britain on 14 September and received the Knight's Cross in recognition. Right and above right: The German Do 17 medium bomber.

Battle over Britain

Jagdgeschwader 26, 16 August 1940

The Luftwaffe began an all-out attack against the RAF on 13 August 1940. German bomber squadrons mounted heavy raids on RAF Fighter Command airfields in southeast England. Major Gotthard Handrick's Jagdgeschwader 26 was deployed to give the bombers fighter cover and to destroy RAF Hurricanes and Spitfires in the air. JG 26 had already scored several successes when, on 16 August, its II Gruppe, based at Marquise, was sent into action in support of a massive two-stage bombing raid. Over the English coast at Deal a dogfight with No. 266 Squadron's Spitfires began.

The raid begins

1225 Twenty-four Dorniers of Kampfgeschwader 2, apparently aiming for the fighter airfield at Hornchurch, are intercepted by No. 56 Squadron Spitfires. Two Bf 109s are shot down and the Dorniers fail to reach Hornchurch.

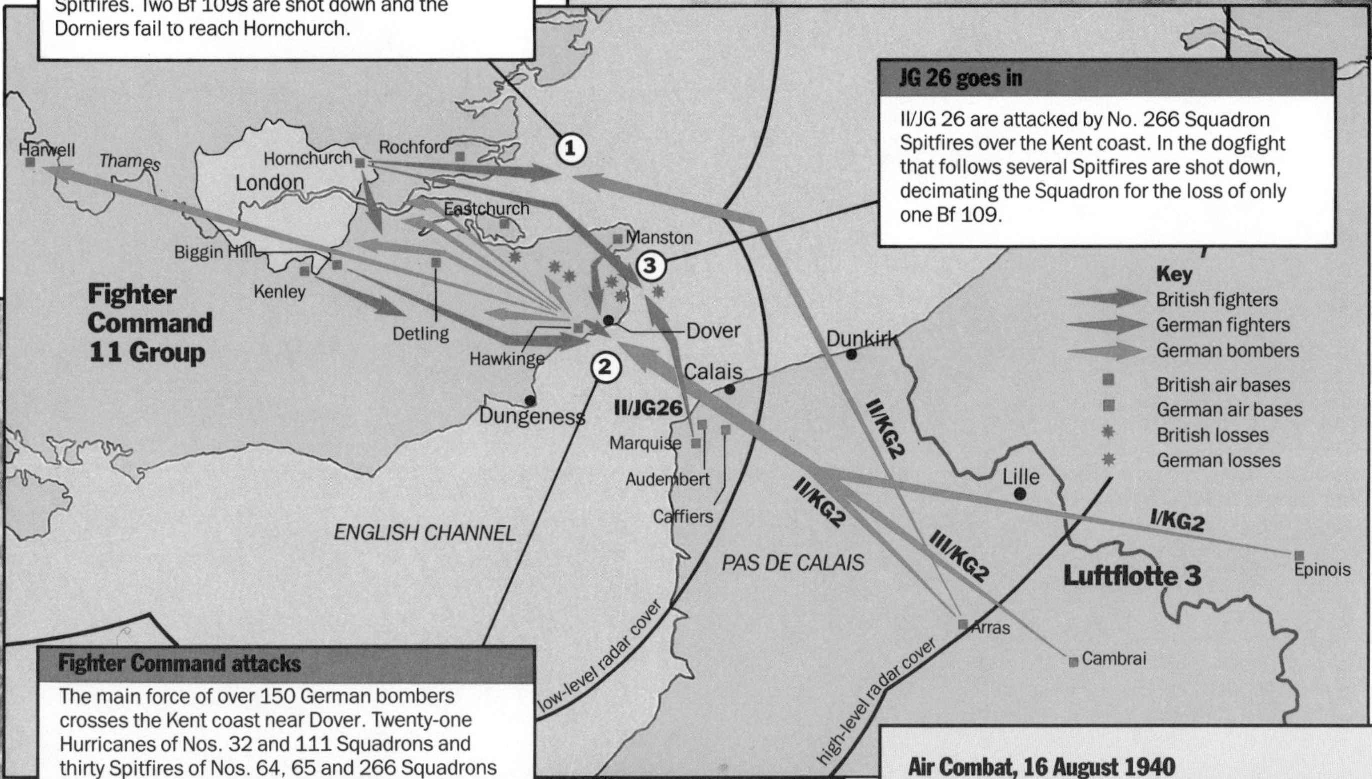

JG 26 goes in

II/JG 26 are attacked by No. 266 Squadron Spitfires over the Kent coast. In the dogfight that follows several Spitfires are shot down, decimating the Squadron for the loss of only one Bf 109.

Key
- British fighters
- German fighters
- German bombers
- British air bases
- German air bases
- British losses
- German losses

Fighter Command 11 Group

Harwell · Thames · Hornchurch · Rochford · London · Eastchurch · Manston · Biggin Hill · Kenley · Detling · Dover · Dunkirk · Hawkinge · Calais · Dungeness · II/JG26 · Marquise · Audembert · Caffiers · Lille · I/KG2 · Epinois · ENGLISH CHANNEL · PAS DE CALAIS · Luftflotte 3 · Arras · Cambrai · low-level radar cover · high-level radar cover · II/KG2 · III/KG2

Fighter Command attacks

The main force of over 150 German bombers crosses the Kent coast near Dover. Twenty-one Hurricanes of Nos. 32 and 111 Squadrons and thirty Spitfires of Nos. 64, 65 and 266 Squadrons are scrambled, scattering the bombers, which fan out and penetrate as far as Harwell.

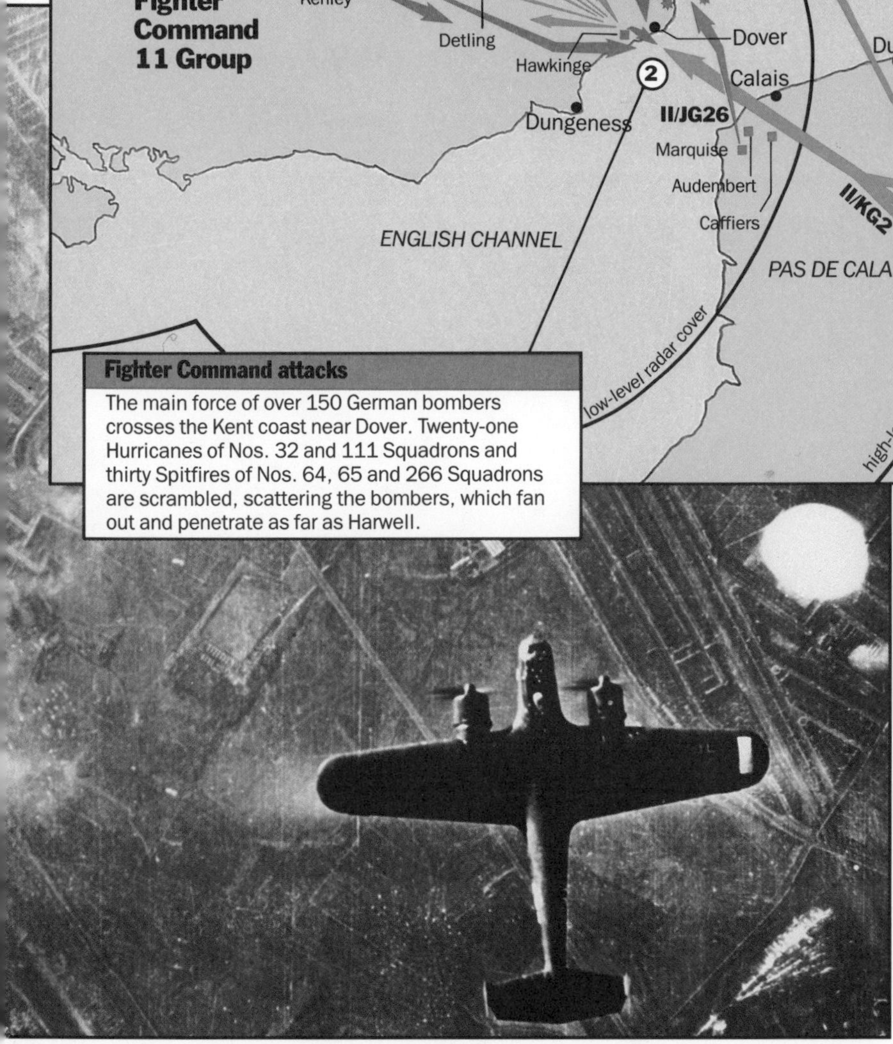

Air Combat, 16 August 1940

Leutnant Karl Borris, a member of the Staff Flight of II/JG 26, was involved in the dogfight against No. 266 Squadron on 16 August 1940. After the RAF squadron had surprised a Staffel of Messerschmitt Bf 109s from the Gruppe, nine more German aircraft joined in the battle over southern England. Borris recorded the action in his diary:

'I was flying at about 7000m behind our Staffelführer and Eckhardt Roch, Leibling and März. Seven Spitfires suddenly attacked us, diving from high on the left forward quarter. We broke up. Over the Channel I spotted a Spitfire on the tail of a Bf 109, the 109 reacted with a quick half loop and roll-out. It was Waldi März.

'I do not think my warning call reached him as the radio was damaged; März landed with 20 bullet holes and an over-heating engine. I saw one Spitfire shot down by Eckhardt Roch, but our section leader Hauptmann Ebbinghausen, did not return.'

Borris stayed with JG 26 throughout the war, ending as the commander of its First Gruppe.

LUFTWAFFE STRATEGY

After the inconclusive skirmishing over the English Channel in the weeks after the evacuation of the British Expeditionary Force from Dunkirk in May/June 1940, the Luftwaffe began its main assault on southern England in mid-August.

Heavy attacks were launched against airfields and coastal radar stations.

The raids on the early-warning stations were potentially the most serious threat to the RAF's survival, as their loss would make the detection of enemy bombers very difficult. Although a significant amount of damage was caused, the Luftwaffe saw little discernible effect and the raids were halted. Attacks on RAF airfields were much less successful. The Luftwaffe relied on high-flying reconnaissance aircraft for gathering information, but they often failed in their mission and the intelligence they gathered was usually of little value. On many occasions, heavy raids were directed against airfields not used by RAF fighters.

Two other phases marked the later stages of the Battle of Britain. The failure to smash RAF bases led the Luftwaffe to switch its attention to London. This fateful policy, begun on 24 August, gave the RAF an invaluable breathing space to recover from the cumulative effects of the Luftwaffe's raids on its airfields. The Bf 109s, flying at the limits of their endurance, failed to provide adequate cover for their bombers and the RAF, with its bases secure from further attack, was able to defeat the massive raids. The final phase, begun in late September, was less critical. The Luftwaffe equipped its fighters with bombs. It was an unhappy compromise; the fighters lost much of their manoeuvrability and their bombload was too small to have any appreciable effect on the British defences. Although German raids continued until April 1941, the Luftwaffe had given up hope of defeating the RAF, and in early May Göring ordered that all Luftwaffe units should prepare for the invasion of Russia.

man would stick to his leader and protect him from surprise attack. In contrast, the British 'vic' formations were more difficult to maintain, less well adapted to keeping a good lookout and liable to break up in combat into single aircraft which were far more vulnerable than mutually-supporting pairs.

In the early phases of the Luftwaffe's assault on Britain, the German fighters would fly Frei Jagd (free chase) sweeps ahead of the bomber formations, with smaller fighter forces flying in visual contact with the bombers to provide direct protection. However, as bomber losses mounted, these flexible tactics were increasingly restricted on the direct orders of the Luftwaffe's Commander-in-Chief Reichsmarschall (First Marshal) Hermann Göring.

Adlertag (Eagle Day) on 13 August marked the start of an all-out attack on RAF Fighter Command, its airfields and the supporting aircraft industry. JG 26, led by its Kommodore, Major Handrick, successfully covered an attack on Detling airfield by the Ju 87s of

IV (Stuka)LG/1. Handrick was a fine athlete, who had won a gold medal in the 1936 Olympic Games, and during the Spanish Civil War he had commanded the Condor Legion's Jagdgruppe 88. On the following day, JG 26 became engaged in a massive dogfight over Dover with four RAF fighter squadrons, claiming eight victories for the loss of only one Messerschmitt. Amongst the successful pilots were Galland, Schöpfel and II Gruppe's Kommandeur, Major Ebbighausen. A Frei Jagd over the same area on 15 August proved to be equally successful, as eight JG 26 pilots submitted victory claims for no loss to themselves. However, the Jagdgeschwader 26 did not have things all its own way, because on the following day II/JG 26's Stabs Schwarm was 'bounced' by Spitfires of No. 266 Squadron and its Kommodore failed to return. Ebbighausen's place was taken by Hauptmann Erich Bode.

It fell to Schöpfel to lead III/JG 26 into action on 18 August, as Galland had been summoned to Berlin for

Below: JG 26 dispersed its fighters at three airfields in the Pas de Calais region of northern France during the Battle of Britain. To prevent the destruction of its BF 109s by marauding RAF fighters, JG 26's aircraft were heavily camouflaged. Bottom: Constant sweeps across the Channel put a great strain on the unit's fighters and groundcrew had to work round the clock to keep them at combat readiness. Below Left: Two members of the groundcrew going through last-minute checks with the pilot of a bomb-carrying Bf 109.

a conference with Göring. The 27-year-old Schöpfel had transferred to the Luftwaffe from the infantry in 1935 and claimed his first victory over Dunkirk. By September 1940 his score had risen to 20 kills and at the end of the war, with some 700 combat missions behind him, he was credited with 40 victories. The mission of 18 August was to be one of his most memorable.

Shortly before 1300 hours Schöpfel led his fighters across the Kent coast on a Frei Jagd to spearhead an attack by bombers from Kampfgeschwader (KG) 76 and KG 1 on Kenley and Biggin Hill airfields. As they neared the first target he noticed the Hurricanes of No. 501 Squadron climbing for height beneath him. Schöpfel dived down and with two short bursts of fire shot down the two Hurricanes acting as 'weavers'

(lookouts) for the formation. He then attacked the rearmost Hurricane and shot it down in flames. 'The Englishmen continued on, having noticed nothing,' Schöpfel remembered, 'so I pulled in behind the fourth machine and took care of him also.' He was so close that wreckage and oil from this victim splattered his Bf 109E. Later the same afternoon, III/JG 26 were again in action, shooting down three Hurricanes of No. 32 Squadron in return for two Bf 109Es lost.

Meanwhile, at Carinhall, Göring's estate outside Berlin, Galland and his fellow fighter commanders faced a barrage of criticism from the Reichsmarschall about German bomber losses. Göring believed that the answer was for the fighters to provide a strong escort tied to the bomber formations, whereas the fighter leaders strenuously opposed this restriction on their tactical freedom. Later in the Battle, Galland's resentment of Göring's ill-founded criticisms of the fighter force was forcefully expressed in a famous retort. Ending a diatribe against the Jagdgeschwader's inability to protect the bombers, Göring asked what it was the fighter leaders required. Galland replied that he should like a Staffel of Spitfires. The immediate outcome of the Carinhall conference, however, was that the older Jagdgeschwader Kommodoren were retired and replaced by younger men. Galland took command of JG 26, while Schöpfel replaced him as Kommandeur of III Gruppe.

'The physical as well as the mental strain on the German pilots was considerable'

There was no let-up in the intensity of the air fighting during late August and early September. 'Two or three sorties daily was the rule,' recalled Galland. 'The physical as well as the mental strain on the pilots was considerable. The ground personnel and the planes themselves were taxed to the limit.' Oberleutnant Heinz Ebeling, the Staffelkapitän of 9/JG 26, was shot down over the Channel on 31 August after his thirteenth victory, but was rescued by the very efficient German air-sea rescue service and was back in action later that day. During the fortnight between 24 August and 7 September JG 26 lost a total of 23 Bf 109Es in combat.

The German pilots were also taking a heavy toll of the RAF. On 28 August Galland led an escort mission in support of bombers attacking the airfields of Rochford and Eastchurch. Shortly after crossing the coast at Folkestone, the German formation was intercepted by the Boulton Paul Defiants of No. 264 Squadron. These cumbersome turret-armed fighters had already suffered heavy losses during the Battle and were no match for the agile Bf 109Es. JG 26 shot down four of them and damaged a further three, Galland himself accounting for one of the kills. This combat marked the end of the Defiant's career as a day fighter and the survivors of No. 264 Squadron were withdrawn from combat on the following day.

A new phase of the Battle of Britain opened on 7 September when the Luftwaffe shifted the weight of its attack onto London. German intelligence believed that Fighter Command had almost exhausted its resources and that the few remaining RAF fighters could be forced into a last stand in defence of the capital. However, the Luftwaffe's fighter pilots soon realized that the vigour of the RAF defence was undiminished and that the longer escort missions to

London exacerbated their range problems. Galland recalled that JG 26 lost 12 fighters in September:

'not by enemy action, but simply because after two hours' flying time the bombers we were escorting had not yet reached the mainland on their return journey. Five of these fighters managed to make a crash landing on the French shore with their last drop of fuel; seven of them landed in the drink.'

'The aircraft spiralled slowly to the ground as though piloted by a ghostly hand'

On 14 September the Staffelkapitän of 7/JG 26, Oberleutnant Joachim Müncheberg, scored his twentieth victory and was awarded the Ritterkreuz (Knight's Cross). By the time of his death in combat on 23 March 1943 he had gained 135 victories.

The climax of the Battle of Britain came on 15 September and Galland remembered his combats on that day:

'On my way back from London, I spotted a squadron of 12 Hurricanes north of Rochester. Attacking from 800m above them and behind, I shot like an arrow between the flights and from ramming distance fired on one of the aircraft in the rear line of the formation, tearing large pieces of metal out of the aircraft. At the last moment I pulled my nose up and leaped over her, then flew right through the centre of the enemy's formation. It was not a pleasant sensation. Again I fired my cannon and machine guns into one of the Hurricanes from close range. Luckily, the British had had a similar or even bigger fright than I. No-one attacked me. As I broke off I saw two parachutes open below the broken formation.

'It was not as simple as this with another Hurricane I shot down west of Dungeness. I had damaged her so badly that she was on fire and ought to have been a certain kill. Yet she did not crash but glided down in gentle curves. My flight companions and I attacked her three times without a final result. As I flew close alongside the flying wreck, by now thoroughly riddled, with smoke belching from her, from a distance of a few yards I saw the dead pilot sitting in his shattered cockpit, while his aircraft spiralled slowly to the ground as though piloted by a ghostly hand.'

By the end of September it was clear that the Luftwaffe had failed in its attempt to wrest air superiority from the RAF over southern England. Yet the German pilots continued to fight effectively and, on 24 September, Galland scored his fortieth combat victory. On that day, JG 26 became engaged in a dogfight with the Hurricanes of No. 17 Squadron over the Thames Estuary. Galland set one of the RAF fighters ablaze with a few well-aimed bursts of fire and watched while the Hurricane pilot abandoned his blazing aircraft by parachute. His victim was Pilot Officer Harold Bird-Wilson, a successful fighter pilot with six victories to his credit, who ended the war with a score of 11 kills and later retired from the RAF with the rank of Air Vice-Marshal.

Galland was ordered to Berlin to receive the Oak Leaves clasp to his Ritterkreuz

Because of this tally, Galland was ordered to Berlin to receive the Eichenlaubs (Oak Leaves) clasp to his Ritterkreuz from the hands of the Führer himself. He was only the third member of the German armed forces to be decorated with this high award. His friend and rival Major Werner Mölders, the Kommodore of JG 51, had received it a few days before. The two men were vying with Major Helmut Wick of JG 2 for the honour of being the top-scoring Luftwaffe fighter pilot.

During October the bomber force switched its main offensive to night attacks but the German fighters continued the daylight battle with high-level fighter sweeps and fighter-bomber raids. Each fighter Gruppe was instructed to convert one of its Staffeln to the fighter-bomber role and their Bf 109Es were accordingly fitted with a centreline rack for a 250kg bomb. 'There was hardly time to give the pilots bombing training', remembered Galland, 'and most of them dropped their first live bomb in a raid on London or on other targets in England.' Each Gruppe was responsible for escorting its own Jabos (fighter-bombers), and in JG 26 they were distributed in small numbers amongst the fighters, so that the RAF could not pick them off so easily. Yet the results of these tactics were negligible. As an experienced fighter

Above left: Oberleutnant Gerhard Schöpfel jumps from the cockpit of his aircraft after a mission. Schöpfel led III/JG 26 into action on 18 August, during the height of the Luftwaffe's sorties against southern England, and despatched four Hurricanes of No. 501 Squadron in a dogfight near Kenley airfield. Below left: The tailplane of Schöpfel's aircraft being moved into its camouflaged hanger after a sortie. Above: Pilots of III/JG 26, with Schöpfel standing in the centre.

ADOLF GALLAND

Born on 19 March 1912 at Westerholt in northern Germany, Galland became determined to be a pilot in the 1920s, while still at school. He became an accomplished glider pilot during this period and, despite his parents' misgivings, applied for, and gained, a place with Lufthansa.

On 1 October 1935, he was commissioned as a Leutnant and sent to a Luftwaffe fighter school as an instructor. Five months later the existence of the Luftwaffe, an organisation forbidden by the Allied Powers after World War I, was formally announced, and Galland joined Jagdgeschwader 132, flying He 51s.

Galland was sent to Spain as part of the Condor Legion in May 1937. He assumed the rank of Oberleutnant during the Spanish Civil War and led the Third Staffel. He was recalled to Germany in August 1938 to help create two ground-support Gruppen.

When Germany invaded Poland on 1 September 1939, Galland was flying He 123 ground-attack aircraft as a Staffelkäpitan in II Gruppe of Lehrgeschwader 2. He flew about 50 sorties during the brief campaign and on 1 October was promoted to the rank of Hauptmann and received the Iron Cross, 2nd Class.

Early in 1940, Galland was finally transferred to fighter duties, becoming the Geschwader-adjutant of JG 27. On 10 May he scored his first victories, shooting down two Belgian Hurricanes.

By 3 June his score had risen to 12 kills.

Galland then transferred to JG 26 and during the opening phases of the Battle of Britain he was in command of its III Gruppe. On 18 July he was promoted to major and, with his score standing at 17 victories, received the Ritterkreuz (Knight's Cross). By the end of the campaign Galland was in command of JG 26 and, with 40 kills to his credit, had gained the Oak Leaves to the Knight's Cross.

In 1941, Galland was promoted to general rank and in this position controlled all fighter affairs in the West, the Balkans, the Mediterranean and on the Russian front. Galland continued to fly and took his total of victories to 94 before being taken off operations on 28 January 1942. At this point, he received the Diamonds to the Knight's Cross.

Throughout 1943 and 1944 Galland was involved in organising Germany's air defences. Galland became very vociferous in his condemnation of Göring's strategy and in late 1944 was relieved of his duties. However, he was soon back in action. At Hitler's request, he was ordered to form and lead a jet-fighter squadron of Me 262s.

Although his unit, Jagdverband 44, fought well, it could not affect the outcome of the war. Galland flew his final mission two weeks before the end of the war when he received a knee injury that kept him out of combat. By the time Galland recovered, the war was over.

Above: Adolf Galland became the youngest general in the Luftwaffe when, in mid-1941, he was promoted to Inspector of Fighters. Below: In July 1941, II/JG 26 was the first unit to receive the Luftwaffe's latest fighter, the FW 190. Known as the 'Butcher Bird', it was much feared by RAF pilots. Bottom: The grim aftermath of a raid by Luftwaffe fighters. The burnt and smashed wreckage of a Spitfire litters the runway of Hornchurch airfield.

pilot Galland knew why:

'The passive behaviour towards enemy fighters, the feeling of inferiority when we were attacked, because of loss of speed, manoeuvrability and rate of climb, added to the unconvincing effect of bombs scattered over wide areas, combined to ruin the morale of the German fighter pilot'.

JG 26 flew its last large-scale mission over England on 5 December.

Despite Germany's defeat in the Battle of Britain, the Jagdegeschwader 26 had fought hard and well and it was fitting that its Kommodore, Adolf Galland, emerged as the top-scoring fighter pilot of the period with a total of 57 victories and one of Germany's highest accolades – the Diamonds to the Knight's Cross.

THE AUTHOR Anthony Robinson was formerly on the staff of the RAF Museum, Hendon and is now a freelance military aviation writer. He has written and edited a large number of books on aviation and military subjects including *American Air Power, Aerial Warfare* and the *Dictionary of Aviation*.

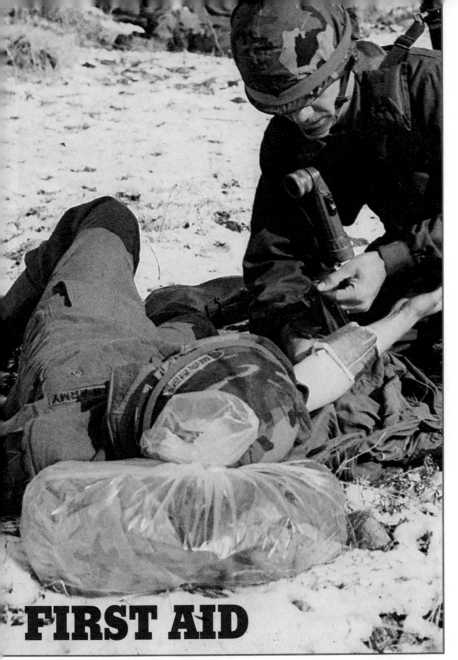

FIRST AID

Basic first aid – how to cope with bullet wounds, fractures, cuts and burns, for example – is an essential aspect of battlefield survival. The field hospital may be miles behind the front lines, and there could be a long delay before wounded personnel can be medevaced out of the combat zone. By reacting quickly and sensibly to any emergency, you may be able to save lives and prevent permanent disabilities and long periods of hospitalisation.

There is another scenario you should be prepared for, however. Although you will normally be in possession of a first-aid kit comprising ampoules of morphine, field dressings and ointments, you may be placed in a situation where only the clothes on your back will defend you against disease and disability. Whether you are being held as a prisoner of war, or using escape and evasion techniques behind enemy lines, follow the basic precepts of first aid and primitive medicine if you want to save lives and stay alive yourself.

There are several recognised rules for the treatment of injuries and wounds. The first of these is to staunch the bleeding. Having checked for both the entry and exit points of a wound (a bullet usually makes a smaller wound where it enters than where it

Above: A waterproof field dressing is applied to an arm wound. In cases where there is serious loss of blood, the nearest main artery must be located and pressure applied to restrict the flow. Only use a tourniquet if all other methods have proved ineffective.

exits), cut and lift any clothing away from the wound in order to expose it. Do not, however, touch or attempt to clean the area. Remove one of the sterilised dressings from your first-aid kit and tie it around the wound with a square knot.

If bleeding continues despite pressure being applied to the wound, raise the injured limb above the level of the heart. Look for any swelling or discolouration of the skin first, however, for this usually indicates a fracture or clean break. If you suspect that this may have happened, make sure that the limb is properly splinted before being moved. Splints can be improvised from sticks and blankets and should extend for at least one foot above and below the injury.

If blood is spurting from the wound, you will have to locate the nearest main artery and apply pressure to cut off the flow. A tourniquet can be applied, but only as a last resort: cutting off the blood supply in this way can lead to gangrene and, ultimately, amputation. Put the tourniquet between the wound and where the injured limb joins the trunk, and never loosen or remove it unless in the presence of qualified medical personnel. If possible, mark a 'T' on the injured man's forehead to make sure he is dealt with quickly at the field hospital.

If the victim is experiencing difficulty with his breathing, lie him on his back in the chin-up position with the head tilted back. Clear the mouth and throat of obstructions with a sharp blow between the shoulder blades and begin mouth-to-mouth resuscitation. If breathing ceases altogether, it may be necessary to restart the heartbeat. Locate the tip of the breastbone and begin external heart massage by squeezing the heart between the breastbone and the backbone. This will provide artificial circulation by forcing blood through the lungs, brain and body. You must begin this technique the instant you cannot feel a pulse – after four to six minutes without oxygen the victim is likely to suffer brain damage.

In the case of a chest wound, it is important to remember that the injury itself may not be as dangerous as the air that might enter through it into the chest cavity and collapse the lungs. Seal the wound and make it airtight by covering it with the plastic or metal-foil side of a first-aid dressing. The casualty should then be laid face down. For an abdominal wound, dress the injury like any other but do not attempt to push any protruding organs back into place. The man should be laid on his side with his head turned to one side, and given nothing to eat or drink. Anyone with a belly wound should be given the highest priority when evacuation becomes possible.

Shock is one of the most subtle killers on the battlefield, and you must be able to recognise the symptoms as early as possible. A pale face, cold

COMBAT SKILLS OF THE ELITE

clammy skin, a rapid but weak pulse and shallow breathing are the warning signs you must look out for. But since shock occurs some time after an injury, it is always advisable to begin treatment before the symptoms become evident. Lay the man on his back, lowering the head and elevating the feet. Loosen his clothing wherever it restricts circulation and quench his thirst with a hot liquid if possible. It is important that you appear calm and self-confident when treating a victim of shock – he will need all the reassurance you can give that help is on the way.

Minor burns, where the skin has not erupted into blisters, should be covered with a sterile dressing or, if none is available, left uncovered. Where severe burns are involved, the victim should be treated for shock and every attempt made to prevent infection setting in. If no sterile dressings are available, cover the area with a sheet or a T-shirt – anything that is clean. Do not try to clean the wound or pull off any clothes – you will only aggravate the injury. Place the victim in the shock position and replace body fluids by giving him salt water.

Whereas first-aid equipment may be available on the battlefield, you may have to follow a different set of rules in the case of an escape-and-evasion or prisoner-of-war scenario. The techniques of primitive medicine may seem unpalatable at times, but they have saved the lives of many a serviceman who would otherwise have died on the battlefield.

Dysentery becomes a severe problem in enemy territory, especially if the sufferers are not equipped with iodine tablets. Once you become infected, you will begin losing water that must be replaced – drink boiled liquids if possible, but at all costs make sure that you do drink. Charcoal can alleviate the condition: find a partially burned piece of wood, scrape off the charred portions and swallow them. Ground chalk, bones and boiled bark can also cure dysentery. Bark contains tannic acid and, although the resultant brew is vile and evil-smelling, the cure is better than the condition.

Worms are an ever-present threat in unhygenic conditions. As one doctor who was held prisoner in Korea has stated: 'Although there are other symptoms, positive proof that you are infested is when a worm crawls out of your nose. That will undoubtedly shake you up a bit. It always does.' In the absence of proper medicines, swallow a couple of tablespoons of kerosene or petrol – it will make you quite sick, but the worms will be a lot sicker!

Under extreme conditions, there are three treatments for a wound. The first is to clean and sterilise it. Hot water is unlikely to be available, so use your own urine. This was often the only method available to American pilots being held captive in Hanoi during the Vietnam War, but should be relied upon only as a last resort.

Another, albeit distasteful, treatment for infected wounds is the use of maggots. These creatures eat only dead tissue and will clean out a wound if surgery is out of the question. Just expose the wound to the air – flies will soon find it and it won't be long before the maggots appear.

Before you enter combat, you will have been instructed in the rudiments of first aid and will be in possession of a basic kit for this purpose. However, you must also face the very real possibility that you will be the only person available to administer to a variety of wounds and ailments. Above all, remember one simple rule – never, unless absolutely necessary, carry out first-aid measures that are beyond your ability.

Above: A battle casualty receives blood plasma through a needle inserted in his arm.

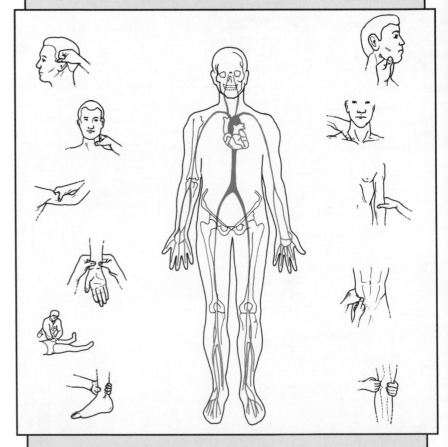